THE WAR OF 1812 IN THE WEST

DAVID KIRKPATRICK

THE WAR OF 1812 IN THE WEST

From Fort Detroit to New Orleans

WESTHOLME
Yardley

Facing title page: Kentucky militia at the Battle of New Orleans. (*Library of Congress*)

Westholme Publishing, LLC
904 Edgewood Road
Yardley, Pennsylvania 19067
Visit our Web site at www.westholmepublishing.com

ISBN: 978-1-59416-309-8
Also available as an eBook.

Printed in the United States of America.

CONTENTS

List of Maps

INTRODUCTION

A S THE LEGISLATURE SAT IN SESSION on January 24, 1867, there were
a number of issues that needed their attention. The Civil War had
concluded two years before and Kentucky, like the nation as a whole,
was still struggling to find a sense of normalcy. Being a border state, the
Commonwealth had seen communities and even families divided by a
conflict that would cost more than half a million lives. Now a people
who seemed irrevocably divided struggled to find a common ground on
which they could work together for the future. It was in this atmosphere
that a resolution was passed through the legislature. Seven years before,
Governor Beriah Magoffin, acting on the instruction of the legislature,
had ordered four gold medals to be struck. They had languished in
Frankfort during the bloodshed that would soon follow and would even
outlast Governor Magoffin himself, who would resign the governorship
in 1862. But now was the time to distribute them to their intended owners. They went to three Kentuckians and one Ohioan who had lived in
Kentucky years before. They were to honor those who represented the
last remnant of a group of men who had fought with Commodore Perry
on the Battle of Lake Erie in 1813.[1] The battle may not resonate with
many modern readers but to the Americans of the mid-nineteenth century, and to Kentuckians in particular, it was the epitome of patriotism
and sacrifice. Despite the division in the state following the Civil War,
the War of 1812 was one subject on which all Kentuckians could reflect
with pride and draw on the resilient, though faint, sense of unity that
was so badly needed during the late 1860s.

The War of 1812 has often been referred to as the forgotten war. But it could more accurately be called the "half remembered war." Unlike the plethora of personalities, battles, and dates from World War II and the Civil War that roll off the tongues of history buffs everywhere, the War of 1812 conjures up fuzzy images and incomplete facts that seem to have little significance to the world today. Music has made sure that the war will never disappear entirely. Most Americans over the age of thirty can recognize the tune to Johnny Horton's ballad "The Battle of New Orleans" even if they can't remember the lyrics. Francis Scott Key's poem "The Defense of Fort McHenry" was imprinted on public memory when it was put to music and christened "The Star-Spangled Banner." But even this well-known memorial suffers from the passage of time, as most Americans can only recall the lyrics to the first of four verses.

Figures like James Madison, Andrew Jackson, the Shawnee Chief Tecumseh, William Henry Harrison, and Davy Crockett, all participants in the War of 1812, are well-known contributors to America's history but our national remembrances of them seem limited to a few disconnected factoids here and there. Phrases like "Tippecanoe and Tyler, too" or "We have met the enemy and they are ours" linger in our memories as unattached proverbs with no historical context. Perhaps the cause of the conflict's identity crisis is that it doesn't seem to be a record breaker. It's not the nation's longest war or the shortest. It is not the most recent, nor the oldest. No great inventions or territorial gains came out of the war. Instead, the conflict remains quietly tucked between the pages of our history books, dawdling in the shadows of larger conflicts like the Civil War, which would come less than fifty years later.

When the War of 1812 is remembered it tends to be confined to the Eastern Seaboard, with the only events worth noting (such as the burning of Washington, the Battle of Fort McHenry, etc.) happening in a single year. But the war was much more than that. It was a battle for national identity and, for those west of the Appalachian Mountains, it was a battle for survival. While the image of the White House engulfed in flames is certainly a dramatic one, the struggles that took place in the states of Kentucky, Tennessee, Louisiana, and Ohio, as well as the territories of Michigan, Illinois, Indiana, had just as great, if not a greater, effect on the lives and developing worldview of its citizens. Yet, their story has, for the most part, remained untold.

Even among contemporary historians who have studied the war, there is a sense of hesitation when describing it. In his 2005 book on the subject, Walter Borneman calls it "a silly little war" but also claims it forged a nation since it was during the war that the United States truly "cast aside its cloak of colonial adolescences."[2] Historian Donald Hickey's work, *The War of 1812: A Forgotten Conflict,* also lament's the war's obscure place in American history. Hickey suggests that because there was no inspiring president at the helm of the republic to serve as a visual symbol of the war, the public tends to let the War of 1812 slip into the mists of time. The same is true when it comes to military leadership. The few generals that many Americans can recall (such as the already mentioned Andrew Jackson) were relegated to what Hickey calls "a secondary theatre of operations."[3] But even this statement is telling and contains a central flaw in our historical reasoning which has made the obscurity of the War of 1812 a self-fulfilling prophecy. Was the war west of the Appalachian Mountains truly a "secondary theatre"? As has already been stated, if we cling to this reasoning we perpetuate the myth that only those battles along the Eastern Seaboard are worth noting and, thus, we unconsciously condense a three-year conflict into twelve months.

In reality, the war in the West would have much more significant long-term repercussions than the war in the East. Not only was the relationship between Anglo-American settlers and native tribes forever altered but the relationship between whites themselves evolved during this period. Historian Alan Taylor suggests that the war was a failure for both sides, as neither was able to sweep the other from the North American continent and that this failure ensured that the two ideologies of republicanism and constitutional monarchy would coexist alongside one another.[4] However, unlike much of the historiography on this conflict, Taylor's work unfolds a new vision of the war in which things did not just return to *pro quo antebellum* (the way they were before the war). Instead, the War of 1812 finally severed the cords of kinship which still bound tenuously the Anglo-American civilization that had developed in North America and forced the various groups who took part in the war to fall on one side or the other of a growing sociopolitical divide. In this sense, the War of 1812 was as great a milestone as the American Revolution since it finished the process that the founders had begun in 1776. Hickey and Taylor represent a growing trend within the historiography of the early republic. This new breed of historian seeks to tease out the details of life for all people during the war rather than recording the experiences of one or two leaders. Hickey, in particular, feels that too much scholarship has been spent on "military and naval engage-ments" at the expense of human experience.[5]

Canadian historiography on the War of 1812 faces many of the same challenges as its American counterpart. Historians such as Sandy Antal, whose work *A Wampum Denied* remains the definitive Canadian history of the western theatre, also struggle to balance the martial and social as-pects of the war. The conflict had extensive social implications, which makes this attempt to reflect social changes alongside the descriptions of battles an essential if thankless task. However, as Antal admits, in a war fought primarily by militia drawn from local communities, it is im-possible to completely separate the battlefield from home and hearth or the soldier from the tradesman or farmer.[6]

This work is an ambitious effort to bridge all of these gaps in the his-toriography of the war as well as cover both the military and social as-pects of the war. This work will not seek to argue that the war is underrepresented in history, as that fact remains the one fact that histo-rians of the period can agree on. Instead, this book will chronicle the contributions of one of these states to the war both on the field and at home. The Commonwealth of Kentucky celebrated its twentieth birth-day in the same year the war was declared, and despite the distance from most of the nation's population, Kentuckians felt themselves to be an integral part of the country and displayed it with a vibrant, almost youth-ful, passion becoming of a new state that was looking to the future. For this reason, when war seemed to be the only way to avenge the honor of an offended nation, they pressed for the start of hostilities with zeal, fought it with valor, and sent one of their most famous citizens, Henry Clay, to negotiate its end.

However, Henry Clay is not the subject of this book. It would be im-possible to write a history of this period without giving credit to him as a guiding influence and a leading voice for war. But there have been nu-merous articles and books on his contributions already. This work is in-tended to relate the story of those lesser-known Kentuckians who fought, suffered, died, and survived the war. From prominent men, like the aging Governor Shelby and the wealthy Green Clay, to the farmers and merchants who made up the infantry and cavalry units in the war, this conflict touched the lives of all Kentuckians. Many of the names in this work will not be familiar and one story often ends just as another is beginning; but when woven together they provide a rich and detailed tapestry that shows, above all, that this was a collective war—one that required the state to sacrifice en masse in order to achieve the goals at stake.

The conflict was made even more complex and interesting by a seemingly endless list of revolutionary symbols that adorned the struggle. The capital of the American Republic bore the name of its commander during the Revolution and the president who would sign the declaration of war was also the senior author of the American Constitution. Many of the governors, legislators, and senior military officers during the War of 1812 had seen service in the Revolution as younger men. On the British side, the same king was sitting on the throne (although power was wielded by his son, George IV, who had been appointed prince regent) and many of the admirals and generals on the British side had also seen service in the Americas during the War for Independence. In the minds of Americans, the war was a new chapter in the same struggle between liberty and tyranny. In the minds of their British counterparts, it was a chance to rectify errors of the past. Unlike the Revolution, the continental powers of Europe would not be participants. Countries such as France and Spain were at first embroiled in the Napoleonic Wars and later left to pick up the pieces of their shattered nations. They would no longer be able to come to the aid of the United States if things became difficult.

Unfortunately, for the Americans, the parallels with the Revolution would continue throughout the war in less popular ways. As with the Revolution, American optimism would be tempered with defeat time and time again. Hunger, the lack of supplies, and defeat snatched from the jaws of victory would be common themes. From the British perspective, history would repeat itself as well. An upstart collection of rebellious former colonies would court disaster by wading into a conflict they seemed to be losing from the start only to rise from the ashes like a phoenix to survive the best efforts of the strongest military in the world.

But while these repetitions would become evident early in the war, not every individual could be so easily placed into one of the two camps. While the war in the West has received less attention than the eastern theatre, recent historiography on the war as a whole has begun to show that these lines blurred, especially along the border between the United States and Canada where residents shared more similarities with each other than they did with London or Washington. Historian Alan Taylor suggests that the American Revolution had been an unfinished work that divided groups of people who had created a common world and culture.[7]

Before the story of the conflict begins there are a few things that I would like to note about this account. Many terms common to the nineteenth century have become antiquated and may not be entirely familiar to the audience. Of the labels related to the conflict that have changed or been discarded over the years, those relating to the native tribes have seen the greatest evolution. In the modern era, efforts are made to accord native tribes respect by citing them by their tribal names rather than using a single blanket phrase. In some ways this was more common during the nineteenth century than today, as different tribes had varying and often opposite relations with the United States and knowledge of each was essential. In such scenarios tribes may be named. However, at other times a single word may be used to describe all native cultures. The moniker "Indian" is used less often in the modern era, and phrases like "savage" have, quite understandably, been discarded as unfair and inaccurate. However, to omit them from any work on the period would be distorting history and would be an injustice to all who lived during the period. With that in mind, they have been retained in this book and the reader is only asked to remember that despite the derogatory connotations that immediately come to mind today, such words were so engrained in the nineteenth century lexicon that their appearance does not necessarily mean they were used in malice by the individuals being referenced or quoted.

While the primary focus of this work is the militia and their campaigns which usually lasted only a few months at a time there are references to some federal units. All in all, three and a half regiments of United States troops were raised solely in Kentucky with, no doubt, a sprinkling of Kentuckians in other units. These men served in the 7th, 17th, 19th, and 28th United States Infantry Regiments and another contingent served in the 2nd United States Rifle Regiment. These men would have had the benefit of standardized uniforms and kit that many in the militia did not have. However, the tradeoff was that federal troops usually signed up for five-year enlistments or until the war ended, which was considerably longer than their counterparts in the militia. [8]

As stated already, this work is about Kentucky's role in the war and, as a result, is told from the point of view of Kentuckians who witnessed the war first hand. In an effort to remain as chronological as possible this story will alternate between the experiences of residents in the state and soldiers in the field. As a result, the experiences of governors, congressmen, officers, enlisted men, and civilians are chronicled herein. This work will mention events elsewhere when they affect Kentuckians or when they provide context to the story, but they will not serve as focal points. The familiar themes of security from Indian attack and asserting American rights on the high seas against a haughty Royal Navy will certainly be discussed as causes for the war, but these causes, as well as the others, were bound together with a common threat—a thirst for honor. It was the sense of national pride that created the keen interest Kentuckians took in events happening on the American Seaboard hundreds of miles away. From their point of view, a slight against the nation's honor in Boston Harbor or on the high seas might as well have happened in Lexington or Louisville.

For many Kentuckians, it was this nationalistic sentiment that justified a declaration of war against the strongest military in the world. To ignore the situation would not only dishonor the nation but would serve as an indictment of its citizens and the republican system they espoused. This philosophy not only guided the nation's policies but effected the actions of individuals. In an era when there were few tangible symbols of American power, a defense of the rights of the people and of national honor represented the essence of what it meant to be an American. It was this mindset that motivated and sustained one state's contribution to a drama that included a cast of millions and unfolded on a global stage.

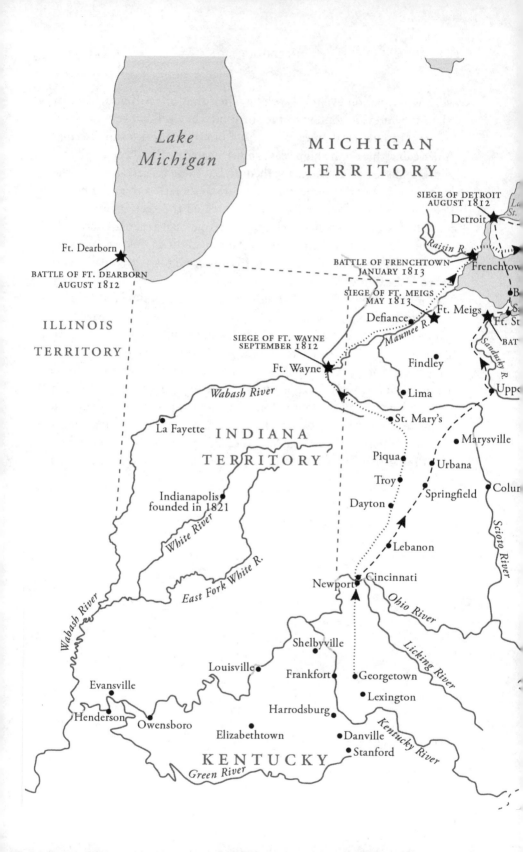

Lake
Michigan

MICHIGAN
TERRITORY

SIEGE OF DETROIT
AUGUST 1812

L.
St.

Detroit

Ft. Dearborn

Raisin R.

BATTLE OF FT. DEARBORN
AUGUST 1812

BATTLE OF FRENCHTOWN
JANUARY 1813

Frenchtow

ILLINOIS

TERRITORY

SIEGE OF FT. MEIGS
MAY 1813

B
S:
Ft. St

Defiance

Ft. Meigs

BAT

SIEGE OF FT. WAYNE
SEPTEMBER 1812

Maumee R.

Sandusky R.

Findley

Ft. Wayne

Upp

Wabash River

Lima

St. Mary's

La Fayette

INDIANA

Marysville

TERRITORY

Piqua

Urbana

Troy

Indianapolis
founded in 1821

Dayton

Springfield

Colu

White River

Lebanon

Scioto River

East Fork White R.

Newport

Cincinnati

Wabash River

Ohio River

Shelbyville

Licking River

Louisville

Frankfort

Georgetown

Evansville

Lexington

Henderson

Owensboro

Harrodsburg

Elizabethtown

Danville

Kentucky River

Stanford

KENTUCKY

Green River

Lake Huron

CANADA

Lake Ontario

Thames R.

St. Catherines

Buffalo

● London

Moraviantown

★ BATTLE OF THE THAMES
OCTOBER 1813

● Chatham

Lake Erie

NEW YORK

land
sky
nson

F FT. STEPHENSON
UGUST 1813

dusky

PENNSYLVANIA

HIO

Pittsburgh

Ohio River

MARYLAND

Washington ●

VIRGINIA

Gov. Isaac Shelby

Gen. James Winchester

American Prisoners

American Prisoners
returning from Frenchtown

𝒩

50 miles

Chapter One

HURTLING TOWARD WAR

JANUARY 29, 1812, dawned like most other days in Frankfort, Kentucky. The curling wisps of smoke that rose above the houses and businesses were signs that the population was stirring and would soon spill into the streets to go about their daily business. While not exactly the kind of city that might have impressed those who had toured the municipalities of the East, like Philadelphia, New York, or Baltimore, there was no denying that Frankfort was a city on the rise. The capital could now boast over one thousand inhabitants and its favorable position along the sometimes hazel and sometimes emerald Kentucky River ensured it was located along a presently busy trade route.[1]

Those who stepped from their doorway into the city streets would have seen a mix of people. Many men and women wore homespun and practical clothing meant to withstand the vigorous chores of day-to-day life as well as keep out the cool winds which blew off the river. The more affluent donned the latest fashions in Europe and it was not uncommon to see ladies carrying their parasols and promenading in the high-waisted Empire dresses that characterized the Napoleonic Era. Many men of the city shared in this indulgence of fashion and made their way to their destinations in suits complete with waistcoats and cravats while others donned the plainer uniform of a farmer or laborer. Regardless of what they wore, early citizens living in and around Frankfort visited the city in order to browse the more than twenty businesses that dotted the streets. Frankfort had three printers and a steady circulation for the city's primary newspaper, the *Palladium*. Mixed with these symbols of civilization that had made their way across the Appalachian Mountains were other, less savory institutions, including slavery. By 1810 over 56 percent of Frankfort families owned slaves.[2] Despite this, the state was still hailed as a land of opportunity and new settlers looking for a better life were arriving every day. Kentuckians had a right to be optimistic about their future. From 1790 and 1800 the population of the state had tripled from just short of 76,700 to over 220,000 and by 1810 there were over 400,000 residents.[3] As the population grew their power and national influence were sure to grow as well.

Though still a city of wood, Frankfort's residents could sleep relatively safe at night knowing they were protected by the six-year-old fire department that stood ready to battle any blaze.[4] Those who could were building brick homes to prevent just such an emergency and adding an additional layer of sophistication for the relatively new town. In addition to these signs of success, new government buildings began to spring up as well. There was the two-storied brick governor's mansion at the corner of Clinton and High Streets[5] as well as the somewhat medieval state penitentiary with its stone towers in front and high walls on all sides. The few windows and doors were covered in iron bars to ensure those inside remained there and served as a warning to anyone who thought about breaking the law.[6] On Sunday residents and visitors could worship in the city's new church, which was shared by Baptist, Presbyterian, and Methodist congregations.[7] There was room enough in town for the righteous, the fallen, and the political.

A lull in violence between Indians and westward bound settlers in the late 1790s was partially responsible for this rapid expansion. Contrary to popular belief, Native Americans were the one group of people who did not have a major settlement in Kentucky. Archeology suggests that centuries before, some native cultures may have lived in the bounds of Kentucky, but by the time of the American Revolution, the state was almost entirely devoid of native settlements with minor exceptions around the southern and western borders. Instead, native populations would use the state for a hunting ground from their homes in surrounding states. While the Cherokee of North Carolina often travelled in the state's southeastern corner, the tribe that expressed the greatest interest in Kentucky were the Shawnee. Situated north of the Ohio River primarily in what is now southern Indiana and Ohio, the Shawnee that remained in the area sided with the British during the American

Revolution in hopes of preventing further expansion, which did not endear them to the settlers of Kentucky.[8]

Even after the end of the American Revolution in 1783, conflict with the Shawnee had persisted and resulted in several embarrassing defeats for the Americans. This all changed in July 1794 when an American force under General "Mad" Anthony Wayne, which included 1,600 mounted volunteers from Kentucky, engaged the Shawnee at Fallen Timbers on the banks of the Maumee River. The battle proved so decisively in favor of the Americans that it marked the high-water mark of Indian incursions into Kentucky.[9]

But despite having no native tribes as permanent residents in central Kentucky, the area had long been a hunting ground for several tribes, and much of the land north of the Ohio River in the Indiana and Illinois Territories was still home to native tribes. The Shawnee and Kickapoo were two tribes who resided near the Ohio River and were a concern to early generations of Kentuckians, but farther north in the Michigan Territory were tribes like the Wyandot, Potawatomi, and Ottawa who influenced public policy as well. These tribes acted independently of each other but shared many cultural and linguistic traits. Many of the tribes in the region had begun to adopt agriculture to supplement their hunts and small Indian communities dotted the Great Lakes region as well as the Ohio Valley. The trading of furs for European goods would continue to fuel the economies of tribes in the area as they had done for more than a century before.[10] The dependence of these trade goods not only ensured constant contact but also future conflict.

These issues and more would have found their way into conversation as the legislature met behind closed doors. Since it was late January the House and Senate were in the middle of their biannual session. They had discussed the usual topics that come with building a new state from the ground up including the founding of schools and regulating river traffic. They were also mired in the middle of "quarrel[s] & Squabbles about Representation Congressional and State..." in which, one member sighed, "every one wants it arranged to suit himself."[11] But the primary topic of discussion, indeed the foremost thought in most political minds, was the looming possibility of war with Great Britain. Measures were already being taken to prepare for war by overhauling the state's militia and passing a resolution that was forwarded to the federal government affirming that the legislature considered the actions of Great Britain as an "insult to our national sovereignty."[12]

At the top of the list of grievances against the British was the accusation that they were selling weapons to the native tribes and encouraging them to attack Americans. Attacks on American settlements in the Old Northwest had been a common occurrence, but the problem had reached its peak two months before in a battle that would come to be known as Tippecanoe and was still fresh in the minds of Kentuckians as they ushered in the year 1812. The two individuals the Americans blamed more than any others were the Shawnee chief Tecumseh and his brother Tenskwatawa. Tecumseh was the older of the two and is suspected to have been born in an Indian village on the Scioto River in Ohio in the late 1760s or early 1770s. His name would be roughly translated as "shooting star."[13] The origin of the name has been debated among historians for some time with explanations ranging from the practical to mystical. Regardless of the actual reason for the name, it seemed to portend great change. Tecumseh's childhood in the volatile Ohio Valley meant he would have grown up with a firsthand knowledge of the tensions between American settlers and native tribes. While subjects of Great Britain, the colonists had been forbidden to settle in the areas west of the mountains by the Proclamation Line of 1763. The vast border meant that it was impossible to stop all settlement in the west, but American independence turned the steady, if small, flow of settlers into a flood.[14]

Fearing the loss of all Indian lands, Tecumseh reached the conclusion that only by uniting against the United States would the various tribes be able to resist further expansion. Tecumseh began to piece together a coalition of Indian nations to present a united front to the United States. His success raised alarm in western settlements and, by 1810, had brought him to the attention of leaders like William Henry Harrison, governor of the Indiana Territory. Harrison had risen rapidly and brought the energetic optimism of youth with him to the office of governor.[15] Tecumseh proved to be a natural leader as well, although nothing about his physical appearance seemed extraordinary with the exception of his height. One Kentuckian described him as a "very plain man, rather above middle size, stout build, a noble set of features and an admirable eye. He is always accompanied by six great chiefs who never go before him."[16]

But Tecumseh was only one half of a team. His brother, Tenskwatawa (or the Prophet as he would come to be known), had also become somewhat of a celebrity among tribes in the Northwest Territory. The Prophet

Portrait of Tecumseh, left, by Benson John Lossing, after a pencil sketch by French trader Pierre Le Dru at Vincennes, taken from life, c. 1808. (*From* The Pictorial Field-Book of the War of 1812 [1868]) Portrait of Tenskwatawa, the Prophet, right, by Charles Bird King, c. 1820. (*National Portrait Gallery*)

emerged as a leader among the Shawnee after falling into a fire where he was so badly wounded that he was not expected to live. After surviving the ordeal, which seemed like a miracle in itself, he began to have visions that shaped his doctrines. The Americans were evil, he taught, and the native peoples needed to purge themselves from all European influence. Clothing, foods, religion, and especially alcohol had been a blight on Indian civilization and needed to be destroyed. But if they would return to their old ways they would soon be restored. While these teachings met resistance from some, the popularity and influence of the Prophet grew.[17] The trend soon came to the notice of American officials who became alarmed that a permanent settlement might spring up in the area around Greenville and they put pressure on the Prophet to move farther west.[18]

This they did and, in 1808, they relocated to a spot near the confluence of the Wabash and Tippecanoe Rivers just north of modern-day West Lafayette, Indiana, in a settlement that came to be known as Prophetstown. A famine in 1809 caused the Prophet to seek assistance from the American government, which it received via Governor Harrison.[19] Despite these brief, hopeful signs of cooperation, by 1810, relations between the two sides had gone from bad to worse and Harrison offered to meet with Tecumseh to quell rumors of possible violence due to the recent purchase of tribal lands by the American government. Arriving at the meeting surrounded by "several hundred warriors" Tecumseh made his presence known. He began by admonishing Harrison for the purchase of the lands stating that they were all held in common by the native nations and could not be bought or sold by a single tribe. Harrison pointed out that the Indians had, like their European and American counterparts, divided into differing tribes with different languages and that they had almost nothing in common. If one tribe wanted to sell the lands they lived and hunted on they could not be prevented from doing so. This angered Tecumseh and he and his warriors rose and grabbed their hatchets and clubs. Harrison sprang to his feet as well and drew his saber. A guard of thirteen men rushed to Harrison's side and for a tense moment it looked like there would be bloodshed. Harrison broke off the negotiations and Tecumseh led his seething warriors away, leaving both sides with the feeling that conflict was now inevitable.[20]

The following year was filled with reports of isolated homesteads being attacked and the inhabitants killed in "Indiana, Illinois and Missouri territories."[21] Additional meetings were held but with few results. Finally, petitions from the scared citizens of the territory found their way to Washington and President James Madison, who placed the 4th United States Infantry under Harrison's command. Harrison was to gather additional militia units and do whatever it took to protect the frontier settlements. This included eliminating Prophetstown, the headquarters of Tecumseh's alliance, if need be. Word spread quickly into Kentucky where a number of volunteers crossed the Ohio to join Harrison, and by late September Harrison was on the march north with around nine hundred men. The party stopped in American territory and sent word through Delaware and Miami emissaries. The appeals they carried were immediately rejected. As things went from bad to worse Harrison began erecting a fort to house the sick and supplies that would become Fort Harrison.[22]

By November 6, the army was within two miles of Prophetstown and preparing for hostilities. Ambassadors from the Prophet, Tecumseh being absent from the town at the time, entered the camp and feigned confusion as to why Harrison was marching on their town. Both sides agreed to meet the next morning and Harrison had his men make camp.[23] At four the next morning, only a few officers and men were awake and preparing for the day when a sentry fired his rifle. The shot was followed by a collective yell from the darkness and immediately a multitude of figures rose from the shadows and rushed the camp. The Prophet had lied about the meeting and now he was launching a surprise attack.[24] Harrison quickly waded into the battle to save his army from annihilation but not before it suffered casualties. The end result was the burning of Prophetstown and retreat of the Prophet and his followers into the wilderness beyond. The battle could hardly be called a great victory for the Americans if it was a victory at all. But to many Americans as well as Indians, it was proof that a great conflict lay on the horizon.

To many in the trans-Appalachian region this was a great victory. For the moment, the greatest threat to their way of life had been checked. The legislature applauded the actions of Harrison and passed a resolution commending those who had participated and commemorating those who had fallen, some of whom were fellow Kentuckians. Praising the "brave deeds of our Officers and Soldiers in the late Battle on the Wabash" the legislature declared that everyone in the chambers would wear "crape on their arms" for the next thirty days.[25]

The fear of Indian attacks would continue to increase. The lull in fighting that had resulted after the campaigns of General Wayne in the 1790s was coming to an end. Now new native threats were arising and many Americans began to suspect that they were being motivated by familiar enemies with their own agenda. Were the British arming the Indians from Canada? Was it possible British officials had been dispersed among the native tribes as agents to incite violence against American settlements? This would certainly slow American expansion and would keep the fledgling, cash-strapped nation busy, leaving Britain to pursue her own aims in the region. The *Kentucky Gazette* printed reports from all quarters of the frontier about Indian disturbances. Kentuckians who bought the April 7 edition would have been appalled to read the report from Fort Madison which assured them:

> The Indians are no doubt stimulated by the BRITISH to acts of such horrid barbarity. Several Americans have escaped death by telling the savages that they were ENGLISHMEN. The Indians have said that the English gave them a HIGH PRICE for every AMERICAN SCALP they would bring them.[26]

This affirmation of British interference circulated more and more frequently and what had been distrustful disdain boiled into calls for

war. To many, the present situation was a simple case of meeting fire
with fire. War was the only answer, and if an outbreak of war was inevitable, could there be a better time? Britain was engaged in a protracted
war with Napoleonic France, which meant they would have their hands
full and would probably sacrifice Canada to defend their interests in Europe. "A War with the United States at this time, would be to the British
the most disastrous thing that could happen; for if they support Russia
against France they cannot efficiently defend Canada" one contributor
to the *Kentucky Gazette* argued.[27]

But Indian attacks were only part of the problem. There was also the
issue of impressment. Following the Revolution, the British had maintained the right to stop American vessels and search them for deserters
from the Royal Navy. This obvious insult to American sovereignty did
not do much to endear the British to the public, but the matter soon
gave rise to even more bitter objections when British sea captains began
using the rule as an excuse to steal American seamen to fill vacancies in
their crew. The whole problem had begun in earnest in 1805 when the
British Admiralty, in an attempt to strangle the French economy, ordered
the capture of all goods being shipped from French colonies in the
Caribbean to anywhere in the world and favored impressments of English sailors who were sailing on foreign ships as deserters from the Royal
Navy.[28] As one of the few independent nations in the Western Hemisphere at the time, this desperately hurt American commerce, further
isolating the new country, and was interpreted by many as an unjust
provocation. The practice of impressment was even more odious to
Americans, as the interpretation of evidence on whether an individual
was "British" or not was left to the captains of each vessel and many interpreted the evidence very loosely indeed. While the law could have
been applied to any nation it was most often practiced on the fledgling
American merchant fleet. As a result, President Thomas Jefferson ordered the construction of a large number of gunboats to defend American harbors from attack.[29]

It was not difficult to see how such an issue could give the wives of
American seamen many sleepless nights or cause any number of merchants and ship owners to anxiously pace their floors until news of the
safe arrival of their cargo and crew made its way back to them. But surely
such an issue would be of little interest to Kentuckians unless they feared
that impressment would harm their ability to get their crops to foreign
ports once they had snaked down the Ohio and Mississippi Rivers to

New Orleans. Public sentiment would soon prove this was not the case. Angry citizens took each impressment as a personal affront to their country, leading the Kentucky state legislature to declare "The state of Kentucky, yielding to none in patriotism" felt the suffering of their fellow Americans too.[30] This sort of sentiment highlighted the changes taking place in Kentucky during the period. This undeveloped and fertile land, which had long been a favorite with the few fur trappers who were brave enough to wander into its uncharted forests and canebrakes, was now a vibrant community.

Pioneer and surveyor John Filson wrote the first history of the state of Kentucky in 1784 entitled *The Discovery, Settlement and Present State of Kentucke*. The book was more of a sales pitch for the area than a history but would become immensely popular. It would even eventually become a hit in Europe. The book described the fertile soil and mild seasons while also introducing the public to the iconic Daniel Boone. Filson's action-packed account not only drew people to the state but also formed the basis for the legend of the frontiersmen as a special breed dedicated to absolute freedom who were independent, hardy, and ready to take justice into their own hands. However, by the turn of the nineteenth century, Kentucky felt very comfortable as a part of the American community and had shed some of its wild and wooly reputation. Those seeking solitude and the wild had moved on. Even the legendary Daniel Boone had left Kentucky for areas west of the Mississippi River.[31] What was left was the framework of a society tied together by the need for a common defense and the desire for a better life. These were not isolated individuals but families that had an interest in the world around them and who had an immense pride in their country. As historian Ellery Hall puts it, the state's people were "naturally independent, and ambitious to expand and make the most of the opportunities about them—and opportunity to most frontiersmen meant land. The pioneers of these open spaces produced a rude but sincere democracy that became enthusiastically nationalistic and expansionist."[32]

It had expanded from the mountains in the east to the Tennessee River in the west and had formed 58 of its eventual 120 counties and each boasted a functioning local government that was issuing marriage licenses, recording deeds and wills, collecting taxes, and trying cases in court. This is not to say that Kentucky did not have its own peculiar brand of justice. Former state laureate Dr. Tom Clark accurately writes that "Early Kentuckians were a simple-living, conscientious people, among whom crimes received immediate punishment." Horse stealing was a capital offense in Kentucky.[33] It was not uncommon for a chicken thief to receive a longer prison sentence than a man who committed murder—provided the murderer had a justifiable reason for doing so. Kentucky society "was based on virtues of bravery, courage, stamina, directness to the point of crudeness, and nonromantic notions about Indians and the destruction of a wilderness by settlement."[34]

Now that sense of union would confront the present increasingly dangerous situation and would well up and burst forth in the highly charged speeches of lawmakers in Frankfort. Newspapers printed articles on the subject while lawyers, farmers, and merchants debated the dangers of the day with their peers. The Revolution had ended less than thirty years before and the mistrust and disdain of the British government still burned in the memory of the public, which only fanned the flames of mistrust. Lengthy letters between American and British representatives were printed in local papers and the occasional remarks on the subject from members of Congress only fueled the rise of patriotism and righteous indignation.

A public consensus seemed to suggest that action had to be taken to stop the British from their hostile attempts to arm the Indians and interfere with American shipping. Kentucky's representatives and other western "war hawks" in Congress increased their call for action against the injustice of British practices. Richard M. Johnson in Congress called on other representatives to protect his constituents from Indian aggression which, he confidently pointed out, was primarily incited by British agents. If skeptics in Congress needed proof, Kentucky "had even now before their eyes widows and orphans who had lost their dearest companions by this influence and hostility."[35] Whether this kind of rhetoric convinced Johnson's fellow congressmen is unclear, however, it certainly played well with the electorate. When the results came in for the election of 1810, 70 members of the 142-person chamber were new, and many had war fever to credit for their victory.[36]

As Kentucky representative Henry Clay entered the halls of Congress it became obvious that the commonwealth was not the only state to feel this way. Many of his fellow representatives, particularly from the South and West, were young and staunch (as well as vocal) supporters of declaring war. This had to provide a sense of satisfaction to Clay who, with other members of the war hawks, had drug the hesitant President Madison slowly toward conflict. Clay's reputation as an orator preceded him

Kentucky representative Henry Clay, left, painted in 1818 by Matthew Harris Jouett. (*Transylvania University*) President James Madison, right, engraved by David Edwin in 1810 from a Thomas Sully portrait. (*New York Public Library*)

and his natural affability soon resulted in his election as Speaker of the House at only thirty-four years old.[37] Despite the reservations of some in Congress and the Madison administration, Kentuckian Aylett Hawes seemed confident that "Hostile measures have almost entirely occupied the attention of Congress. Unless Great Britain relinquishes her orders in Council, War seems to be almost unavoidable."[38]

Clay had wasted no time preparing for war as he strategically placed fellow war hawks in key positions in various committees that would speed the nation's push to action.[39] In April 1812, Congress took the first concrete step toward conflict with Great Britain by passing an embargo against British shipping and had authorized a detachment of up to one hundred thousand militia for six months. President Madison responded by requesting up to 1,200 Ohio militia men who were to rendezvous at Vincennes by the twenty-ninth of the month.[40]

The militia system was the pride and joy of early American society and one of the few social obligations that held the community together. The idea of the citizen leaving his plough behind to rescue his countrymen and then returning to it once more seemed like the ideal defense. After all, who would fight harder for their homes than the inhabitants themselves? Still, even the sons of liberty would need training. With this in mind every part of the state was laid off into regiments and as soon as a young man turned eighteen he was expected to participate.[41] The

only exceptions to this included judges, state officials, professors at sem-
inaries, clergy, and a few other very small groups.[42] Militia training made
regular appearances on the calendar of every Kentuckian. Each company
of soldiers would muster four times a year (April, June, August, and September) where they would drill for three hours a day. In May of each
year the companies within a battalion would meet to drill and in October
the whole regiment would meet.[43]

While the American rifleman remains the iconic symbol of the defenders of the early republic in the west, the standard firearm for an
American at the time was actually the much cheaper "model of 1795"
musket. It had a smaller caliber than the musket used by the British but
it was lighter for those long marches on dirt roads or forest trails and it
was more accurate—a quality prized by the American who favored firing
one accurate shot and then falling back, while the British favored several
shots en masse.[44] There were also differences in training and battlefield
formation. British infantry would often form in two ranks where the
Americans formed in three. This was partly due to the fact that the
United States was still using Baron von Steuben's 1799 "Blue Book."
Steuben had trained Washington's Revolutionary Army and had created
a reputation that few could match. But while the Americans remained
constant, British tactics were adapting and evolving constantly on the
battlefields of Europe.[45]

In America, military costume had evolved much more than tactics.
Military service was seen as a valuable responsibility of every free man
in the community and, as such, it was celebrated with a level of patriotic
pomp that rivaled the esprit de corps of any professional army in Europe.
The parading of the local militia would have been a sight worth seeing
for most nineteenth-century Americans and was often described in great
detail by newspapers. Generals in their blue coats with broad tan (or
"buff" to use the terminology of the day), gold epaulets, black hats with
cockade and plume, and ceremonial swords would have watched as field
officers in suits of blue with red lapels and silver epaulets barked orders
to their men and attempted to correct their failings. Other kinds of units
including riflemen, light infantry, cavalry, and artillery were allowed to
wear the uniform decided on by their unit, which varied greatly.[46]

In Lexington in 1811, drills took place in front of the hotel at 10 a.m.
sharp. The regiment would assemble and, in front of the onlookers, companies would be formed before the drills commenced. The aim was to
get the gaggle of farmers, merchantmen, and laborers to move in unison,

which was as difficult then as it would be today. Men repeatedly practiced marching in columns, forming lines of battle, firing their weapons
on command, and adding their bayonets in preparation of a charge
against the enemy. The cavalcade of humanity shuffled along as officers
called out "Support arms! Halt! Carry arms" and several other commands. Of course there was also the necessity of maintaining some
morale, and thus uniforms were inspected and the positions in which to
hold a sword were critiqued.[47]

Of course, this system also had its downside. Each state's force oper-
ated under its own commanders and its own rules with the governor at
its head. Many states could not order their militias across state lines unless they had the consent of the soldiers themselves. While all adult free
men were expected to participate in the militia drills they were permitted
to hire substitutes to go in their places when battle called. This practice
meant the lines were often filled with men whose motivation was the
payment of a debt rather than the defense of their community. Others
felt the militia was an excellent tool to advance their political careers. In
an age when martial status was so important, sharing the same dangers
and hardships of the men who would be voting in the next election was
an important prerequisite to holding office. The result was an army that
could be assembled quickly at low costs to handle local threats, but that
was also a far cry from the mechanical war machines of Napoleonic Europe.[48]

But with enough drilling, even the most uncoordinated members of
the community could improve and, with this training and the mythol-
ogized role of the militia in the Revolution, many Americans were confident they would be able to strike at Britain, or any other enemy for
that matter, when the time came. Of course, if war with Britain did come
it would have to be conducted against her weaker more vulnerable
colonies and not the island fortress itself. Even the most optimistic
American would acknowledge that sailing three thousand miles across
the ocean to engage the world's most powerful military in its own back-
yard would be a disaster and of little help in quelling the unrest among
the natives. If war commenced it would be fought in Canada. After all,
it was from there that Britain was selling weapons to the tribes that were
hostile to the United States, and the removal of Britain's largest remaining colonial possession in the Western Hemisphere, with all its natural
resources, particularly the wood that would be so useful in mainlining
the Royal Navy, would be far more devastating to the Crown in the long

term than the sinking of any man-of-war. In addition, the fact that the Union Jack flew over Canada had left a bad taste in American mouths since the Revolution. It fluttered like a defiant reminder that the Revolution had not been entirely successful in sweeping despotism and monarchy from North America. Had the battle of Quebec been successful during the Revolution it was likely that Canada would have also been part of the growing American confederation.

Americans, Canadians, and the British all understood that Canada lay in the crosshairs should hostilities break out and the first target was just as obvious: Ontario. Sharing a very long border with the United States that stretched from New York to the Michigan Territory, it seemed logical to strike at this agriculturally rich area, cutting the British off from powerful tribes living around the Great Lakes, especially Tecumseh and his growing confederation, and providing a staging ground for the capture of places like Quebec.

This meant that a good deal of the conflict would be settled in the state of Ohio as well as the Indiana, Illinois, and Michigan Territories, collectively known as the Old Northwest. It would need a commander who could be respected and whose charisma would rally men with a sense of purpose even when fighting so far from home. President Madison, who had a well-deserved reputation as a bookworm and thorough researcher, considered his choices carefully. One Kentucky legislator had commented on the uncanny resemblance between Madison and his writings. Both were "short, pithy, sensible & distinguished."[49] There was some truth to the lighthearted description. Madison approached each challenge like a master chess player, paying attention to minute details. After considerable thought, Madison made his move, tapping former revolutionary William Hull. From this strategic and clinical point of view Hull seemed like a good choice. He had served in the American Revolution at battles known to every American schoolboy, including Trenton and Saratoga.[50] Who better to continue fighting the British than someone who had experience doing so in the past? Of course, Hull was much older now and the days of his active service were a distant memory. Nevertheless, the old general packed up his family and began the long journey back to the Michigan Territory. It was a daunting task that lay before him. He would be the first line of defense against British aggression.

Hull had been assured that American control of Lake Erie would be firmly established and that his small army would receive reinforcements before war was declared so his task would not be as daunting as it at first seemed. This second assurance seemed to bear fruit as he picked up to 1,200 militia from Governor Meigs of Ohio at Dayton and 300 troops from the 4th United States Infantry.[51] Having arrived in Dayton, Ohio, five days earlier, General Hull took command of three regiments of Ohio militia, totaling 1,200 men. These men would form the basis for the army that would conquer Upper Canada. On June 1, Hull's force marched from Dayton through Urbana toward Maumee Rapids.[52]

As news of these advances to war reached Kentucky, support for the war reached its zenith and Governor Charles Scott worked to organize the state for the coming conflict. At the age of seventy-three, Charles Scott had a lot to recommend him for the position he held. Born in eastern Virginia in 1739, and orphaned at a young age, Scott had come to rely on his own judgment early in life. Joining the French and Indian War at age sixteen, he had distinguished himself as an able commander. When the drums of war sounded again in 1775, Scott left his farm to join the rebels in fighting for independence. His military prowess earned him a colonelcy in the Fifth Virginia Regiment. After the war, Scott moved to Kentucky and, in 1808, was elected governor. However, like Hull, those early days of military glory were buried in the past, and Scott was now an old man. Still sound in mind but weaker in body, Scott had taken a bad fall on the steps of the governor's mansion, which left him on crutches. Despite the frustration of his lack of mobility, he was now called on to wield his pen instead of his sword as the state geared up for war.[53]

His address to the legislature the year before had been one of resigned determination rather than fiery passion. "While half the inhabitants of our Globe are in arms, staining the earth with each other's blood, it was perhaps to[o] much to expect their convulsive spasms should not, in some degree, be felt on our remote and peaceful shores" he lamented. "Justice, as well as policy, dictated the pacific course our Government has endeavored to pursue." But France and Britain had been trying to draw America into their incessant conflict and both had done harm to the young nation. What other course was left America except to raise her sword in defense? America had two choices: "Force" or "unqualified submission."[54] It was bad enough that American trade had suffered from the harassment of the Royal Navy on distant shores, but they have grown so brazen as to attack vessels within sight of the American mainland. Then there were the poor captured sailors who were "taken and condemned, like Galley Slaves, to man their ships and to slaughter their brethren."[55]

Recalling the recent battle of Tippecanoe, Scott had yet another threat to fear. Echoing the sentiments of the legislature Scott reminded his listeners that the governor of Indiana "was attacked treacherously on the night of the 6th of November last, by a large party of Indians." They had repulsed them but at a cost that was heavy.[56] All else had been tried and there were no other alternatives. "The Spirit of '76 has too long slumbered—Let it again breathe in our councils & animate the children of worthy sires." Yes, the battle would be difficult, but it would divide "the chaff from the wheat."[57] As for his own career, he admitted "I look forward to the end of my public course; and indeed to the termination of my earthly career, which cannot be far distant, with a tranquility not unmingled with anxiety for the future destinies of my country."[58]

However, he had one final bit of advice. He had asked the adjutant general of the state's militia to make suggestions on how to improve the system. The report that he had received was discouraging. It was almost impossible to know where to begin. Every man between age eighteen and forty-five was designated a member of the militia. However, this only served to drain whole communities of their manpower during drills. Would it not be better to divide the militia into groups by age and only force those in the prime of their lives to meet and drill regularly? This would be quicker and more efficient. Aside from this issue there was the severe lack of arms and military equipment and the failure of officers to submit accurate returns. The necessary paperwork for running a successful army was becoming a victim of an extensive chain of command that governed the militia.[59]

The legislature applauded Scott's attention to the militia and acknowledged in a grandiose fashion that "The time has perhaps arrived when some of the people of Kentucky will have to exchange the plowshare for the musket—the peaceful happy fireside for the soldier's tent—domestic joys and comforts for the dangers and vicissitudes of war." They had not been able to make all of the changes advised by Scott and the adjutant general but they had made some and that would surely be an improvement. Either way they would have to do.[60]

On the twenty-sixth of April, an American general by the name of James Winchester arrived in Lexington with orders to recruit men to defend the Old Northwest.[61] Frankfort may have been the state capital, but Lexington was a much larger community with more to offer. Around four times larger than Frankfort, Lexington could boast the state's first university (Transylvania University), churches, and a number of shops that sold anything the nineteenth century palate could desire, including cheese, raisins, chocolate, oysters, cinnamon, mustard, nutmeg, coffee, and lime juice. For those under the weather there were options as well. A sickly customer could choose between the infamous castor oil and the more pleasant essence of peppermint. It was also becoming easier to acquire real luxury symbols like glass panes for windows.[62] By 1789, Lexington had a racetrack and by 1800 the citizens could enjoy a "theatrical perform-

Charles Scott, at the time of the American Revolution. (*New York Public Library*)

ance" on the steps of the courthouse. For the athletic type, there were dancing and fencing schools while the more academic members of the community could take courses at Transylvania University.[63] And as a true symbol of their urban status, Lexingtonians received what may be the state's first restriction on pets within city limits when an early ordinance for the city "Prohibited citizens of the town from keeping pet panthers."[64]

From this center of commerce and people, Winchester should have had no trouble recruiting soldiers. He soon found that, with support for the war being so vehement, all he had to do was wait and let them come to him. Recruiting officers throughout the state began sending recruits to meet him. In May 1812, the guidelines for recruitment and the requirements to enlist were printed in the *Kentucky Gazette*. All volunteers had to be free of sicknesses like "sore legs, scurvy, scalled heads, ruptures, and other infirmities," but as long as they were healthy, boys as young as fourteen could be enlisted if they had parental consent.[65]

By late May, there were suggestions of war on every corner. On May 21, the 42nd Kentucky Militia marched through Lexington before being addressed in a fiery speech by John Crittenden. As the speech came to an end, the roll of drums commenced as a sign for volunteers to step forward to defend their country. Ninety-four men were needed to fill the quota. Two hundred and twelve volunteered. On the twenty-sixth of May, readers of the *Kentucky Gazette* could hear about the dangerous Indian movements in the Illinois Territory, the activation of militia to battle hostile Indians in Tennessee, and a letter from Governor William

Henry Harrison, of the Indiana Territory, to Governor Scott of Kentucky stating that the American settlement of Vincennes was in danger of being overrun. Each new speech, toast, or article either warned of danger all around or extolled the virtues of those who would rise to defend their country.[66] Even the weary traveler, wishing to take in some entertainment and forget about the impending war, would have been disappointed to find that the featured Saturday night entertainment in Lexington was a play entitled *John Bull*, which was a satirical comedy being put on by the volunteers from a light infantry regiment who were using the admission to purchases arms and supplies for their unit.[67]

But not everyone was as keen on the idea of war. Ironically, President James Madison, the man whose name would forever be connected with the war, had worked tirelessly to prevent it. A series of letters flew back and forth across the Atlantic carrying negotiations between the Madison administration and the Crown. As long as there was any hope of a peaceful resolution, Madison clung to it, turning a deaf ear temporarily to the war hawks who claimed that impressment was only a precursor to enslavement. But his efforts had been in vain. By late March, Madison had received word that the British intended to continue stopping American ships at sea. An exasperated Madison finally gave in and began to prepare for war.[68]

Congress seemed receptive to declaring war but not necessarily to paying for it. For one thing, the United States would need to beef up its defenses. With almost every man of fighting age being enrolled in their local militia, manpower did not appear to be a problem, even if there was some debate about whether the militia could be ordered on to the British soil of Canada. American sea power, however, was another story. With a coastline stretching from the rocky shores of modern-day Maine to the white sands and swampy enclaves of the Gulf Coast, a sizeable navy would be necessary to keep the British navy at bay. There were smaller vessels, of course, but these would be swept aside by a British man-of-war. The navy would need to expand and expand rapidly. Congress took up a bill for twelve "ships of the line" and ten frigates. But when the estimated cost of this expansion came in at $50 million the plan was doomed. In the spring of 1812, the United States had a total of five frigates ready to sail and five more which, with significant work, could be made seaworthy again. But even here, the budget for repairs was cut by more than 60 percent.[69]

On June 13, a letter arrived for the president. It was from Lord Castlereagh, Britain's secretary of state for foreign affairs. As Madison read though each line, the answer to his latest entreaties became clear. There would be no compromise.[70] Despite severe opposition from New England, Congress voted for war on June 18, and President Madison signed the bill the same day. The United States was at war.[71] Around three in the afternoon the news was released to the public. However, it was not until July 7 that it reached many citizens of Kentucky through Lexington's *Kentucky Gazette*. The message from Madison was characteristically matter of fact and very detailed, beginning somewhat unceremoniously. "I communicate to Congress certain documents," Madison had stated, "being a continuation of those heretofore laid before them, on the subject of our affairs with Great Britain." Madison continued to lay the groundwork for the grievances the United States had with Britain.[72]

The impressment of sailors led the list. Not only was it a violation of American sovereignty for British ships to stop American vessels to search for deserters from the British navy, but it was enraging to consider that many of the individuals taken from American ships were Americans. "The practice, therefore, is so far from affecting British subjects alone, that under the pretext of searching for these, thousands of American citizens, under the safeguard of public law, and of their national flag, have been torn from their country and from everything dear to them."[73]

Madison went on to argue that the poor unfortunate sailor who was forced onto a British ship of the line would find his hardships just beginning. They would be forced to work in difficult conditions, suffer severe punishments, and fight for a foreign nation at the most remote corners of the globe. Madison highlighted that, if the same outrageous actions were taken against the British, they would have instantly moved to punish the guilty. The United States, however, had held back time and time again only to be rewarded with more of the same. To make the situation worse, the British navy had become so brazen as to linger just off shore of America's busiest ports to intimidate merchant vessels as they came and went. Madison turned his attention to the American frontiers. Indian attacks were on the rise, and it was suspected that British representatives to the tribes were encouraging the attacks. The attacks were not just waged against American militia but old and young, men and women found themselves victims of these atrocities.[74] Word of the conflict would take weeks to reach Great Britain. Without knowledge that war had begun, Britain's Parliament repealed the orders-in-council on the twentieth of June. Impressment, the primary justification for war, had been removed before the first shot was fired.[75]

On June 30, the news finally wound its way to Kentucky and was instantly celebrated. Anyone not in the immediate area when the news arrived could have guessed it by the constant musket and cannon fire that echoed through the towns of the bluegrass into the evening hours. The *Lexington Gazette* summed up the attitude of the nation and certainly the state of Kentucky by exclaiming that "the citizens saw their country a SECOND time declared independent."[76] Kentucky's representatives in the House had voted unanimously for the war. In the Senate, however, John Pope achieved the distinction of being the only member of the commonwealth's delegation to vote against the war, arguing that it should also have been declared against France, which was equally guilty of violating America's sovereignty.[77] Pope's reasoning did not sway his fellow Kentuckians and his decision to oppose the war led his popularity among his fellow Kentuckians to plummet. By mid-July his anti-war stance had led to his effigy being shot and burned in the city of Mount Sterling.[78]

Despite support for the war in the western states and territories, Madison's government began attempts at reconciliation immediately. In a letter to his British counterpart, Secretary of State James Monroe explained that "If the orders in council are repealed, and no illegal blockades are substituted for them, and orders are given to discontinue the impressment of seamen from our vessels, and to restore those already impressed, there is no reason why hostilities should not immediately cease."[79] The government in Washington had no way of knowing the Orders in Council had been repealed already and, thus, one of the main causes of the war had been resolved before the conflict had started. When word reached Governor General in Council George Prevost in Quebec he instituted a ceasefire in an attempt to give the conflict time to resolve itself.[80]

Fearing that the peace would not hold, both sides continued their preparations for war. This was no easy task for Governor Scott. He had plenty of volunteers to fill the ranks, but supplying them was another matter. Word from the federal arsenal in Newport arrived in August that there were few supplies stored up, and camp equipage for the Kentucky militia who would, presumably, march north very soon, would have to be made from scratch. The Revolutionary War veteran must have re-called the infrequent and irregular supplies from battles almost forty years before and winced. The fact that war was inevitable had been clear, at least to those in the west, for months now. Was it possible that the federal government had neglected to make basic preparations for necessities like kettles and tents?[81]

The reality was there had never been enough supplies to begin with. General James Taylor had been designated as the quartermaster and pay-master for troops around the Newport Barracks, which served as a major supply hub for supplies in the west. Situated strategically at the conver-gence of the Licking and Ohio Rivers, the barracks/arsenal could easily transport supplies down into Kentucky, Ohio, Indiana, Illinois, and east-ern Missouri. When war broke out and the call for troops went forward Taylor took survey of his miniscule inventory. He had almost nothing in the way of supplies and the arms stored at the barracks were poorly constructed. Taylor tried to remedy the situation by sending word to Lexington that he would purchase ammunition and lots of sturdy cloth to have tents made.[82] War had seemed like a foregone conclusion to many for well over a year and little had been done to prepare for it.

As the armistice ended on the eighth of September, the Americans found themselves little more prepared than they had been the month before. The British were still far away in Canada, but their allies were not and the thought that an Indian war party might cross the Ohio into Kentucky at any time was a nerve-wracking one. The war would now begin in earnest and the British would not be taken unaware. Sensing that things were escalating, the Canadian Parliament had approved the raising of two thousand militia in May 1812, but the total was later raised to four thousand by Governor General George Prevost. A portion of the force would be sent home each year where they would form a reserve. Their position would be filled by new men who would be trained and would act alongside veteran militia. This prevented the military require-ment from becoming too onerous and diffused knowledge on martial practices throughout the general population. Should the reserve units need to be called up at any time, the experience would not be new to them.[83]

In Prevost, the British had a leader who could boast some experience in the New World. Prevost was Swiss born but his father had faithfully served the Crown in several minor offices in the British government. Prevost himself had served in Dominica and Martinique and held the post of Lieutenant-Governor of Nova Scotia before ascending to the rank of Governor-General of Canada in 1811.[84] If the Americans were coming, he would do everything in his power to make sure he was ready for them.

Chapter Two

DANGER IN DETROIT

T HINGS WERE LOOKING UP for William Beall for the first time since leaving Kentucky. When war was announced Beall had signed up to fight and enthusiastically left behind his home in Newport to serve in the Army of the Northwest on its way to join the aging General Hull. He was quickly promoted to assistant quartermaster general and took his place in the columns of Kentucky troops snaking their way north through the Ohio countryside with uncontainable optimism. Canada was ripe for the picking; all they had to do was get there. But marching through the undeveloped wilderness of the Ohio backcountry was no easy task. Like Kentucky, Ohio had grown rapidly in the previous decades but could still only boast a population of slightly over 230,000 residents.[1] In between these small communities lay thickly wooded countryside. Beall found himself partially responsible for getting supplies for the coming campaign over the many miles that lay ahead with few or no roads to guide him or even provide much of a welcome break from thick underbrush. As the column trudged on they arrived in Ohio's northwestern corner not far from the Michigan Territory. The ground was becoming swampy, which would have made each footfall that much heavier. Slogging through the marshes was hard enough on its own, but when the army sought fresh water to replenish their strength, all they could find was water that "flowed as yellow as saffron."[2]

Despite the unending and seemingly unchanging scenery there were sparks of martial glamour. Any time a town appeared in the distance, the column swiftly struck up the fifes in true military fashion for the benefit of the citizens.[3] Yes, soldiering had its good points. If misery loves company Beall did at least have the comfort of knowing he was not the only member of his community stuck in the limbo between home and military glory. Among those marching north from Newport was James Taylor, Beall's superior and one of his hometown's more well-connected neighbors. Taylor had left his unenviable post at Newport's arsenal at the request of Ohio governor Return Johnathan Meigs and had accepted the position of quartermaster general.[4] By July 1, they had met up with Hull's army and were preparing for the last leg of their march to Detroit. The most difficult part of the march was behind them. Their perseverance meant they had discarded the seemingly omnipresent smell of stagnant water and the unchanging view of untamed wilderness for the fresh breezes and stunning vistas provided by the shore of Lake Erie. If Beall and Taylor felt any sense of accomplishment at having made their rendezvous it must have been tempered by the cost. A quick glance over the columns revealed not only their exhausted fellow soldiers but the weakened draft animals as well. They needed a rest if they were going to make it to Detroit alive.[5]

Not long after their arrival on the shores of Erie, Taylor found himself summoned to General Hull. He probably responded without much thought. As quartermaster, it was necessary for Taylor to stay in constant contact with Hull as they worked to supply the army. But if Taylor had expected this meeting to be like the others, he was mistaken. Weaving his way through the rows of tents and exhausted soldiers, Taylor found Hull in the middle of a conversation with someone he did not know. Noticing Taylor's arrival, Hull explained that the man was an old acquaintance of his named Captain Chapin. Chapin owned a small ship on Lake Erie and he had come to meet Hull and to strike up a business deal. Hull explained to Taylor that he thought it best to send as much baggage as possible to Detroit by water. The sick could go, too. This would allow the army to move faster, lighten the load of the poor worn-out animals, and give the ill time to rest. Taylor was to be in charge of arranging the contract. Hull and Chapin must have been surprised when a somewhat stunned Taylor refused immediately. Place the majority of the army's supplies and baggage—along with its sick and helpless—on an unarmed merchant vessel with the British just a few miles across the lake on the Canadian shore and with the possibility of war at any moment? That would surely invite disaster.[6] Either out of annoyance at

being challenged by one of his officers or out
of a truly naïve optimism, Hull waved off
Taylor's concern's nonchalantly. As long as
the vessel stayed near the American side of
Lake Erie it would be fine. Taylor disagreed
again, pointing out that the British were not
without spies and were probably already
aware of their presence. To sail onto the lake
unprotected would be sailing into the mouth
of the lion.[7]

"I know Capt. Chapin well," Hull in-
sisted, "and the boat can pass on the American [side] of the Grosskill." The Grosskill
was the largest of a series of islands located
off the American shoreline in Lake Erie.
Hull was confident they afforded plenty of

William Hull by Gilbert Stuart, c. 1823. (*National Portrait
Gallery*)

protection from the prying eyes of British ships if, indeed, there were
any in the area to begin with. Taylor refused a third time and a somewhat
displeased Hull became fed up with the conversation. Turning to one of
his aides-de-camp Hull ordered him to work out the details, and with
that the decision was made. Before long a steady parade of supplies
began making their way on Chapin's ship. Hull had almost everything
not carried on the back of the soldiers placed on board, from raw steel,
tools, medical supplies, to the personal effects of officers. If Taylor had
been watching the action he would have observed his own baggage being
loaded on board with the rest, and while he had retained enough clothing and supplies to make the march to Detroit, the other comforts he
had brought from home slowly made their way onto the vessel. Lament-
ing the situation before him, Taylor must have observed the bitter irony
of having carefully packed certain luxuries from Kentucky and seeing
them safely carried across the entire state of Ohio only to be wrested
from him in an unnecessary gamble by an overly careless general. Running through the inventory in his mind (and later in his journal) Taylor
remembered the "groceries, tea, coffee, chocolate, sugar, spices, and half
bushel of parched corn meal . . . keg of spirits and vinegar . . . and another
trunk of clothes" that all disappeared into the hull of Chapin's boat. But
Taylor was not giving up that easily. His uneasiness refused to leave and
he finally ordered his assistant Beall to accompany the supplies.[8]

It took some time to finish preparing the vessel, but by two in the morning everything was in place and Captain Chapin urged his boat away from the shore and onto the placid waves of the lake. Taylor and the rest of the army under Hull's command were in their tents trying to rest as much as they could before resuming their march the next morning. But the thin canvas tents offered little protection against anything except mosquitos, and the sounds of the outside world pressed their way through. Taylor's senses focused when he heard the sharp challenge of one of the camp's sentinels. There was an unexpected visitor. Getting up to see what was the matter, Taylor found the sentry talking to a single man who claimed to be a messenger for General Hull. He had important dispatches that needed to be delivered immediately. Perhaps sensing something ominous, Taylor personally led the messenger through the maze of tents, boxes, and stands of arms that had not been ordered on to the ship until he reached Hull's tent. The messenger produced a letter that the general opened immediately. Reading the dispatch, Hull immediately barked out orders to convene his officers. The United States was at war.[9]

The camp was alerted and the proper precautions taken in case a British force might be lurking in the darkness, but it was too late to warn Chapin. His ship had already silently glided into the night. The question now was, did the enemy know that hostilities had begun? If they did not, then Chapin would probably get through. If they had received word, the scenario would most likely have a very different outcome.

Beall awoke on the morning of July 2, 1812, to find himself amidst a mix of people and boxes. It would take several days to reach Detroit and he had plenty of time to think and observe the ship. Chapin's vessel was a "packet"—a small three-masted vessel—named the *Cayahoga*, more than capable of gliding along the waves of the lakes. This new experience was not an unwelcome one. Beall had not emerged entirely unscathed from the swampy terrain, long marches, and an unsavory army diet. Now, instead of helping break camp and steeling himself for another long march he was sailing unencumbered toward Detroit. There were over thirty other soldiers and a few women who had been ordered on board, so there was no lack of familiar faces to keep him company.[10]

The day passed lazily as the wind pushed the *Cayahoga* northwest. By the end of the day they had already traveled eight miles. Near midnight the vessel became stuck on a shoal in shallow water but was freed within hours and Beall and his fellow passengers were back on track and enjoying the effects of a full day's rest. The sight of so much open water was a new experience for a soldier who had probably never laid eyes on a larger body of water than the Ohio River near his home. Beall was moved somewhat by the view. Taking out a journal he scratched "I had never seen such majestic waves."[11] Putting his surroundings to good use, Beall pulled out his copy of *The Lady of the Lake* by Walter Scott (only two years old at this point) and memorized a few lines while there on deck.[12] In the early morning hours of July 3, Beal was awakened from a fitful sleep by the crew of the *Cayahoga* and told they were nearing Amherstburg, Canada. This meant the *Cayahoga* was beginning its exit from the openness of the lake and entering the funnel that would eventually collapse into the Detroit River. It also meant that British territory was dangerously close. Gazing over the railing to the shore, Beall could clearly see the small town crowned by Fort Malden, which stood on the higher ground nearby. In the morning light it offered a striking contrast to the deep blue waters of Lake Erie and to Beall, "appeared beautiful . . . with its "green wheatfields . . . waving in the wind in a lovely and superior imitation of Lake Erie, and everything appeared to wear the smiles of peace and plenty."[13]

His gaze was drawn back to the water and a long slender dark object moved along its surface. Its shape suggested an Indian canoe, a common sight near the lakes, and Beall and his fellow sightseers dismissed it and returned to basking in the beauty of the summer morning. But as the vessel drew closer its shape became more defined under the morning sun and they could see it was not a canoe but a longboat manned by six sailors and a British officer. Captain Chapin noticed it too but continued on his course. It was not uncommon for ships in these remote parts to pause to exchange news with one another and Chapin welcomed the chance to parley. As the sailors stopped rowing and pulled alongside the *Cuyahoga* the passengers prepared to hail the newcomers. Looking over the side they watched the soldiers lay their oars down. When their hands reemerged into view they were holding muskets. Immediately, the soldiers took aim at Beall and the others. The officer called out to Chapin to lower the main sail immediately. The stunned Americans all stood on board unmoving and confused. What was happening? As the two sides stared at each other in silence, the British officer raised his pistol to the air and fired. The flash of the muzzle and the sound of the shot jarred the Americans to their senses and immediately the crew began lowering the sail.[14]

Even if the British had not had the element of surprise there was little Chapin and his passengers could have done. They had few arms on board and those they did have were locked away safely for the journey. In the distance a second vessel with sixty British sailors was fast approaching. There was no escape.[15] Climbing into Chapin's vessel, the British officer identified himself as Captain Rollet and immediately "expressed his regret at being compelled" to capture them. The British had received "rumors" that war had been declared but were still skeptical. Until the truth could be ascertained Rollet lamented that he would have to hold them under arrest. However, if the rumors proved false he would release them immediately. If true, they would be prisoners of war. Once on land, Rollet arranged for the women, boys, and some of the baggage (though certainly not all) to be forwarded under a flag of truce to Hull in Detroit. Beall and the other men were taken across the lake to Canada.[16] Hull and his army had arrived safely in Detroit on July 5. The loss of the men and supplies on the *Cuyahoga* was certainly lamentable, not to mention embarrassing. However, on the bright side, the rest of the Northwest Army had reached Detroit with their arms and with relatively few losses. For the moment, they were safe.[17]

Still in its infancy, Detroit was a growing settlement. It could now boast a population of 700 residents and 160 homes, not to mention the public buildings. Overshadowing the village was Fort Detroit. Perched on higher ground behind the town like a medieval castle, it gave a sweeping view of the Detroit River, which glistened a few hundred yards to the west and marked the border with Canada. The troops found that, while not overly large (the fort only contained around two acres), it was certainly formidable in its defenses. Any force attacking the fort would be forced to charge up the incline while the force inside harassed them with cannon and small arms. Before reaching the fort, they would have to cross a ditch that was bristling with pickets. Any enemy able to reach the other side of the ditch in the face of these obstacles and the constant fire from the fort would be forced to contend with a second row of pickets ringing the fort. [18]

Soldiers resting inside the walls of Fort Detroit had a right to be confident. It would take more than a few Canadian militia or British infantrymen with muskets and rifles to force their way in. But if the fort itself offered some comfort, the sweeping view outside the walls would have given a very different feeling. To the east lay the Detroit River and then the edge of enemy territory. It was true that many Canadians along the border may welcome being made part of the United States, but many would not, and there were still the British regulars to contend with. To the north and west lay an almost limitless, barely explored wilderness that stretched to the Pacific Ocean. But there was hope to the south. Reinforcements would be sent now that war had been declared, but they would have to be gathered from scattered settlements and then marched through the same unforgiving territory that Hull's men had just crossed. It was a daunting situation and it was very possible that the seemingly infinite land surrounding the outpost was actually isolating it.

A week after his arrival, Hull was ready to seize Upper Canada. The wait was over. The Kentuckians had marched more than 260 miles and many men from Ohio and other regiments had faced a similar journey. They had survived rain, difficult terrain, and critically low supplies to reach this moment. But, for the first time since Jefferson had ordered the navy to Tripoli, an American military force would land on foreign soil. Hull gave the order and the fort sprang to life. On the morning of Sunday, July 12, several vessels launched from the Michigan shore. The American force dug their oars deep into the cool waters of the Detroit River and were soon pulling their boats onto the Canadian shore. An earlier feint against nearby Malden made the cautious, and exceedingly small, British force fall back and now they were nowhere to be found. Bumping into the Canadian shoreline Hull's men clambered out as quickly as they could and the American flag was immediately unfurled and planted on Canadian soil. Cheering erupted, not just from the soldiers but also the citizens of Detroit who watched from the other side of the river. General Hull immediately set up his headquarters in a nearby brick home and very quickly issued a proclamation to the Canadian residents in the area.[19]

"Inhabitants of Canada!" it began. "After thirty years of peace and prosperity, the United States has been driven to arms." Hull went on to assure the people that he knew they had no part in the actions that had caused the war and that, far from conquering them, he had come to set them free and protect them from the "tyranny" and "injustice" of the British monarchy. Extolling the prosperity the United States had experienced since independence, he encouraged the Canadians to remain in their homes and go about their normal business. As an acknowledgment (and perhaps a subtle reminder) of the frequent border crossings, Hull declared, "Many of your fathers fought for the freedom and independence we now enjoy," and those American transplants living in Canada were entitled to the benefits of that freedom since they are "part of the same family." He promised to respect the rights and personal property of all Canadians who were peaceful.[20]

However, if these reassurances and promised freedoms were not enough of an enticement to cooperate, Hull then issued a warning. Anyone found assisting the British would be treated as an enemy combatant and anyone fighting alongside the native tribes of the region would be executed. As a further warning, Hull declared that if Britain allowed her Indian allies to attack American civilians, "this will be a war of extermination. The first stroke of the tomahawk, the first attempt with the scalping knife, will be the signal for one indiscriminate scene of desolation." The declaration seemed to work and many of the inhabitants who had fled to the surrounding forest reluctantly returned to their homes.[21]

The triumphant landing in Canada seemed to promise the quick and easy success foretold by the war hawks in Congress. The majority of the British army was tied down in Europe fighting Napoleon and the regulars who were actually in Canada would spend most of their manpower protecting the Niagara frontier. In the days that followed, Hull sent out scouts to check for hostile forces. Many of these returned with reports of sizeable parties of Indians. On occasion they would pursue them, but the native warriors knew the lay of the land and quickly melted into the forest before they could be caught. A few lingering Canadian militia were captured, disarmed, and paroled, and several boats containing flour, blankets, and weapons were captured and taken behind the American lines.[22]

The advance continued under Colonel Lewis Cass and a detachment of Hull's regulars who advanced south along the Canard River. This was around twelve miles distant and marked the only natural impediment between Hull and the strategically important city of Amherstburg. The Canard flows into the Detroit at an angle and, while not impassable, holding the bridge across it would make it difficult for British and Canadian forces to cross rapidly in any counterattack. With his right flank protected, Hull could drive deeper into Canada with the river at his back and right flank. But was it worth the risk? The small advance force had moved, rapidly leaving themselves dangerously unsupported and there was always the chance that the British could be preparing a counterattack. Hull's officers were divided on whether to hold the bridge against an increasing enemy force or to fall back. After a council was called, those in favor of holding the position were overruled and the detachment

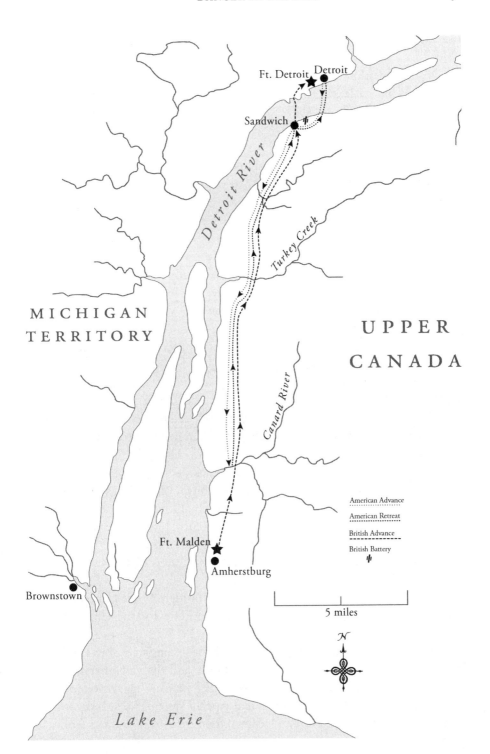

MICHIGAN
TERRITORY

UPPER
CANADA

Ft. Detroit Detroit

Sandwich

Detroit River

Turkey Creek

Canard River

Ft. Malden
Amherstburg

Brownstown

Lake Erie

American Advance
American Retreat
British Advance
British Battery

5 miles

N

was forced to fall back to the town of Sandwich and the rest of the army.[23]

This battle, or more accurately, skirmish, for the bridge over the Canard River had at least proven that American troops could drive the British and Canadians back, even on their own soil. Once the army was ready to march forward the bridge would be retaken and a march of the peninsula would be commenced. But all was not well. The army lingered awaiting orders and optimism turned to confusion. When an announcement did come from Hull, five days had passed. Rather than ordering the army to continue, Hull announced that he was crossing the Detroit River back into the United States on business.[24] His stunned army remained alert and anxious in the knowledge that the British forces in Canada must be planning a counterattack. Almost a week had gone by since they had battled at the Canard River. Not only was the element of surprise gone but the British would probably have had plenty of time to plan for their next move. What was Hull doing? In Washington, the appointment of the graying Revolutionary War hero had seemed an obvious choice. Now, he seemed to have either lost his courage, or perhaps something even graver was wrong.

By July 28, Hull's army still remained in Sandwich and his men were beginning to become concerned. For his part, the general seemed to be suffering from an increased sense of foreboding and lack of confidence. His anxiety and indecision were heightened when he received word that the American fort on Mackinac Island, over two hundred miles to the north, had been forced to surrender. Fort Mackinac was the northernmost post in the Michigan Territory. Situated on an island near the conjunction of Lakes Huron and Michigan, the small force had only a few defenders but its loss was a significant psychological blow to the already waning American morale. Hull seemed to dissolve into panic at the announcement, exclaiming, "The whole northern hordes of Indians will be let loose upon us."[25]

After receiving the news of Mackinac, Hull ordered Fort Dearborn (near modern-day Chicago) to be evacuated. The fort at Chicago boasted no more than one hundred people in 1812. Of those, a little more than half were men of fighting age. The rest consisted of women and children. Hull's order was obeyed instantly and the small band of settlers began packing what they could for the journey east to safety. Their preparations were brought to a halt when a large party of Indians arrived on their doorstep. The band seemed friendly enough and supplies from the fort were brought out to make sure it stayed that way. If the settlers could have remained behind the walls of their fort they might have relaxed in relative safety. But in doing so they would be completely cut off from outside aid. They had to get to Fort Wayne in the Indiana Territory, which was a grueling 160 miles away. When an American officer named Heald arrived with his own party of Indians to escort them to their destination the final preparations were made. The day came to leave the fort behind and it was decided to place a body of Indians in the front and rear of the force. There had been no reason to doubt the friendly overtures of the tribes in the region, but once out of the safety of the fort, things could turn ugly very quickly. The American residents of Fort Dearborn would march in the middle of these two contingents of warriors with the men guarding the women and children under the command of Captain Heald. Marching along the shore of Lake Michigan the party marched about a mile and a half without incident. Then, without warning, the quiet of the lapping lake erupted with gunfire. Parties of warriors emerged from behind sand dunes and rushed the Americans. The ambush proved effective and a number of defenders collapsed to the ground injured or dead. Mrs. Heald had the bridle of her horse seized and was carried off as an Indian prisoner of war. Within fifteen minutes only three women and twelve children were to be found with Captain Heald. He led them out of range of the gunfire, but in the end they were captured. Heald and his wife were later reunited and, despite being wounded, both were taken to Buffalo by the British and surrendered there as prisoners of war.[26] One of the most promising settlements in the Illinois Territory had been exterminated.

When word arrived at Detroit it must have unsettled Hull even further as he writhed in indecision. The rest of July passed without a hint of what the army would do next. By the beginning of August, something was in the wind and the troops found out they would finally decamp from Sandwich. The men prepared to resume their long overdue march into Canada. As predicted, the order to break camp did arrive but its details left the troops speechless. On August 7, Hull had ordered an immediate *withdrawal* from Canada. The retreat was made all the more bittersweet by the fact that most of the army crossed the river under cover of darkness in contrast to the triumphant landing of a few weeks before. Perhaps the most surprised actors in the unfolding drama were not the befuddled American soldiers but the Canadians that had either heralded the American landing or cooperated with them once they arrived. They were all left to face whatever retribution the British officials would deem appropriate after their return.[27] While it is difficult to explain Hull's motives for recrossing the river, the Battle of Brownstown two days before may have been a factor. The battle, which was really more a skirmish between a combined British and Indian force and an American relief column on its way to Detroit, resulted in few casualties but may have served to further convince Hull that he was isolated and that his supply lines could not be maintained.[28]

Regardless of the reasons behind the withdrawal, the arrival of the British regulars would not be long in coming. From the time that Hull had landed, Canada's governor-in-chief George Prevost had been planning the recapture of the area. He could rest a little easier with the knowledge that the forces on their way to meet the Americans were in experienced hands. Indeed, it would have been difficult to find a better commander for the defense of Canada than British general Isaac Brock. Now in his early forties and full of confidence, Brock was at the height of his career, having been transferred from Europe where he had received plenty of battle experience against the French. By the start of the war, Brock had already been in Canada for a decade and had wasted no time in squeezing what resources he could out of a very cash-strapped Royal Army. But his greatest weapon was his tactical abilities and his willingness to act offensively.[29]

In response to Hull's magnanimous invitation for the Canadians to join the United States, Brock issued one of his own. Calling the declaration of war "unprovoked," Brock added "The Officer Commanding that detachment has thought it proper to invite His Majesty's subjects, not merely to a quiet and unresisting submission, but insults them with a call to seek voluntary protection of his Government."[30] Scoffing at Hull's suggestion that their rights were violated he pointed out that the area had been settled by many former residents of the American colonies whose only crime was loyalty to their king. The myriad economic benefits of being British subjects speaks for itself. "And what is offered you in exchange? To become a territory of the United States, and share with them that exclusion from the ocean which the policy of their present government enforces."[31] Brock had made his point. Canada would not surrender without a fight and he was just the man to lead it.

Back in Detroit, Hull had been sensing the displeasure of his men and had begun to look on his own officers suspiciously. Hull summoned Taylor to his tent, and when he arrived, Hull chastised him for his lack

of support concerning the evacuation and
accused Taylor of being opposed to his plans
no matter what they were. Taylor countered
that he was not the only officer to disap-
prove of the withdrawal. Besides, Hull had
asked for his opinion and he had freely given
it. And what about the Canadians who had
been loyal to the Americans? Hull had
"promised protection to the Canadians, had
induced the whole provincial force to desert
from Malden" and then left them. Taylor
then sardonically "asked if he [Hull] thought
they would ever again confide to the appearances of any General invading Canada."
Hull replied that the Americans maintaining
the side of the river were more important

Isaac Brock, a posthumous
portrait based on an earlier
drawing. (*Provincial Archives
of Ontario*)

and before long he was sure Governor Scott of Kentucky, being a fellow
revolutionary, would send thousands of men his way to reinforce him.[32]

A troubled and frustrated Taylor left the general's tent and immediately sought out several fellow officers to hear their opinions of their situation. To his surprise, and even greater concern, he found that Hull
had discussed his plans with them individually and had given different
objectives to each of them.[33] It now seemed more likely than ever that
the elderly Hull was no longer capable of command. There was always
the chance that he could be right about reinforcement. Troops might
arrive soon and the army could cross the river again. But what if he were
wrong? The fate of an entire army hung in the balance.

While Hull wasted time worrying, British general Brock had worked
tirelessly to counteract the American advance. In addition to his small
contingent of regulars, Brock also collected three hundred militia men
and set off down the Thames on the eighth, arriving five days later. Relating all of this in a letter to Sir George Prevost on August 17, Brock
added "I found that the judicious arrangement which has been adopted
immediately upon the arrival of Colonel Procter (one of Brock's subordinates who would later play a major part in the war), had compelled
the enemy to retreat, and take shelter under the guns of his fort."[34]

Despite his optimism, it must have come as quite a surprise to Brock
when he arrived in Amherstburg to discover the American force he had
come to defeat had been accommodating enough to surrender the last

square inch of Canadian soil without his army having fired a shot. The fort at Malden by Brock's own admission "could not have sustained a siege of any duration" and the fact that Hull had not tried to take it was a mystery. Rectangular in shape, it had four bastions and picketed walls with holes to permit musket fire. The buildings inside the fort, with the exception of the magazine, were all made of wood with crude pine shingles—all of this accompanied by a single dry ditch and a low breastwork.[35] Sensing the confusion behind American lines, Brock decided to seize the initiative and go on the offensive. By August 13, his army had arrived at Sandwich and could be seen building large earthworks where a howitzer and two eighteen-pounder cannons were then mounted. The American force inside Fort Detroit was forced to watch helplessly from the opposite bank.[36]

Hull seems to have settled on waiting out any British attack from inside the fort until reinforcements arrived, but waiting had its price as well. Supplies began to run low and the situation was becoming dire. In an effort to secure what he could, Hull ordered 350 men to march south to Frenchtown (modern-day Monroe, Michigan) on August 14 to bring back what supplies they could. Sending such a large force weakened the fort significantly, but recent Indian activity required a substantial body of men to prevent their being overtaken.[37]

With this contingent still on their way to Frenchtown, Brock set his attack in motion with psychological warfare. At one o'clock in the afternoon a British messenger rode up to the gates of Fort Detroit under a flag of truce.[38] He bore a single letter to General Hull from Brock. It read,

> Sir—The force at my disposal authorizes me to require of you the surrender of Fort Detroit. It is far from my inclination to join in a war of extermination; but you must be aware that the numerous body of Indians, who have attached themselves to my troops, will be beyond my control the moment the contest commences. You will find me disposed to enter into such conditions as will satisfy the most scrupulous sense of honor. Lieutenant colonel M'Donnell, and major Glegg are fully authorized to conclude any arrangement that may prevent the unnecessary effusion of blood.[39]

Hull wrote his reply and dispatched it with the messenger to the British force that was now waiting dangerously close to the fort. Brock read over it. "Sir—I have received you letter of this date. I have no other reply to make, than to inform you that I am ready to meet any force which may be at your disposal, and any consequences which may result from its execution in any way you may think proper to use it."[40] It seemed General Hull had regained the fire in his belly. The walls of Fort Detroit were certainly suitable for a siege. Perhaps Hull hoped that the promise of a lengthy blockade to reduce the fort would be seen as too costly by the British and their allies. But Brock was not ready to discount the general's fear of massacre so easily.

At four that afternoon, the British cannon sprang to life from the earthen wall at Sandwich, firing volley after volley into the fort. The American batteries returned fire and the two sides lit up the sky for seven hours as the thunder of the opposing cannons echoed through the countryside. When the cannonade ended late that night, little damage had been done to either side. At sunrise the next morning the artillery duel resumed, and the main body of Brock's army crossed onto American soil three miles below Detroit.[41] A captain who had seen service at the Battle of Tippecanoe rushed to Hull and volunteered to lead his men out to oppose the landing British "pledging his life upon success." Hull rejected the idea and the captain retook his spot among the anguished and confused.[42] The American force was waiting outside of the fort as the British approached. The artillery duel played on in the background as Brock's force of regulars and Canadian militia came into view.[43]

The lines of soldiers approached the motionless Americans. The battle about to be fought was not ideal for Hull's men, especially when they remembered having the upper hand on the other side of the river, but at least it would be a fight. With the fort at their back and plenty of ammunition, they were as ready to meet the enemy as they could make themselves. The British lines approached to within five hundred yards of the American force and both sides braced for the first volley of musket fire, when the American troops were ordered back inside the fort by General Hull. This move seemed inexplicable and unforgivable. The Americans had the high ground and were able to fight from a secure position while the cannons of Fort Detroit provided substantial cover. What could be Hull's reason for such a counterintuitive order? If the troops expected to shell the oncoming enemy force with guns situated along the fort walls they were mistaken. Inside the fort, Hull ordered the guns not to fire. At this, the murmuring of the men erupted in "one universal burst of indignation." Ignoring this, Hull had a white flag hung from the wall in view of the British.[44]

Envoys from Brock approached to see the reason for the flag. General Hull with a white handkerchief tied to a staff dashed to the gate and opened it himself. To the surprise and anxiety of his men, he stepped outside the fort to confer with the British. From the walls, the American force watched Hull walk the approximate one hundred yards to the waiting British envoy. An inaudible conversation ensued and, within ten minutes, Hull returned to the fort clasping a piece of paper that would decide their fate.[45]

All of this remained unknown to the people of Kentucky. When word of the declaration of war had initially reached the state whole towns erupted in celebration. Troops paraded through their county seats and ballads were written and sung that talked of the glorious days of 1776. A favorite format was to simply rewrite the words of "Yankee Doodle." This included verses such as:

> The clarion loud, of war is blown,
> Oppression fills its cup, sir,
> The British have the gauntlet thrown,
> And we have took it up, sir,
> Sound the trumphet, beat the drum,
> Now's the time for action,
> How oft we wish'd this day to come
> To Crush the British faction[46]

Most believed that they would soon be the masters of Canada and drive the British from the North American mainland. The symbolism of the war was obvious. Another chorus composed to the same melody as "Yankee Doodle" stated "Saratoga to them all, Bunker-Hill confound them, Soon the Canadas will fall, When Freedom's Sons surround them."[47]

In Frankfort, Governor Charles Scott had very little time left in his term in office, but that did not prevent him from doing everything in his power to move arms and men to the front. Though now an elder statesman, Scott was no stranger to military conflict and had served with honor during the French and Indian War as well as the Revolution and countless campaigns against hostile tribes.[48] Now he worked to make sure the troops were prepared to meet the old enemy. However, his time was running out. The election results for the next governor of Kentucky had been published in Lexington's *Kentucky Gazette*, and with very few votes remaining, Isaac Shelby was the inevitable winner.[49] Shelby had been the state's first governor and had guided the commonwealth through its infancy before retiring to his farm named Traveler's Rest in modern Lincoln County. But as the prospect of war drew closer, Shelby had been encouraged to run by many across the state. One friend wrote that the citizens of Barren, Adair, and Warren Counties were heavily in favor of Shelby.[50] Another wrote that "war seems now inevitable. It is important to this state and to the genl government to have at the head of the state of Kentucky a man under whom all can rally with confidence."[51] He warned Shelby that it was not enough to say he would serve if chosen since this was too noncommittal. He needed to declare his hat in the ring.[52]

Shelby, however, had refused to budge but made a modest statement acknowledging that he was willing to be governor if elected but declared that he did so out of a willingness to serve and not due to party affiliation or to keep someone else out of office. He simply was willing to serve. The opinion of most Kentuckians, however, was made clear when, just two columns over from this brief statement in the *Kentucky Gazette*, an article claiming to detail Shelby's character offered a glowing review of his abilities. The use of revolutionary jargon when describing Shelby's career to date only convinced the public further that he was the right man for the job; calling him a "patriot of '76" and someone who was reliable "in times that try men's souls."[53]

But patriotic sentiment aside, the citizens of Kentucky had good reason to have faith in Shelby's abilities. First and foremost, he had experience fighting the British at the Battle of King's Mountain in the American Revolution. This battle had become legendary in the West Country and Shelby had played a significant part when he led a contingent of backwoodsmen and defeated British major Patrick Ferguson and his army of over a thousand loyalist militia. Shelby had also fought numerous engagements with a number of Indian tribes during the Revolution, providing him experience with the two foes the young United States would have to face. His participation in the state's constitutional convention and his service as first governor proved he was a consensus builder and someone who could accomplish much with very little.[54]

The one individual who did not share in this opinion was Shelby's opponent, Gabriel Slaughter. Slaughter was a rising name in Kentucky politics and, sensing the way the political winds were blowing, had approached Shelby months before the election to ask if he would run. Shelby intimated that he would not run for public office again unless a national emergency required him to do so. A relieved Slaughter had departed from Traveler's Rest, feeling he had successfully removed the only impediment to his election. But his relief turned to indignation when, in March, Shelby decided that the state really did need him at the helm and announced his candidacy. The intense campaign that Slaughter waged in the following weeks grew heated but hardly dented the reputation of the former governor.[55] It would be later that month before a real sense of how significant Shelby's victory was. By August 25, the vote count for Cumberland and Muhlenberg Counties had still not made their way to Frankfort, but the rest of the votes had been counted and the results were already clear. Shelby had received more than twenty-nine thousand votes while Slaughter had drawn just under twelve thousand.[56]

However, Scott could ill afford to wait for these results to be reached. His most pressing concern was to gather and equip eleven hundred men who were gathering at Georgetown for the march to Newport by August 12. This was more than likely in direct response to General James Winchester, who had already spent some time in Kentucky recruiting, and had requested a force of eleven hundred men to assist in the defense of Detroit and the Michigan Territory. At Newport, they would rendezvous with Colonel Wells of the United States Army and four hundred men from the 17th US Infantry Regiment. Despite being a federal formation (which meant having standard uniforms and weapons) the regiment was made up almost entirely of Kentuckians.[57]

Kentucky had ample volunteers for military ventures, but supplying them was another matter. While working to arm the men arriving at Georgetown, Scott was also trying to get supplies to Louisville to assist in defending the Indiana and Illinois Territories.[58] On August 5, an express rider from General Hull's headquarters had arrived in Frankfort with a message for the governor. His name was Thomas Davis Carneal and he had left Hull's headquarters in Sandwich, Canada, on July 29. He explained the army's situation and the dangerous position Hull was in since Fort Mackinac had fallen.[59] This only served to reinforce the urgency that Scott was feeling. But the process would still take time.

Slowly the militia from across the state began to trickle in and they were organized into regiments. The 1st Kentucky led by Colonel John M. Scott and the 5th Kentucky led by Colonel William Lewis were infantry formations that carried standard issue muskets. The 1st Kentucky Rifle Regiment was commanded by Colonel John Allen. These three regiments would eventually be accompanied by men from the 17th United States Infantry under Colonel Sam Wells, which consisted almost exclusively of Kentuckians. The whole body of men would be under the command of General John Payne.[60] The festivities that accompanied the various units as they converged on Georgetown were celebratory in nature. As Lewis's men left Lexington the street was lined with cheering families and neighbors. The army only marched three miles outside of the city before it was compelled to stop for "refreshments" and a stirring speech by Henry Clay.[61] Now they just needed to cover the vast distances of the Northwest Territories in time to save Hull and his army.

Chapter Three

FORTS WAYNE
AND HARRISON

THE CALL FOR TROOPS to rendezvous at Georgetown would extend beyond the inner bluegrass until it reached the more isolated villages and farms of central Kentucky. When it did arrive it spread like wildfire until it reached the ears of enthusiastic supporters such as the young William Northcutt. On the day the news arrived the twenty-two-year-old Northcutt was battling both August heat and the long list of farm chores that monopolized his day. The declaration of war had, so far, done little to alter the predictable cycle of farm life for Northcutt and others like him, and the arrival of the news on the tenth of August found him stacking wheat instead of performing military drills.[1] Northcutt had moved to Kentucky with his father and siblings from Virginia early in the year of 1797.[2] In the spring of 1812 he had been a student in a small school, but classes were indefinitely dismissed when the school's teacher resigned and joined the army. Being drawn to the glamour of a military life himself, Northcutt had earlier joined a company of light dragoons. These homemade units were often more appealing than the regular state militia, as they were able to design their own company uniform and select their own name.[3]

Northcutt's company was headed by Captain William Garrard and called itself the "Bourbon Blues."[4] The downside was these units had to outfit and equip themselves at their own expense. The Bourbon Blues had a uniform of the "finest Blue broadcloth, trimed with white lace and

Red Scarlet vest with a Jacked, Leather cap, Black Cockade, Black plume tipt with Red."[5] The uniform and equipment cost Northcutt every cent he had, but when he picked up the finished product from the tailors he was finally ready to be called to active service. As of yet, there had been no real occasion to wear the uniform. But as he glanced up from his work to see his sergeant approaching he knew the time had come. They had been activated, he was told, and would march from Georgetown north to Newport and then into Ohio where they would join the fight.[6]

As soon as the men could be gathered and their affairs set in order, the Bourbon Blues began their march to Georgetown. They arrived to find the air around the city electrified. The small town had received an infusion of over a thousand militiamen from across the state as well as several well-known personalities, including Governor Scott himself and Congressman Henry Clay. Early on the morning of the sixteenth, the men were organized and paraded before the governor. At ten that morning they were paraded again. A local minister named Blythe delivered a sermon to the troops and was followed in a speech by the fiery Clay.[7] Some local estimates suggested a crowd of spectators that topped twenty thousand, though this may be an overzealous estimate by excited eyewitnesses.[8]

After a few additional days in Georgetown sorting out details, the men began their march forward on the nineteenth of August. Each company would leave in intervals to keep from clogging the roads. According to one of Northcutt's fellow soldiers, a man named Elias Darnell, the men were in "high spirits," but the sky soon filled with storm clouds and the men were forced to make most of the five-day march in the rain. Darnell admitted "these hardships tended a little to quench the excessive patriotic flame that had blazed so conspicuously at the different musters and barbecues."[9]

If that patriotic flame had begun to flicker, it would be nearly extinguished by the news awaiting them in Newport. On August 16, the day they had left Georgetown, General Hull surrendered the fort at Detroit after just ten minutes of negotiating with the British. The loss of the fort would have been bad enough, but the surrender of 400 cannon shot, 100,000 small arms cartridges, and 2,500 stands of arms, and more than two weeks' worth of provisions exacerbated the situation for the supply-strapped American army in the West.[10]

Hull had not only agreed to surrender the men in the fort but ceded the entire Michigan Territory to the British, making the northern edge of the Indiana Territory the new international border and bringing the war a lot closer to home. Among the arms and supplies taken by the British at Detroit was one particular item that the Americans would have been chagrined to lose and the British all too happy to accept: one small three-pounder cannon. At first it probably did not stand out. It was brass and moved on a wooden caisson like the other guns that peered over the walls at Detroit. However, this cannon bore an inscription. It had been taken from the British army during the American Revolution at the Battle of Saratoga—a major American victory and turning point in the war.[11]

The cannon served as a metaphor for the whole conflict. To the Americans, it was like the independence and freedom they now possessed. It had been won on the field of battle through the blood, sweat, and tears of the preceding generation. Once in their possession they were to use it in defense of their rights as free men. To the British, its loss, like the colonies, was an embarrassing blow to a powerful empire that happened more out of chance and the bungled leadership of a few men rather than efforts on the part of Americans. But the tide had now turned, and thirty-five years later it had returned to the Crown almost without a fight. More than a few people must have wondered if Britain's former colonies would do the same. The information must have come as quite a shock to General Payne who, up to that point, thought that Hull's army was still in Canada. At three in the morning on the twenty-fifth, a sleepless Payne opened his inkwell to write to Governor Scott.

"Sir, you will receive copies of Such Inclosures as will astonish you. I have Some hopes that it is not to the extent so Desperate as it appears." The whole thing could have been a trick by the British, but what if it were true? Regardless of the truth, Payne admitted "the State of Ohio is in great alarm." Promising to send future dispatches on to the governor, Payne determined to march north as quickly as possible. He ended with determined assurance that "Our troops from Kentucky are in good spirits & you will not hear of their capitulation until some blood is spilt."[12]

As news of the loss of the Michigan Territory spread, its effects were immediately felt. Ohio governor Return Johnathan Meigs (perhaps the most creatively named governor in Ohio history) had been at Piqua in council with representatives of the United States government and members of native tribes in the area in an attempt to preserve the uneasy peace between the two. Members of the Shawnee, Wyandot, Mingo,

Delaware, Ottawa, and Miami had planned to attend. Both sides professed a desire for peace, but an air of suspicion hung over the entire meeting. This mistrust was aided by word that a large portion of Miamis on their way to the meeting received word of the fall of Detroit and the massacre at Fort Dearborn and, sensing which way the wind was blowing, immediately moved toward Fort Wayne, which they laid siege to.[13]

At Newport, Northcutt's Bourbon Blues received a second bit of bad news when they were informed that the cavalry arms they had been promised were not available yet and they could either arm themselves with muskets and continue on as mounted infantry or they could return home.[14] The men thought it over and decided to go ahead. Having to dismount and fight on foot was not as glamorous as the dashing cavalry charge, but the thrill of danger and patriotic pride spurred them on. Of the 106 men in the unit, the vast majority were between the ages of sixteen and twenty-two and only two were married. Many were prominent doctors, attorneys, or aspiring entrepreneurs who had little to tie them down and more than enough zeal to spur them on.[15]

Circumstances meant the mission had now changed from offensive to defensive. Brock had wasted no time in securing Detroit and moving farther south. General Payne received word from General John Gano at Lebanon, Ohio, that the men guarding the supplies at the Raisin River were forced to flee to Urbana. British officers arrived in the camp with news of the fall of Detroit and a copy of Hull's capitulation. They immediately demanded the surrender of the men and their supplies. The officer in charge "confined" these officers, ordered the livestock that had been brought for beef to be released, and ordered the men to get away in any way they could. While the actions may have been a breach of military etiquette they resulted in most of the men escaping to fight another day. Beneath the general's signature was another paragraph. "This moment I have received another express," it began. The troops stationed at the Rapids on the Maumee River had been captured and Fort Wayne was in danger. In typical regency understatement, Gano adds "this judicates something Serious as to the fate of our frontiers and would it not be adviseable to march your forces forward as soon as practicable."[16] The reality was a significant force of Potawatomi warriors (who were probably accompanied by a few other tribes), buoyed by the news of British success in Michigan, had surrounded the fort with the intent of replicating the victories of their allies.[17]

A second rider arrived with word from brigade quartermaster Joseph Pierce, beseeching the general and the approaching army to send all the arms they possibly could. An express rider had just arrived in his camp from Piqua, Pierce said, and he was sending wagons to collect what could be spared. "There cannot be a doubt but the Savages & British have planted the British flag at the Rapids; the fall of Detroit is confirmed beyond a doubt and Fort Wayne the only remaining barrier is in the most imminent danger…" Seventy-five men had been sent on to Piqua and six more companies had been formed and were ready to march if they only had arms.[18]

With these urgent requests flooding in Payne's Kentuckians soon got underway but with a new target in mind. If the reports were true, Detroit was lost for the moment. Fort Wayne in the Indiana Territory was the new boundary and it had to be defended at all costs. Their path would take them through Lebanon and Dayton, Ohio, and then straight northwest to Fort Wayne. The only question was, could the fort hold out?[19] The men on their march north soon rallied despite the bad news of Hull's surrender and were more confident than ever. Observers in Cincinnati seemed impressed by the little army, with one eyewitness claiming, "They are hardy, brave looking troops in high spirits, and anxious to avenge their countrymen."[20] The army paused for the night at Hutchinson's tavern just north of Cincinnati and were pleased to find a number of civilians had come out to see them. One older gentleman, either in nostalgic, ill-timed patriotic fervor or in jest, gave a loud cheer for King George, which quickly drew the attention of the camp. He was immediately picked out of the crowd and drug to the nearest watering trough where the soldiers "pumped water in him until they had cooled him of[f]."[21]

At the same spot, the young group of soldiers caused further commotion when a man selling melons arrived in the camp. Gathering around to see his product they deemed his prices far too high and decided to relieve him of some of his load. While several soldiers gathered around the merchant to argue over the prices a few soldiers would spirit some of the fruit off the cart. Finally, realizing that his supply of melons was being pilfered the merchant tried to move out quickly to save what he could, but in his haste he overturned his load, sending melons rolling in all directions.[22]

The army soon pulled out, but the merriment (and rowdiness) continued and the officers found it somewhat difficult to control their unruly troops. The men moved on a forced march through Dayton and Pickaway where they were given ammunition and flints.[23] Despite making good time on the march, there was some dissatisfaction among the army when they learned they were not to be led by General William Henry Harrison as they had expected. Instead, the hero of Tippecanoe would yield control of the army to General James Winchester of Tennessee. The Kentucky militia had sought Harrison so long that Governor Scott walked danger- ously close to unconstitutionality by confer- ring on Harrison, who was obviously not a resident of the commonwealth, the ability to command Kentucky troops by executive order on August 25.[24]

William Henry Harrison. (*Library of Congress*)

Now that had all been cast aside by the orders of the federal govern- ment. The problem was not that Winchester was known to be inept; rather, it was that he was not known at all. Like many senior officers in the army and militia, Winchester's military credentials dated to his serv- ice during the American Revolution and then as a member of the Ten- nessee militia. But he had not fought any sizeable engagement in years. Besides that, he was unfamiliar with the territory he was now tasked with crossing. Would it not make more sense to appoint General Har- rison, who had spent years living and defending the territories of the Northwest and had actually fought at Tippecanoe, as commander in- stead of an aging general with little to no knowledge of the terrain that spread out before him?[25]

On the thirty-first of August when the army was less than a day's march from Dayton, General Harrison rode into camp. His appearance caused the men to erupt in three cheers. The army's arrival in Dayton the next day must have added to the sense of confidence. The men inside the settlement fired a cannon in salute as the army approached. By the third of September, the army had reached Piqua. The 106-mile journey had taken six days. Despite marching an average of over seventeen miles a day, there was little time to rest. The latest news to arrive was that Fort Wayne was becoming desperate. A contingent of the army under Colonel Allen had pressed farther north to Saint Mary's and, being much nearer to the fort, chose to ride on hastily.[26]

Harrison prepared to follow in short order. He had the men parade before explaining the dire situation at Fort Wayne. A forced march to relieve it was a necessity. At noon the next day (September 6) the army marched northward. Baggage and the sick were left behind to make the march faster. One mile from the fortification known as St. Mary's Block-house, Harrison ordered the flour ration cut in half to allow the army to move even more quickly. This had the desired effect of lightening the load the men had to carry but also prevented them from having enough supplies to be comfortable. Soldier Elias Darnell complained that the area was "badly watered; the water in the wagon-ruts was the only drink we could get to cool our scorched thirst, but very little of that."[27] The water shortage reached crisis levels and an order was issued that when water was discovered on the march, a guard was to be posted immediately, not to protect the users from ambushes but to prevent the militia from watering their horses or soaking their sore feet in it. The army was ordered to be clothed and to have their arms with them at all times, which only added to their misery.[28]

As the army approached Fort Wayne, the caution expressed by its commanders and anxiety shown by its enlisted men highlighted that a battle was expected very soon. The men were ordered to sleep dressed and with their arms. False alarms had become prevalent with the men awakened numerous times in the night. Consequently, it was decreed that any shot fired should be followed by the shout of "all's well" for false alarms or by two more shots fired in rapid succession if there was a real emergency.[29] To afford the best protection during the march, the infantry were divided into three columns. The middle column consisted of wag-onloads of supplies and the infantry and rifle regiments made up the outside columns. Mounted units guarded both flanks, as well as front and rear guards. A half mile to the front and on either side of the army were spies (or scouts) tasked with spotting the enemy as quickly as possible.[30]

A day's ride outside of Fort Wayne the column stumbled across some Indian spies in camp. A small fight broke out, but the native warriors escaped into the woods. The column hastened forward and at three in the afternoon on September 9 they arrived at the fort. No battle was fought, as the body of Indians that had been besieging the fort had fled the night before. This brief respite of good news must have been a welcome change to the recent fortunes of the United States. The corn crop and several buildings had been burned by the warriors before their departure, but the enemy had been repulsed and, for the moment at least, the advance southward had been stopped.[31] Despite relieving the fort, the men were forced to be constantly on their guard, as native warriors would steal horses at night or fire into their tents.[32] Once inside the fort, cautious officers refused to let up on discipline. Fearing a future attack, it was ordered that muskets were not to be carried in wagons (presumably so they could be carried by soldiers) and when pausing to work only half the men should work at one time with the other half standing at the ready with their muskets primed.[33]

While the Kentucky militia under Payne congratulated themselves on a successful march to Fort Wayne another American outpost was a little less celebratory. On the night of September 2, twenty-eight-year-old Zachary Taylor lay on his bed inside the wood walls of Fort Harrison, which was entrusted to his command. The fort lay just north of modern Terre Haute (many miles south of Fort Wayne) and the Virginia-born Kentuckian was determined to keep it out of enemy hands. The fort had been built by Harrison in 1811 on his march to meet the Prophet at Tippecanoe. It was a fairly unimpressive structure whose picketed walls took the shape of a rectangle anchored on three corners by blockhouses.[34] While still very young, Taylor had already been an officer for four years.[35] His command post was well south of hot spots like the Michigan Territory and Lake Erie. While in contact with local tribes the fort had never been truly threatened—at least until now. The day before friendly Miamis had warned him of a possible attack and shots fired in the distance seemed to confirm the rumor.[36] Taylor knew that two young men had been cutting hay about four hundred yards from the fort. The gunfire had echoed from their direction. Its message was loud and clear. At eight o'clock the next morning, Taylor dispatched several men to investigate. Before long one of the men returned. His intuition had proven all too true. The bodies had been recovered and the rest of the detachment were waiting for orders. Taylor sent an oxcart to the scene and had the bodies brought back where they could be buried. Both corpses had been scalped and mutilated.[37]

That same evening, a group of twenty-five Indian leaders approached the fort under a white flag and asked for a council the next morning. Taylor remained suspicious of the party's intentions, but there was little he could do to prepare. A fever had recently thrashed his men and had left many of them unfit for duty. Taylor himself had only recently recovered and was still too weak to remain on watch all night like he had wanted. Sinking into his bed that evening, Taylor sank into sleep with the knowledge that he had only enough men to guard a portion of the fort's walls. The remaining portion would be in the hands of a single sentry who walked constantly back and forth, peering into the darkness in search of menacing silhouettes that might prove dangerous.[38] Taylor and his men had no way of knowing, but they were being slowly surrounded by a confederation of Potawatomi, Shawnee, Kickapoo, Wea, and Winnebago warriors that numbered around six hundred.[39]

Despite the stress of the day and his weak body, Taylor was roused instantly by the sound of a single gunshot somewhere in the inky distance. Leaping out of bed and running out of his cabin, he ordered the men to get up and to their posts. Within a few seconds more shots were fired and then an incessant volley from both sides soon followed, showing his men were awake and in position. Above the roar of the chorus of muskets, a sergeant shouted that one of the two blockhouses was on fire. Immediately realizing that the building was full of supplies that would turn the fire into an unquenchable blaze, Taylor diverted some of his men to form a bucket brigade. Despite their efforts the weakened men were slow in responding, and by the time they reached the blockhouse with buckets in hand the fire had spread to the whiskey stored inside. The flames shot higher and soon the roof was engulfed in an inferno that could not be extinguished by several sickly soldiers and their buckets.[40]

At the growing flames pierced the night and licked away at the wooden walls, panic ensued. The blockhouse formed a significant portion of one of the fort's walls and, once reduced to ashes, would provide an entrance for the hundreds of warriors outside to pour through. After the battle, Taylor would recall that "what with the raging of the fire, the yelling and howling of several hundred Indians, the cries of 9 women and children… and the desponding of so many of the men, which was worst of all, I can assure you that it was one of the most awful situations that a man could be placed in." Two of Taylor's healthy soldiers gave the fort up for lost and leapt over the side of the wall, disappearing into the darkness in an attempt to run to safety.[41]

Taylor barked his orders as best he could, but it took some time to restore complete discipline to the panic stricken. He dispatched part of the men to rip the roof off the end of the barracks closest to the blockhouse and to pour water over it to keep the fire from spreading. If the flames could be contained to the one blockhouse, the resulting gap in

Fort Harrison in 1812 from across the Wabash River. An 1848 etching based on an earlier sketch. (*Library of Congress*)

the wall would be no more than twenty feet wide, and a temporary replacement might be built to fill the gap. Thousands of balls from muskets took aim at the defenders and an endless stream of arrows arced over the walls and landed in the middle of the fort throughout the night. Around an hour before daybreak a voice cried out in English from the indistinguishable grays and shadows beyond the walls, begging to be let in. The voice sounded unfamiliar and, suspecting a trap, Taylor ordered the voice ignored, stating that if he (whoever he was) approached the gates to shoot him immediately. The begging continued until a soldier took aim at the individual and narrowly missed him. Running to a different part of the wall, the unknown petitioner continued to beg for admittance. It was only then that the voice was recognized. It was one of the two men who had deserted during the confusion over the blockhouse fire. He was ordered to lay behind a barrel against the wall of the fort until daybreak.[42]

By six the next morning, dawn was offering enough light to allow the Americans to more accurately pick out targets. Being forced to fall back under the increased accuracy of the American force, the Indians took revenge on the horses of the nearby citizens, killing sixty of them. When the eight-hour battle was over, a fatigued Taylor could take stock of the situation. Despite only having around fifteen men who were completely healthy at the onset of the battle, he had one dead and two injured, not including the poor soul who had sought refuge between the walls and a wooden barrel. When it was finally safe enough to admit him, the men found that one of his arms had been mangled by an Indian who had found him during his attempted escape. He had somehow managed to escape the punishing treatment and return to the fort, but it was doubtful that, even inside the walls, he would survive. The hastily constructed breastwork had filled the gap admirably, but the loss of the blockhouse meant the loss of all supplies. The only thing left to eat until supplies arrived was ripened green corn.[43]

Back in the north, Harrison and the army seemed to be having more success, but the men were far from happy. They had rested briefly and were now on the offensive. But the biggest blow to the army's morale did not come from the British but from the War Department in Washington. On September 19, the official change in command of the Northwest Army took place. With no orders to the contrary arriving from his superiors Harrison decided it was time to surrender command to General Winchester as promised.[44] The transfer was, as anticipated, not taken well by the men. One Kentucky militiaman had put it best when he wrote that he had several men who were willing to fight. "We go where you may choose to direct," he stated confidently before adding, "provided Genl. Harrison commands."[45] Despite the grumbles from the men, the reality was Winchester was in charge until orders came from Washington and that meant Winchester's order's had to be obeyed. He wasted little time in issuing them, too, and before long the men left Fort Wayne for the Maumee Rapids.[46] The Rapids (situated just southwest of modern-day Toledo) are just short of ninety miles from Fort Wayne. If a well-armed garrison could be maintained there, any incursions down the Maumee River into the Indiana Territory by the British would prove impossible. It would serve nicely as a launching point for the recapture of places like Frenchtown, Michigan, and, eventually, Detroit.

Subsequent successes against hostile Indian villages by the Northwest Army had left the army in a confident mood. But the boisterous behavior of the militia did not endear them to the aging Winchester. Their lack of discipline would prove to be more than an annoyance; it was dangerous. False alarms during the night became the rule instead of the exception, and the killing of a soldier due to accident happened all too frequently.[47] There was no denying the gravity of these mishaps, but this did little to curb the practice of firing a musket out of sheer boredom or other pranks by restless troops. It was explained that to do so not only wasted ammunition but gave away the army's position in a hostile country. But such warnings were quickly forgotten. As the columns of troops made their way north, there was little one could do to pass away the time. One bored private glanced up to see a porcupine resting on a tree branch. It was a target too tempting to resist. Raising his barrel he took aim. He pulled the trigger and when the smoke cleared the porcupine toppled from the tree. "Accident!" he called out to the column, which had now turned its attention in his direction. Immediately an officer on horseback thundered to the scene. The real course of events was clear. Glaring at the offender, he drew his saber and made it clear that "he wanted no more such accidents."[48]

By September 26, the army was more than thirty miles from Fort Wayne and Winchester's concern for their safety began to show. He ordered the men to sleep with their arms and as soon as cooking was completed fires were ordered extinguished. No man, no matter his rank, would be allowed outside the flanking columns for any reason.[49] The next day the orders were amended so that fifteen minutes after the drums beat to awaken the men, half of them would stand guard while the others finished preparing for the day. Winchester reminded the men that their "suttle and savage enemy" was near, and "the moment we are off our guard he may strike."[50] But, trying to sound upbeat, he ended by reminding the men that "this army is composed of materials to be easily conquered."[51]

Near Defiance and the convergence of the Auglaize and Maumee Rivers, Winchester detached around six hundred men to build four blockhouses. Each would be two stories tall with the exterior walls of the second story extending an additional several feet from the bottom level, creating an overhang and preventing anyone from scaling the wall. They were to be a daunting fifteen to sixteen feet high. Next a storehouse, "watch house," and hospital would be built. The buildings would be picketed in between. Then "a sergeant from each Reg. and a private from each company shall be turned out for soap and candle makers." The order to only fire when permitted was repeated, but this time officers were ordered to arrest anyone who violated the law.[52]

On October 3 word reached the camp near Defiance that Harrison had finally been placed in charge of the Northwest Army officially.[53]

However, any excitement over this was destroyed when, on the same day, Harrison ordered the detachments of the 17th and 19th Infantry (which were made up largely of Kentuckians), and the regiments under "Jennings, Poage, Lewis, Barbee & Allen," all of whom were in the Kentucky militia, to make up the left wing of the Northwest Army. The commander of the left wing, per Harrison's orders, would be none other than General Winchester.[54]

Hunger and inaction combined to slowly erode discipline in the army. On October 17, Winchester had reprimanded a portion of his army for their "tardy and unmilitary manner."[55] Four days later he was forced to issue another reprimand, this time to the men on guard duty who had had been lax in their duties by sitting or sleeping at their post or even lighting fires that only helped in making them easy targets.[56] Hunger began to get the best of the men as well and a few weeks later he would be forced to put an extra guard around the provisions with orders to shoot anyone found in the area who did not stop when challenged.[57] On November 2, Winchester moved his men once again and they crossed the frigid river to build a third fort.[58] On the sixteenth and seventeenth, sentries saw Indian scouts observing their camp from the woods just beyond. They never fired on the sentries nor attempted to steal any horses, which led Winchester to believe they were being reinforced for a general attack on the fort. The troops were ordered to "lay on their arms" and to listen for the drum which would call them to defend the fort if need be.[59] The men continued their isolated vigil, but the enemy never attacked.

By late November, the area was firmly in the grasp of winter. This was an encouraging sign to both Winchester and Harrison. For one thing the lake was frozen and the British could no longer use the navy they had defending the lakes. Frozen ground also made it easier to get supplies on the move. Between Jennings' blockhouse, Saint Mary's, and Piqua were more than 200 hogs and more than 1,700 barrels of flour just waiting to move.[60]

Packages from home had begun to trickle in and "watch coats" were assigned to the men on duty to protect them from the cold. Because there were so few, they would be shared. When one watch ended, the coat's owner would relinquish it to the next man and hurry for cover.[61] While not able to move just yet, Winchester ordered the camp picketed so fewer men would have to take night duty. Thus the men cut nine-foot-long posts and buried them one foot in the ground (or at least at-

tempted to).[62] The frozen ground made it
hard to bury the posts and many were ordered redone.[63] The portion of the army that
suffered most in the winter conditions were
the draft horses. Some grew so weak that, on
December 10, each company was ordered to
make a pirogue to "transport its own baggage" and men had to "make themselves mo-
chasons out of green hides."[64]

But hardships were no reason to delay action. If anything they were a motivator to
keep moving. Harrison continued his preparations to secure the areas north of the Ohio
River for good before recovering Detroit.
The chief of which would be to eliminate
Indian villages in the area. To modern ears

William Winchester by
Ralph Earl, 1817. (*NSCDAT,
Tennessee Portrait Project*)

such a scorched earth tactic seems a bit strange but was an integral part
to how both sides would prosecute the war. Settlements of any kind, be
they American blockhouses or Native American villages, represented a
concentration of manpower, supplies, and ammunition. To win the war
would require one side to either capture or eliminate their enemy's settlements. Without them, armies could not be supplied and opposition
would disintegrate. But because both sides understood this, both sides
would be on their guard. If Harrison ordered his men to undertake such
a mission they could be sure it would not be accomplished without opposition.

Hundreds of miles away in Frankfort, a change of watch had transpired a month before that would have important consequences for the
war. Governor Scott's term had expired and the aging patriot returned
to his home. The local militia worked hard to prepare a proper welcome
for the familiar face that was to appear on the scene. Two companies
stood on the road to Frankfort, about a mile outside of town, waiting.
Around three o'clock in the warm September afternoon their charge appeared on the road before them. Governor-elect Isaac Shelby was approaching Frankfort for his inauguration. The two companies of militia
and many citizens from across the state escorted Shelby into the city.
Giving a modest speech, thanking his fellow citizens for the honor of
returning the office he had held once before, Shelby took the oath of
office.[65]

The workload waiting for Shelby would have left little time for cel-
ebrating or sightseeing. Three regiments of Kentucky militia were mus-
tering for active service. The news of war had spread to the wilderness
and requests began pouring in for assistance. On August 26, the newly
inaugurated governor took his pen in hand and began issuing orders.
First, two regiments under the command of Colonels William Jennings
and Joshua Barbee were ordered to march to Newport where they were
to wait for orders from either General William Henry Harrison or himself.[66]

However, new intelligence led Shelby to alter his orders the next day.
If Detroit had fallen (or even if it hadn't) there would be no time for
these troops to catch up with the force that was on its way to relieve or
retake it. It would be better for Barbee and Jennings to rendezvous at
Frankfort, and the regiment at Henderson under Colonel Barbour was
ordered to Kaskaskia, Illinois, based on intelligence recently received
from there. If the two regiments at Frankfort were needed as a reserve
to the force advancing on Detroit or if they were needed in the Illinois
Territory or along the Wabash River in Indiana they would be close
enough to march either direction without much delay.[67]

Soon the details were sorted out and Barbee and Jennings' men were
on their way to Harrison via Georgetown and then Newport. Regiments
under Colonels Wilcox and Miller were on their way to Vincennes, Indiana, and Colonel Barbour's regiment was headed to distant Kaskaskia,
Illinois.[68] Shelby now turned to the men already in the field. The term
of service for much of the Kentucky militia under Harrison was about
to expire and the army was desperate to retain them. If the army shrank
too much Harrison would be severely outnumbered and without hope
of immediate reinforcement. The legislature appealed to the "well known
patriotism" of Kentuckians to remain in the army. Shelby also issued a
proclamation asking the men to stay on, reminding them of what they
had set out to accomplish. "Gain was not your object—you gloried in
the precious inheritance so nobly won by the revolution."[69] They had
entered the conflict determined to avenge the failure of Hull and to
eventually "plant the standard which bears your Country's Eagle, on the
wall of Malden." They had suffered much, but their fellow Kentuckians
back home had not forgotten them and had sent as much aid as they
could. "You have shewn that you are Kentuckians, firm and invincible."
Yes, they could return to the comfort of home now, but that knowledge
that they left just when they were needed would always remain.[70]

The requests for help did not just arrive
in dispatches from the far-distant settlements and the Canadian border. Letters
from local militia commanders around the
state's borders also found their way to the
governor's mansion. General Ramsay of
western Kentucky wrote to Shelby about the
concerned citizens in Livingston and Caldwell Counties, which were situated on the
Tennessee River. Just to the west of their
homes lay Chickasaw land and the narrow
strip of land that would later be called "the
purchase" was the only land east of the Mississippi River that could connect the tribes
of the south, like the Creeks, to Tecumseh's
allies in the north. This made the narrow

Isaac Shelby, the first and
fifth governor of Kentucky.
(*New York Public Library*)

causeway of land very well travelled and the people who lived there very
nervous. "I have had a guard of a few men on that frontier for several
months part by order of the late Governor, but at this time I have discharged them, not being willing that the state should incur the expenses."[71] Sending the militia to meet an enemy force was one thing,
but defending the state's borders was another. It would be impossible
for the state to keep guards posted around the state's borders for the duration of the war and yet, without them, Ramsey warned, those settlers
between the Cumberland and Tennessee Rivers would flee their
homes.[72]

At 4 a.m. on the fifth of September, an express rider tore through the
streets of Frankfort with a message for the governor. Rising to meet the
messenger who, at this hour, could only be bearing bad news, he found
it to be from a local militia leader in Shelbyville, just over twenty miles
to the west of Frankfort. It read,

> Dear Sir—I this moment have received news, which cannot be
> doubted, that the INDIANS are within fifteen miles of us (Henry
> court house) and the people are crossing the Ohio by hundreds!
> We wish you to send through the neighborhood, and to the meet-
> ing; and get all the men and ammunition you can. We will start
> for Westport by times in the morning. Mr. Bonta is the bearer of
> this news, don't fail to send assistance.

The messenger had even more grisly news he was carrying by word of mouth. One brave defender attempted to hold off the attack and was able to kill two attackers. Upon further inspection of the dead men, it was discovered that one had two scalps in his possession. Witnesses claimed they looked like they belonged to a female and an infant. [73]

The raid even sent the city of Louisville into a panic. One resident complained that "every two hours" additional news reached them. Word of houses burning in Charlestown twenty-four miles away and additional Indian crossings were said to leave several people dead at Westport. "The town at present is in the greatest possible tumult and bustle."[74]

A few days later a letter arrived from the concerned citizens of Washington County informing the governor that veterans of the Revolutionary War had formed their own militia unit to combat slaves, Tories, and Indians within a fifteen-mile radius of their home base. While it seemed unlikely that any invading force would reach so far into Kentucky as to threaten communities like Springfield, the fear of domestic uprisings proved substantial enough to draw these men from retirement. "It is to be understood, that this company is form'd of old veterans who fought in Defence of their Country in the Last war, and are now too old, & infirm to Render more Servise than what may be wanting in the Space above mentioned, but Should more be Required of us, we trust, that as it Has always been our wish, to Render all in our power for the welfare of our Country that we Shall Exert Our Selves to the utmost of our abilities in preserving those Rights which was purchased by our Fellow veterans in the Last war."[75]

Petitions from other states also called on the governor to send the already-stretched militia to protect them. One petition arrived from the inhabitants of Vevay, Indiana, expressing their reluctance to leave their homes but fearing they were not strong enough to repel an attack made against them. "We take the liberty," the petition reads, "to state that we remember the generous offer you made us last spring of sending over some troops in case of danger."[76]

Doing what he could, Shelby briefly turned his efforts from the north and west to the east. In a letter addressed to the secretary of war, Shelby asked that a suggestion be made to the president. The west was so far removed from Washington that "it appears to me impossible for the President to adopt with certainty a line of operations to be observed by any officer, appointed to command in this section of the United States... " This not only applied to tactical issues but was also especially true when it came to supplies. "Inattention, or any other misconduct, in quarter masters, contractors, commissaries and paymasters, or either of them, in the western country, so distant from you may produce irremediable misfortune."[77]

"I will take the liberty of suggesting to the President, the propriety of appointing a board of respectable characters, resident in the western country, responsible to him in any way which it shall be his pleasure to direct, with power to call into service, under the laws of congress, the militia, which may be required from time to time, from the states of Kentucky, Ohio, and the territories of Indiana and Illinois to direct their operations either of offence or defence." This board would be in charge of requesting arms and supplies from the War Department instead of having each state request their own, and would be responsible for "subordinate agents" in their districts. The board would make regular reports to the War Department, allowing Washington to steer the committee as needed.[78]

Shelby closed with a grizzly example of the results of inaction. "Before I had concluded this letter, information was received that a number of families had been killed by the Indians, on the waters of White river, twelve or fifteen miles from the Ohio, in the Indiana territory; and that the inhabitants thereof, are crossing into this state by the hundreds."[79]

Several weeks later Governor Shelby received a reply from Secretary of War Eustis dated September 17. The letter was cordial and offered thanks for the suggestion. The secretary went on to acknowledge that such a board would be useful, however, "Whether they could be clothed with the powers suggested, is a question requiring consideration." After all, Harrison had the authority to do what was needed and supply shortages were inevitable but would eventually be fixed. By the time the governor's eyes fell on the signature at the bottom he must have realized that he was receiving a polite but rather dismissive "no."

This must have exasperated Shelby, who was versed in frontier warfare. His own experiences as a soldier should have been recommendation enough of his qualifications, but he could also point to his first term as governor as proof that he knew what he was talking about. In 1794 when he was serving his first term he had written to then secretary of war Henry Knox and asked him to communicate to President George Washington concerning the "Defenseless situation of the frontiers of this state."[80] He had felt comfortable in his duties as governor particularly when it came to protecting his fellow Kentuckians. But orders from

Philadelphia (the District of Columbia being not yet built) transferred much of that authority to the army. "I consider the powers with which I was invested by the President to make provision for the defense of this State, as having been superseded by the orders which General Wayne has sent into this Country," Shelby complained. "It is by no means a desirable thing to me to be vested with such powers, but the particular situation of this Country renders it indispensably necessary that discretionary powers of that kind should be lodged somewhere within the State to be exercised as time and Circumstances may require."[81] In other words, the federal government's well-intentioned meddling would only increase the vulnerability of his fellow Kentuckians. Now, eighteen years later, he was fighting the same battle with the same results.

Chapter Four

BATTLE FOR THE
NORTHWEST

I F THE MEN MARCHING NORTH felt isolated during the long days and
nights in the wilderness that were so rife with uncertainty, they could
at least take heart in the fact that other columns of their fellow soldiers
were moving at the same time to various posts across the Old Northwest.
Harrison's plan to secure the region involved a two-pronged attack
against native villages that harbored hostile warriors and supplies.[1] Once
these camps were removed, his forces could march north without fear
of attack. The American force was divided with Kentucky's General
Payne and Harrison marching to attack the Miami towns at the forks
of the Wabash River while General Wells and his regulars focused on
Pottawatomie settlements at Elkhart on St. Joseph's River.

The Bourbon Blues were assigned to John Allen's regiment and were
given the task of riding up the Wabash River and destroying any Indian
villages they could find. The Bourbon Blues met with some success in
eliminating native supply bases and were credited with destroying native
population centers like "White Loon Town" while capturing or destroying their supplies before returning to Fort Wayne on September 17.
Reaching camp they found a battle of a different kind was brewing. One
regiment of Kentucky militia was bordering on revolt due to General
Winchester being placed back in command of the Kentucky volunteers.
It was only when Harrison intervened that the men were convinced to
stay in camp and obey orders.[2] On the twentieth of September, Win-

chester set out with three regiments of Kentucky militia, the Bourbon Blues, and Colonel Wells' regiment of United States regulars for Fort Defiance as tensions remained high.[3]

The move would not only gather intelligence and continue the practice of destroying hostile bases of operation but would also give the restless and dissatisfied men something to do. The first village they entered was only a two days' march from Fort Wayne and was utterly deserted. It lay in eerie silence broken only by the scratching of a few chickens who had been left behind to greet them. Moving cautiously among the bark walls of the wigwams they discovered a pile of sticks mounded high. Closer investigation revealed it to be the burial site of an elderly Indian who lay inside the crude casket wrapped in a blanket with his rifle.[4]

Finding empty villages was a common occurrence, as Indian scouts often warned residents of the approaching American army. (And even if they did not, the multiple columns of militia crashing through the woods and randomly firing muskets would have given it away.) But that did not ease the nerves of the soldiers who were going from home to home. In each instance, the Americans would fan out and inspect buildings to make sure they were empty before destroying them. In the village of Five Medals, some of Harrison's men entered a hut to find they were not quite alone. There in the gloom of the hut they came eye to eye with the icy, blank stare of an elderly woman. She was dead but her body had been placed sitting erect in a chair. A basket of bird beaks, talons, and bones combined with various roots and plants suggested that she was an Indian healer. While such a sight was sure to leave an impression on the memory of anyone who found it, the more chilling discoveries were located elsewhere in the camp. Poking among the remains that had been left in the village, one soldier uncovered a newspaper. Flipping through its leaves, the words *Liberty Hall* identified it as one of Cincinnati's local papers. Its columns contained valuable accounts of Harrison's troop movements, which were supposed to bring news to anxious family members on the home front, but obviously they had served another inadvertent purpose. The enemy was keeping an eye out for them. Looking further they discovered bags with the words "Malden" and "London" printed on them that looked like they had been used to carry ammunition.[5] The discoveries only helped to underscore the already painfully obvious. The British and their native allies were expecting them and they would be ready for them when they arrived. The real question was, how did the paper make its way so far north? Was it taken off a dead soldier? Was it found carelessly discarded in the woods or perhaps passed on by someone who shared the same sympathies as the elderly man who had cheered King George on their march north of Cincinnati?

Anxiety and unanswered questions were also echoing through the minds of those safely back in Kentucky, especially the governor. On the eighth of September, Shelby had issued a proclamation describing the siege of Fort Wayne as well as the danger to Fort Harrison and Vincennes. He had announced that General Harrison had requested mounted volunteers to relieve these places and troops were gathering at the rendezvous points before meeting at Louisville in just ten days' time. Each man had been instructed to bring a month's provisions. The proclamation ended with the confident boast: "Kentuckians! Ever eminent for their patriotism, bravery, and good conduct, will I am persuaded, on this occasion give to the world a new evidence of their love for their country, and a determination, at every hazard to rescue their fellow-men from the murders and devastations of a cruel and barbarous enemy." True to Shelby's predictions his call yielded two thousand volunteers, and the number would have been greater if volunteers had not been turned back at Frankfort and Louisville for fear of raising more troops than they could handle and provision.[6]

On the same day, the governor wrote a slightly more personal letter. This one was addressed to General Samuel Hopkins.[7] If this venture was to succeed, it needed a veteran who knew something about command to lead it. Like so many other commanders, Hopkins was a veteran of the Revolutionary War and had distinguished himself by having served in well-known battles like the siege of Charleston, where he had been taken prisoner. Having lived in Kentucky for almost twenty years, Hopkins had served as both attorney and judge. He was a man who was used to making decisions and had previous experience in the field.[8]

Hopkins' military experience also meant Shelby did not need to mince words. "It appeared from the enclosed copy of a letter which I have just received from Governor Harrison, that great danger is apprehended from the attack of the British and Indians upon the weak and defenseless Settlements of Indiana and Illinois Territories and particularly as to the Safety of Fort Harrison and Vincennes."[9] It cannot be said with any degree of certainty whether Hopkins wanted the command or not, but Shelby wrote cryptically, "From what passed between you and myself when I had the honour to see you here, I have thought it Proper to name you as the Officer to command the enterprise." Either the governor was extremely presumptuous or the subject had come up before. Shelby explains the need for experienced officers and, as a testimony to his faith in Hopkins' abilities he candidly admitted, "Although this is not just such a command as I should be pleased to see you at the head of, it is perhaps the only one in which you can serve your country this present season."[10] With the campaign under Hopkins secure in his mind, the governor left Frankfort on the eighteenth of September for Louisville to supervise the securing of troops who would attack hostile Indian towns along the Wabash River.[11]

From the beginning, problems began to arise. Stragglers arrived late at Vincennes on a regular basis, which added to the confusion of trying to organize the men into regiments for the march north. To make matters worse, the elderly Hopkins was too ill to organize the men himself and was forced to leave the task to subordinates. Finally the men were organized into four regiments under Colonels Sam Caldwell, John Thomas, James Allen, and Young Ewing. The regiments were grouped by twos into brigades led by Generals James Ray and Johnathon Ewing.[12]

The first leg of the journey from Vincennes to Fort Harrison went smoothly enough. After drawing ten days' worth of provisions, Hopkins planned to march his men to the Illinois River in order to attack villages belonging to the Kickapoo Indians. The journey would be an eighty-five-mile trek. Around twenty-five miles into the trip, an Indian path was discovered. Following this path seemed like the logical solution to the endless sea of brush and branches that pulled at the men with each tree they passed. After several days, the path turned abruptly to the west. At this point, the guides leading the army decided to abandon the trail; claiming to have a better knowledge of the country, they pressed Hopkins to continue north. As proof of the accuracy of their claims, one guide reported that he could see an Indian town in the distance. At this urging, the army, somewhat reluctantly, left the trail and turned north.[13] When the army arrived at the "town" their fears became reality. The town, or rather the rising smoke they thought originated from a town, was nothing more than a prairie fire. There were no settlements anywhere in sight. The poor, beleaguered militia were incensed and many were losing confidence in their aging commander. Sensing he was losing control of the situation, and becoming as impatient as his men, Hopkins took control and led the men in the direction the path had taken.[14]

As the sun set on Hopkins' army dissatisfaction in the ranks was more than evident. Not only had the campaign been a bust so far but even now they had traveled several miles out of their way. Through the dwindling twilight a grove of trees sheltering enough water for the army was spotted. The weary men trudged to the oasis and set up their camp in the darkness before unceremoniously laying down to sleep. Before long the uneasy silence was broken as a few soldiers (probably those on guard duty) began to notice a shimmering golden blaze in the distance. Upon investigation they found that the Indians had followed them and, after they had made camp, set the whole prairie on fire. The camp was soon up in arms as men rose from their beds to burn a fire line around the camp. It was the only chance they had to prevent the fire from engulfing the few supplies they had left. The efforts worked and the flames were kept from their beds, but it had been a close call.[15]

The next day, however, Hopkins discovered that the fire had been the last straw. His men were on the verge of open rebellion. Convening the officers, Hopkins pointed out the pros and cons of continuing the expedition. Acknowledging the lack of supplies and the unhealthy state of the horses, Hopkins attempted to paint the situation in the best light possible and called for just five hundred men to follow him forward to victory. It didn't work and the decision was made to return. Trying to retain some sense of control, Hopkins agreed to return and had the men formed, taking his place at their head. As the army moved forward Hopkins was mortified to look behind him and see the army marching in a different direction. Sending word to the officers ordering them to correct the situation Hopkins' officers replied helplessly that the men were no longer listening to them. "The army has taken their course, and would pursue it." Hopkins rode to the rear of the army, fearing an attack would be made on the disorganized rear echelons. (In reality he was probably trying to explain away the embarrassment of having the army's "commander" follow the army instead of the other way around.) All in all, Hopkins concluded that the appearance of such a large force so far north would at least instill some measure of fear in the local tribes and might make them think before aiding the enemy. This, at least, would prevent the expedition from being a total failure.[16]

Both the armies under Hopkins and Harrison were kept busy during the second half of 1812, but little news of their actions made its way home to Kentucky. The disruption of what little connection the frontier regions of the Old Northwest had with Kentucky and the rest of the United Stated meant the men might as well be fighting on the dark side of the moon. Back in Frankfort autumn was in full swing and Governor

Shelby was starting to become restless. Organizing, equipping, and dispatching men to different states and territories was time consuming. But once a venture had been launched, there was nothing to do but wait. Shelby had hoped that dispatches would arrive at regular intervals to keep him abreast of the army's progress. But the arrival of messengers on the steps of the governor's mansion was a rarer occurrence than Shelby preferred. He had watched thousands of his fellow Kentuckians march off to engage the enemy, but where were they now? Had they been defeated? Had they even engaged the enemy? The memory of the disaster at Detroit could only exacerbate his apprehension.

On the evening of the twenty-fifth, a letter finally arrived in Frankfort. Shelby eagerly opened it and found it was from Harrison. Reading over the dispatch and discovering, to his relief, that things were still progressing fine, the annoyed governor put his pen to paper in an obvious rebuke. "I was honored last evening with the receipt of your Excellency's favour of the 18th Instt," he began before adding with some asperity, "Which was the first intimation we have had of your position in twenty days." Having added this subtle reminder, Shelby went on to express his "highest gratification" to hear that the Kentucky troops had performed to the general's liking. Shelby replied to Harrison's letter by describing the expedition under General Hopkins, whose troubles had not yet reached him, hoping that Harrison could make use of them as well.[17]

> . . . his [Hopkins] whole force would not in my opinion be less than two thousand or upwards of mounted volunteers of the most respectable citizens that perhaps ever was embodied either from this or any other state in the union. Having gone to Louisville to personally see the men off, Shelby reports "I have never seen such a body of men in the western country or any where else."[18]

But the governor would soon learn that his vote of confidence in Hopkins had been premature. In late October, a dispatch arrived in Frankfort from General Hopkins himself, and Shelby reviewed it with great interest. But each line revealed that, instead of being a resounding success, the mission had been a disaster. The letter stated that the men were on their way to Bufferton to be discharged. "Yes Sir, this army has returned without hardly obtaining the sight of the enemy. . . . Hopkins army had crossed the Wabash on 14th instant and marched about three miles and encamped."[19] From there Hopkins had announced to the officers that they were going after the Kickapoo, whose primary villages were eighty to one hundred miles away. They were the most formidable tribe in the area and, thus, the most immediate threat. Some of the officers told Hopkins they would meet and discuss it and wanted to meet the man who had given him this intelligence. There was a better attitude among the men than at Vincennes, where there had been "discontents and murmurings." This only increased at Bufferton, and by the time they had reached Fort Harrison there was a spike in desertions "although no army was ever better, or more amply supplied with rations and forage than at this place."[20]

The confidence expressed by the governor in the men under Hopkins had been in excess of anything he had related about the other formations marching out of Kentucky. The surprise generated by the enterprise must have been second only to the fall of Detroit some months earlier. Harrison's aide-de-camp was in town and Shelby took the opportunity to pass along the details. The matter was made worse by the knowledge that a force of regulars and militia had been marching to meet Hopkins at Peoria in what was to be a pincer movement. Now one whole wing of that pincer was missing. "Thus has ended an enterprise," Shelby lamented, "on which the flower of Kentucky had enlisted themselves and are now returning home deeply mortified by disappointment."[21] While deeply chagrined and embarrassed by the conduct of the army, Shelby never lost faith in Hopkins. In a later letter to General Harrison he asserted, "Various Gentlemen with whom I have conversed and whose duty it was to be near General Hopkins admit that his conduct throughout the whole expedition, was that of an Attentive Vigilant good Officer."[22]

On the ninth of November, Shelby sat down to write Hopkins. "My dear General," he began. The failure of the expedition was a disappointment, he admitted, and Shelby seemed shocked "That so formidable a body of respectable men, as the volunteers under your Command possessing so much good sense zeal and patriotism with which they embarked on the expedition, should afterwards without any Just Cause be so entirely influenced by a Spirit of discord and discontent... is to me one of the most unaccountable events that has ever passed my observation."[23]

Shelby saved his most scathing criticism for the men of high social rank that had marched with the expedition. In his mind, it had been their job to rally the men behind Hopkins, to see that the objective was achieved. Their silent acquiescence made them guilty of the offense. It

is even possible that some of these respectable men had been the insti-
gators of the cabal. With a true Kentucky euphemism, Shelby declared,
"I most devotedly wish that the truth may leak out, and the saddle be
fixed upon the right back."[24]

The army under Hopkins had reminded Shelby of his Revolutionary
War days at places like Kings Mountain and only underscored the con-
cerns Shelby had voiced to the secretary of war in his letter. It was not
enough to respond with small-scale tête-à-tête attacks on the enemy or
to fight an entirely defensive war. A nineteenth-century version of shock
and awe was needed to turn the tide. While Harrison gathered his army
for the march to Detroit, Hopkins' expedition was to sweep large areas
of the Northwest Territory of hostile Indians. Instead, it had fallen apart
at the seams. Assuring Hopkins that the cause of the failure was beyond
his control, Shelby confessed that he had several of Hopkins' letters deal-
ing with the expedition published for the general public to prove the
fault was not his.[25]

While Hopkins was rallying a second force for another expedition,
the disgruntled militia under Winchester had been continuing north.
By the time the troops crossed the Auglaize River they were put on half
rations and were constantly pausing to form the battle line to ward off
parties of warriors who would appear out of nowhere and then disappear
in the woods just as quickly. Exasperated, five of the men offered to scout
ahead to prevent any more surprises. They were given permission and
disappeared into the woods. They never returned. Night fell and the
army stopped for the night. By the next evening they had only progressed five miles. As the forest dimmed in the twilight the men in the
front of the column stumbled onto a gruesome discovery. The scouts
had met the enemy, but it had not ended well. Their corpses all had bul-
let holes and tomahawk wounds. Their bloodied heads had been
scalped.[26]

The grief at the loss of their compatriots mingled with frustration as
the slow-moving army was slowed even more when several baggage wagons broke down and the army was forced to halt while repairs were
made. There was nothing left to do but wait. There was, at least, a river
nearby, and after weeks on army rations, fresh fish sounded like a welcomed diversion. Peering longingly into the cool waters of the Auglaize,
several soldiers stared longingly at the fish waiting to be caught. Ignoring
the repeated orders not to discharge their weapons, one soldier loaded
his musket, stuck the barrel in the water, and pulled the trigger. The heat

from the discharge inside the water-cooled barrel split the barrel and badly injured the soldier in yet one more episode in a long string of disappointments.[27]

As the march to Fort Defiance continued, the men became more cautious. At one point during the march several men on horseback were spotted in the distance. The front units of the army gave chase and, seeing they were discovered, the men on horseback beat a hasty retreat. After a considerable time the gap between pursuer and prey was closed enough for the gallant militia units to realize they had been chasing their own scouts who had been sent out earlier. The men around the campfire that night laughed at the mistake, though it highlighted how easily details can be confused during war time.[28] By September 30, Winchester's men had been just a mile from the key post of Fort Defiance. The situation was deemed dangerous enough that a breastwork was built here. On October 1, 380 men under the command of Colonel Lewis were dispatched seven or eight miles down the river in search of rumored British and Indian forces. While it was clear the enemy had been there it was also clear they had moved on. Colonel Lewis returned to camp with the news and the unspoken question of whether the enemy had truly retreated or if they might appear again on the American flank.[29]

The next day General Harrison arrived in camp with around one hundred mounted troops and two things that were of great interest to the army. The first was two days' worth of flour. It had been four days since the men had run out and fresh bread was heartily welcomed. The second item was a document confirming once and for all that he was commander of the Northwest Army. Three additional regiments arrived the next day and the situation finally appeared to be improving. Harrison had received word of a combined British and Indian force on its way, and he was preparing to meet it. Before long, their force would be joined by men from Virginia and Pennsylvania, which would bring their troop levels to around ten thousand men. Perhaps just as vital as the reinforcements was the additional promise of supplies from St. Mary's. The flour Harrison had brought would soon be gone and, without extra rations, the army would have to dissolve.[30]

But inactivity continued to fuel dissension in the ranks and the arrival of the clothing left at Piqua did little to ease tensions in the camp. One expedition was cancelled when the men refused to march due to lack of faith in the officer in charge. Security and discipline had been tightened as well. When one poor sentry was found asleep at his post he was arrested and tried by court martial. He was found guilty and ordered to be shot. When the day of his execution arrived, Winchester's men were ordered into formation. Then, before the columns of soldiers, the unfortunate prisoner was marched to the place of execution as "solemn music" began wafting over the otherwise silent procession. Reaching the selected spot, the man was blindfolded and the guards that had brought him to the scene stepped away. The only task left was for the firing detail to pull the trigger. The silence was finally broken when a reprieve arrived from General Harrison. The sleepy sentry had been spared, but the message was clear. The enemy was near and breach of orders would not be tolerated.[31]

The rainy weather continued to menace the army throughout autumn and the vibrant enthusiasm of the soldiers had begun to fade, replaced by sickness and persistent cold. The army that had marched north several weeks early had done so with the cheers of the neighbors ringing in their ears to save Detroit. Instead, they were slogging through mire constantly on the alert for an enemy that could appear at any time and fade away without warning. Darnell's exuberance had died down some as well, as he noted in his journal that "Four of this army have gone to the silent tomb, never more to visit their friends in Kentucky." It was clear to everyone that as long as the fever spread, it was inevitable that casualties would continue to climb.[32]

But the creeping pace of the army was not entirely the fault of the weather. It was also partially due to design. Harrison knew (as evidenced by the fall of Detroit) that an isolated army was sure to be defeated eventually. The key to success lay in establishing a chain of blockhouses and forts throughout the Northwest. Doing so would provide refuges for settlers, a safe dry place to store supplies, and a defensive position that did not require as many men to be concentrated in one area to prevent their being cut off from help. With this in mind Harrison dispatched 240 men to rebuild Fort Defiance. But this would take time.[33]

While Harrison struggled to forge a chain of defense and supply, the army's left wing and the unpopular General Winchester were scraping the bottom of the barrel when it came to supplies. The shortage was not due to a lack of planning. A shipment had been sent to Winchester's men under the command of Kentucky Militia colonel William Jennings. This included a significant amount of food. But, hearing rumors that the British were waiting to intercept the Americans, Jennings had stopped and built a blockhouse by the Auglaize River to protect the supplies from the enemy until the rumor proved false or alternative orders were sent.[34] This short-term fix dragged on and by mid-October the supplies slated for Winchester's hungry soldiers remained neatly stored within the log walls, waiting to be picked up for the last leg of their journey. Meanwhile, the soldiers in the area of Fort Defiance began to feel the pinch. Winchester's camp had been placed in an uproar when one grim and famished soldier glanced at the plate of his neighbor. He accused the man of getting more than he deserved, which brought a swift response. Before long the argument escalated into a full-scale fight. The contest quickly drew the attention of everyone nearby who not only heard the conversation but also the blows. A nearby corporal pulled his knife and rushed in to break up the fight, but his haphazard efforts almost struck a bystander, who took offense and the fight expanded. Finally the other soldiers broke up the fight and the men, but as the crowd dispersed it had become more obvious than ever that something had to be done to alleviate the supply shortage.[35]

A detachment of men from the ever-shrinking pool of healthy troops was dispatched to make the forty-mile trek south to the stranded supplies. Northcutt was among them. Their journey turned out to be a miserable one. As night fell after a long day's march the men set up camp. There was no food to be had, but the presence of an innumerable supply of mosquitos caused them to build a fire anyway. If they could not eat themselves, at least they could prevent themselves from being dinner for the host of insects in the area. The blazing fire offered warmth and respite from the mosquitos, but the men soon discovered that the fire was attracting the attention of nearby wolves. Presented with a choice between the buzzing of mosquitos or the howling of wolves the men grudgingly extinguished this last comfort and lay down for a long cold night. But the sun eventually rose and the band of men found themselves at the door of the blockhouse the next day.[36]

Now equipped with full bellies and loads of supplies the men began the return trip. But, in keeping with the already soggy autumn, the skies opened up on their return and drenched the men. Northcutt would complain that his "boots got full of water at least one dozen times" that first day. The next morning the men awoke to find the rain had mercifully ended, though everything remained very damp. Soggy clothes were an annoyance, but soggy gunpowder could mean the difference between life and death. One by one the men primed their guns for firing, but each time one of them pulled the trigger he was rewarded with a rather substandard metallic click instead of the loud crack of a weapon firing correctly. There was nothing to do but pack up and return to camp while hoping to avoid war parties in the area. By nightfall they were back in camp with the supplies. The army would hold together, at least for a little while longer.[37]

Back in camp the food helped raise the spirits of the men toward their duties as well as one another, but it did little to increase their regard for General Winchester. To say so out loud was a breach of military etiquette. Instead, some of the men decided to show their displeasure through more anonymous, if creative, methods. During one of the many long nights that must have seemed to run together after a while, General Winchester made his way through the dark to the latrine. The general found out too late that his makeshift toilet had been covered with a porcupine skin complete with quills. On a separate occasion his personal toilet was again sabotaged by being sawed nearly in half. The result was the structure gave way under his weight and Winchester went toppling "backwards into no very decent place." The next morning the unnamed perpetrators knew their scheme had been successful when they woke to find the General's "rigementals hanging high upon a pole the next day taking in the fresh air."[38] Through this long period of inaction there was some shuffling of men and material, including Northcutt and the rest of Garrard's Bourbon Blues who were soon transferred to Franklinton where they joined Colonel James Ball's United States Dragoons to go on more raids against native villages.[39] The rest of the army remained behind waiting for spring and the chance to take action. As the Bourbon Blues rode away from the camp they had no way of knowing that their path and that of their companions would end very differently.

Around the fifth of November the Bourbon Blues rode into Franklinton to join the regulars. They would spend the next three weeks there gathering supplies and preparing for their next mission into the forests. There were no tents so they would have to camp in the local courthouse, although there was one benefit to this assignment. Northcutt and his company could finally turn in their infantry muskets for cavalryman's pistol, sword, and a shorter rifle called a Yauger, which could be more easily wielded from horseback. From now on they would fight on horseback instead of foot.[40]

Fear of Indian attacks had seized the area causing local citizens to picket the courthouse and remain inside to prevent attack, which must have made for a crowded three weeks. On November 20, they departed for Xenia, Ohio. Outside of an incident involving some stolen pistols (which led to the perpetrator being forced to ride a very uncomfortable rail around the camp before being discharged) the journey was a smooth one. The men moved from Xenia through the freshly fallen snow to Dayton where they left their baggage and wrapped their feet with cloth to prevent frostbite.[41]

The harsh night march had brought the men to within a mile of their intended target by sunrise. To this point they had been undetected, but as the sun penetrated the forest canopy and shadows formed recognizable shapes they were spotted by an Indian scout who quickly alerted his village. The dragoons formed a line half a mile long and charged through the thick underbrush engulfing the town. Nine villagers were killed and forty-two taken prisoner. A contingent of the men crossed the stream that lay behind the village and continued the battle while those on the near side set the huts and wigwams on fire. The men repeated this three miles down the river at another village, but this time there was no resistance as the inhabitants had fled. Forty horses were captured and taken back with them. This would inhibit the warriors' mobility and would lessen the likelihood of being outmaneuvered at some point in the future.[42]

The sun soon dipped below the trees and the men settled down for another cold night. At two hours before dawn a false alarm roused them from their beds and the relatively little warmth they had left them shivering in the darkness. Rather than returning to their tents only to be roused again in two hours the men began preparing their breakfast. There was some captured beef from the day before and some leftover biscuits that would provide a simple but filling fare. A bucket of water heating over the fire would soon be transformed into steaming hot coffee to make the morning chill more bearable.[43]

As the majority of the army huddled around their campfires the sentries stood peering into the darkness a short distance from camp. The night had been quiet and those unfortunate enough to be standing watch undoubtedly looked forward to daybreak and a chance to get warm. Then, in the distance, a sentry spotted human forms gliding silently toward him. A line of warriors was streaming through the trees with an obvious objective. Too frightened to yell he raised his musket and cocked the hammer and squeezed the trigger to sound the alarm. The muzzle remained silent and only the snap of the hammer signaled that the gun had misfired. He instantly drew the hammer back again and fired with the same result. The panic-stricken soldier repeated this feat several times until mercifully a nearby sentry also spotted the column. Yelling and firing his gun the camp was instantly on its feet, but the natives were also prepared. The front warrior fired his own musket and a collective yell rose through the trees as native warriors formed a line and came crashing through the trees toward the camp.[44]

The surprised Americans doused their fires and fell back in an effort to organize and return fire. The warriors seemed to have the upper hand and the men were forced to fall behind their horses for cover. Casualties in men and horses mounted quickly and the smoke from muskets and rifles rose into one collective mass until the only way to know where the enemy was (or if they were still there) was by watching the muzzle flashes. Slowly the Indians fell back and some of the men managed to mount their horses and charge the native rear guard, only to be cut down.[45] The whole time the captured prisoners from the day before were yelling and cheering their comrades on.[46]

With that the battle ended and the smoke began to clear. The warriors had managed to carry away their wounded, but forty dead were left on the field. Eight Americans were dead and four more would die later. Perhaps most significantly, more than sixty were wounded and would have to be transferred back to camp somehow.[47] The decision was made to bury the dead in the cabin where the prisoners had been kept and then to burn the building in order to prevent their being discovered and dug up. Then the men cut long slender poles and sewed canvass around them. This would serve as a makeshift cot for the wounded. One end of the two rods would be attached to a horse and the other two would drag on the ground, allowing the wounded to recline on the way back but also to feel the jolt of every bump they hit on the way home.[48]

The slow march back to base meant the army was a prime target, and a number of false alarms continued to plague the army. Northcutt disdainfully declared that he would not be so easily fooled, and when his turn came for guard duty he was determined to prove it but found the promise difficult to keep. Like the sentry from a few nights before, he found the monotony of his watch interrupted by a shadowy shape moving toward him through the brush. He raised his weapon and cocked the hammers in dreaded anticipation. He was further convinced this was more than his imagination when he heard the clicking of at least two more sentries down the line who had obviously spotted something as well. In the silence Northcutt waited for his target to break through the foliage. When it finally emerged he could clearly see that his adversary was a lost horse who had broken free and was now wandering back into camp after a night in the woods.[49]

Not all expeditions turned out to be so eventful and the Bourbon Blues soon learned that their greatest enemy could be the weather. On one trip Northcutt found himself bounced drowsily along in the saddle of his horse through the dark night on the chilly sixteenth of December. The weather was bitterly cold, especially after sunset. An exhausting day's ride coupled with the penetrating cold had deadened Northcutt's senses until he nodded off. Suddenly out of the darkness something tore at his face and clothes and he was instantly awake from the stinging sensation it caused. His enemy, however, proved to be nothing more than a malevolent tree branch that hung low over the path his company was taking. It was not the first time it happened that night and the repeated attacks by the local flora did little to improve his mood. Despite the aggravating night Northcutt was better off than some of his fellow soldiers who had dismounted and walked alongside their horses to stamp out some of the cold. Their efforts were rewarded by perspiring feet that later cooled when they remounted, causing horrible frostbite.[50]

As Harrison sought to disrupt enemy tribes and build his army and supply lines Governor Shelby had been working to combat the cold. In early October the governor had dispatched riders carrying a special request to the various corners of the state. But this time was different than the requests for volunteers that had gone out before. Shelby was not requesting additional manpower. In fact, his correspondence did not include men at all but reached out to the other half of the state's citizenry. The leaves were shedding their green hues for shades of gold and red; it was becoming more obvious to the old soldier that Harrison would be forced to retire his army to winter quarters before they could act. The army would need winter clothing (something they had neglected to pack that sunny August when they had marched from Georgetown). The result was a circular that was distributed throughout the state and addressed to the "Patriotic Females of Kentucky." What the men needed now was not arms or ammunition but coats and blankets, and who better to supply them than the "benevolent and humane patriotic fair sex of Kentucky"? Beneath the proclamation were two columns for the names of the participants and the items they intended to donate. Linen shirts and knitted socks were some of the most popular items (and for good reason), but items like mittens, overalls, pantaloons, gloves, roundabouts, shoes, and short coats also made the list as wives, daughters, mothers, and neighbors signed up to make and donate what they could.[51]

The response to Shelby's request had been immediate and favorable. Places like Louisville, Georgetown, and Falmouth were receiving shipments within weeks. By the fourteenth of October, the citizens of Shelbyville were estimating that two wagonloads could be filled before the end of the month.[52] The subject was brought to the forefront again when a letter from General Harrison to Shelby was published in the *Kentucky Gazette* promising to have the clothes brought north as quickly as possible using government funds. The clothes would be boxed and then labeled so it would be known what regiment was to receive what. Like the care packages compiled for troops in the modern era, this gave the project a more personal air. The socks, jackets, and shirts were not disappearing into some nebulous government bureaucracy. They were being sent directly to family members and neighbors.[53]

Collecting the clothing had turned out to be the easy part. Getting wagonloads of goods through the soggy terrain of Indiana and Ohio without being mired in a seasonal morass or being attacked by Indians was another. Abraham Hite of Jefferson County was placed in charge of collecting clothing in Louisville to be forwarded on to Vincennes. Making his way to Louisville from his home in farmland south of the city, Hite soon found the project in a state of confusion. For starters, a captain was already in Louisville collecting supplies for General Hopkins' army by order of the quartermaster. Interpreting this to include clothing, a portion of the donations had already been collected by him and departed on a boat for Hopkins' men. Unfortunately, the journey proved to be a rather short one, as the boat grounded on some unknown object less than a mile from Louisville. The crates of clothes had to be moved to another vessel but, after a brief delay, were now on their way again.[54]

Efforts to locate transportation in Lexington were not meeting with much success. With no river running through town, items would have to be sent over land. Thomas Bodley, who had been appointed quartermaster of the Northwest Army's left wing, was attempting to gather supplies in the city to be sent to Winchester's men. He soon discovered that teams of oxen and packhorses could be acquired, if the price was right that is, but finding drivers willing to leave their own hearth to travel through hostile territory during the frosty autumn was another matter entirely. Bodley lamented that "every exertion has been made to get drivers for the teams & packhorses, but the advanced state of the Season &

the prospect of bad weather & roads; alarms them & prevents them from engaging."[55]

One major issue that hindered the recruitment of drivers was whether it would be counted as military service or not. Marching off, rifle in hand, to meet the British certainly counted as a tour of duty, but was the same true of driving a team of oxen pulling a wagonload of laundry?[56] The answer was unclear but important. If this was not counted as military service a volunteer could spend weeks driving supplies north to Vincennes and suffering the same privations and dangers as the troops only to return and find himself drafted in the next wave of volunteers who left the state to serve their country. October and November were prime time for gathering stores for winter. The last vestiges of the harvest had to be gathered or go to market; the cool autumn weather made this time of the year the best time to slaughter hogs and to lay in wood for the coming winter. It would take more than a negligible wage and the thanks of their country to draw many farmers from their works at such a crucial time unless they could be assured they would not be called on again in the near future. As the weeks had passed the shipment had slowly come together, and as the end of the year approached Shelby worked to get the needed supplies to the front.

But Winchester's men knew nothing of the confusion back in Kentucky. They had continued to chop, saw, dig, and hammer uninterrupted, and by October 19, their new fort, modestly named Fort Winchester, was completed.[57] The last picket was added just in time too. Encounters with hostile Indians were becoming more frequent and more deadly, suggesting that more and more British allies were moving into the area. It was becoming more risky to send out reconnaissance missions, too. Captain James Logan led one of the few groups to try it. Logan was an excellent scout. He was a native Shawnee chief who had allied himself with the American cause. Leading a band of native scouts out of the new fort Logan and his men scanned the forests for clues of nearby danger. Around November 22, he and two fellow scouts stumbled onto a British officer and five enemy warriors. The two sides clearly saw one another and Logan had to think fast. He and his men were outnumbered and outgunned, which left them with only three options: run, surrender, or try to bluff their way out. Logan chose the latter. The Shawnee were allies of the British so it would not be out of place for him to bring intelligence to the British. Sauntering up to the British officer, Logan and his men pretended to be on their way to the British line with news about the American force at Fort Winchester. Not quite buying the story, the British officer and his allies determined to follow the three men to the British camp. After all, it was safer to travel in as large a group as possible. And if Logan and his men happened to be lying and were foolish enough to try and run through the forest, it would be no problem for the mounted natives to shoot them or run them down. With no other alternative Logan and his men agreed and began their march toward the British lines. Having been allowed to keep their arms, Logan and his men walked several miles with the small band behind them, waiting for the most opportune time when the enemy would become complacent. It was a difficult call. The longer he waited to act the more complacent the enemy would become, but each step also brought them closer to British troops and farther away from their own army. Finally, Logan felt he could wait no longer. Without warning he wheeled around and opened fire. Both sides exchanged several shots and the mounted Indians dismounted to seek cover.[58]

Having driven the enemy away from their horses Logan and one of his men darted toward the free horses, leapt into the saddles of two of the animals, and rode to camp. Riding through the underbrush they made it safely away from their captors and soon arrived at camp. The third scout returned on foot the next morning with a bloody scalp to testify to the battle. Their intelligence proved the British were in the area. But it came with a price. Logan had been wounded. The men did what they could, but the wound was mortal. After two days of intense pain Logan died.[59]

Logan's mission proved that building Fort Winchester as soon as possible was a wise decision. If the men and supplies were to be able to withstand a siege they would need walls to offer protection. But in truth, this was all the fort could offer. Fort Winchester was not meant to permanently house large armies but rather to offer temporary shelter. A more permanent defense against the enemy and the weather was needed. By crossing to the opposite bank, the army could spread out some and would have easier access to firewood, since most wood on the other side had already been consumed in building the fort. Eventually a second and then third campsite was selected. Finally, at camp number three, the men began to build huts to ward off the approaching winter, which would have found its way through the thin tents that had sheltered them through the summer and fall.[60] Eight-foot pickets were placed around the camp and the men settled in.[61]

Winchester could offer little comfort to his men so far removed from civilization, and the situation continued to deteriorate as the last of Jennings' supplies ran out and additional shipments were late in coming. At one point, the army had been six days without flour. By the eighteenth of December Captain Hickman went in search of the long-absent supplies.[62] While he was travelling south, Bodley and his canoes full of supplies were moving upriver, but navigating through the natural debris that clogged the river and having to break through ice that was too thin to walk on but thick enough to stop the canoes slowed him down considerably.[63] Slowly supplies began to trickle in. By the twenty-second, three hundred hogs had arrived and enough flour had made it to camp for a three-fourths ration to be distributed. This only left food for the horses, which remained almost nonexistent. When the time came to make the final leg of the journey to the Maumee Rapids, sleds full of supplies had to be pulled by men because the packhorses were too weak. By Christmas Eve, more than one hundred men were dead and three hundred were sick.[64]

Meanwhile, Harrison was developing his strategy. With summer gone and autumn fading quickly the best possible alternative was an early and bitter winter. If the temperatures could drop the marshlands that made up the area would freeze over, making the terrain passible. The road to Fort Defiance was described as "one continual swamp, knee deep on the packhorses and up to the hubs of the wagons."[65] Without a hard freeze, the army would have almost no mobility, but once the ground was hard they could move easily.

Writing to the secretary of war, Harrison confided that freezing temperatures were key to the recovery of Detroit. While it might seem like he was being inactive, waiting for the bitter cold was necessary. In words that would almost prove prophetic he warned against any attempt to recover Detroit with an enemy army waiting at Malden. The army would stick out like a sore thumb with supply lines that were tantalizingly long and easy to disrupt (especially by British forces on Lake Erie). The only answer was to have a second force stationed nearby that would be used to cover the flanks of the army that would recover Detroit and to meet the enemy anywhere they tried to land.[66]

The one thing Harrison could do was seek out more supplies. Though somewhat dismayed by how little the contractors had prepared, he began to amass supplies at Sandusky for the march north. In the meantime, he would keep his army spread out in three groups. This would allow his army to protect a greater area and would discourage hostile warriors from making attacks on settlements, as there would always be a considerable force nearby to intercept or pursue them.[67] Harrison's strategy of building chains of forts and blockhouses was slow and tedious but effective. If everything proceeded according to plan, Detroit and the Michigan Territory would soon be back in American hands.

There was one thing that must have given Harrison hope. He would not have to contend with Brock. In an attempt to deflect an American attack along the Niagara River in October, Brock had been killed in battle.[68] With the military prowess of Brock out of the way Harrison would have to deal with Colonel Henry Procter. The question was, what kind of man was he and what strategies would he employ?

Chapter Five

THE RIVER RAISIN

F OR WINCHESTER'S MEN Christmas passed in gloom and inactivity.
On the 27th of December some of the long-awaited clothing from
Kentucky arrived and was a welcome respite from the winter weather.[1]
In mid-January a snowstorm dropped up to two feet of snow in the area
surrounding the Maumee River and encased the army in a heavy white
blanket.[2] General Payne would later send his thanks to Governor Shelby
and the citizens of the state for sending the homespun clothing. By the
time the clothes were counted Kentucky's ladies had made an estimated
"2552 pairs of pantaloons, 814 vests, 1160 blankets, 8146 pairs of socks,
3510 pairs of mittens, 1176 roundabouts and hunting shirts, 192 shirts,
80 caps, 2038 pairs of socks."[3] Perhaps benefitting personally from some
of the shipment Payne sent an open letter to the *Kentucky Gazette* stating,

> It is a source of heartfelt satisfaction to express a proper sense of
> the obligations under which the *patriotism* of the sons of Kentucky
> have placed her volunteers, *that* pleasure is conceivably enhanced
> when they reflect that to the *daughters* of Kentucky they are in-
> debted for most of the comforts rendered imperiously necessity
> to withstand the keen blasts of a northern winter.[4]

Harrison's supply base at Sandusky was prospering as well, and the
general had every reason to be optimistic. Within weeks the lakes would
be frozen over and the formidable British ships, which were one of the
greatest symbols of Britain's imperial ambitions, would be helplessly

locked in their harbors. Once that was assured, the army would move north to recapture the territory that Hull had so easily relinquished before plotting greater action in the spring.[5]

On January 10, Winchester and the left wing reached the Maumee Rapids where they made camp and built a fort. General Payne had taken 670 Kentucky militia some time before and they were ready and waiting when the rest of Winchester's army arrived. They immediately began work on what would come to be known as Fort Meigs and would later play an important role in the outcome of the war.[6] All the pieces of Harrison's plan had fallen into place. He had amassed a large enough army to defeat the British and he had successfully split them into three wings that were far enough apart for the areas around them to sustain them in the cold months ahead. But one obstacle to victory still remained—one so important it threatened the success of the whole campaign. The Kentucky militia's six-month tour of duty would be over in February. If enough men could not be induced to remain, the entire plan would unravel, and the restless, bored, half-starved, and half-frozen militia was ready to leave. Time was not on Harrison's side.[7]

Back at the Rapids it is not unlikely that Winchester had anticipated the dissipation of his command as well. The refusal to obey orders and the several incidents of sabotage could not have failed to indicate the army's overall opinion of its commander. But any thoughts on this score were interrupted on January 13. While milling around camp with little to do, some of the men glanced up to see two men emerge from the woods and approach their camp. They were not Indians and they were not in uniform, which suggested they were not hostile, so Winchester's men allowed their approach. Once in camp it was made clear that the men were French descendants from the Michigan Territory, which now lay only a few miles to the north. They had traveled from the aptly named Frenchtown and were asking for protection from the Indians.[8] The men and the intelligence they could supply were a welcome sight. Many settlers in the Great Lakes area were of French origin and most were still unhappy with the British conquest of Canada during the French and Indian War. They much preferred to throw their lot in with the Americans. This meant the surrender of Michigan by Hull was a blow to them as well. Winchester sought what information he could from his two informants, and while trying to decide on a course of action five more Frenchmen arrived in camp four days later. The British were destroying Frenchtown, they claimed, in anticipation of the American approach.

Their very homes were being destroyed. The army was already restless and, as these reports circulated, they became even more anxious to take action. Would their tour really end without meeting the British at all, especially with them lying so nearby? Militiaman Robert Logan wrote to his sister that he hoped the men under Lewis could "protect the poore defenseless inhabitants from entire destruction—I think you may expect to hear of a bloody work shortly."[9] If they were not there to protect Americans from Indian and British attacks then what were they there for?

Winchester sought feedback from some of his officers. They had two options: remain where they were until Harrison was able to arrive with reinforcements in order to capture Detroit, or launch a preemptive attack on the British and Indian forces already at Frenchtown. The first option was safer and, perhaps more importantly, it was what they were ordered to do. Still, the second could save a strategic settlement in the region and garner even greater admiration from the primarily French settlers who, understandably, were not happy at the prospect of seeing their homes burned down. Asking Harrison what to do was out of the question since it would take too long to get an answer. The way Winchester saw it, a decision had to be made now.[10]

As the meeting adjourned and the officers returned to their units they brought word to their men. If the people of Frenchtown needed help then they had to go. Winchester detached 550 men with three days' rations. The men struck their tents, packed their gear, and urgently marched north. Later that night an additional 110 riflemen under Colonel Allen were sent to join them. The men marched in anticipation of finally getting to meet the enemy. As the sun sank beneath the horizon, the small command stopped for the night at a small island known as Presque Isle. At some point during their preparations for the night an express rider appeared out of the woods and rode into camp. If there was any doubt about the presence of British troops in Frenchtown he could lay their fears to rest. There were, indeed, two companies of British troops in the village with more on the way. With this information it was clear. The race was on. If the Kentuckians could get there first they would take the town for sure and hopefully turn back the advancing British column. But if they arrived later the fight would be that much tougher and success would be nowise guaranteed. The small army struck camp early the next morning and marched toward the small village and the waiting British regulars. Travelling on the ice they moved forward, determined to "conquer or die."[11]

When the men arrived within sight of the small town on January 18 they found the British ready and waiting. To this point, they had only fought small bands of Indians and swarms of mosquitos. Now, for the first time, they would meet professional British soldiers. The officers halted their men a quarter mile outside of the town to form into battle lines. The confrontation they had been seeking had arrived. As the militia formed battle lines they could see the shapes of men and buildings that stood at a distance. A bright flash followed by the echo of cannons sounded. The British knew they were here. Two more volleys were fired, but in each of the three times they did little damage. The army, now formed in battle lines, stood ready. The orders were given and the men started forward with a shout. Rushing over the snow-covered ground the men could see the flash and hear the firing of British rifles as they came into range.[12]

The Americans held their fire and continued their rapid advance. Just before reaching the British lines the order to halt was given and the men unleashed a volley of fire in unison. Immediately, the British fell back and the Kentucky militia rapidly advanced into the town itself. The relentless push by the militia soon forced the British and their native allies to the edge of town with a few pausing periodically to try and return fire. The Kentuckians pressed their advantage until the British had left the town entirely and sought refuge in the woods.[13]

The battle had begun around three in the afternoon and the winter sun soon fell behind the horizon. With it too dark to see the battle broke off and the Americans slowly filtered back into the town. Twelve men had been killed and fifty-five were wounded. There were at least fifteen confirmed dead among the British. Despite similar numbers killed, the battle had been an astounding success. The British and Indian forces had offered little resistance and the town was safe in American hands. Colonel Lewis, commander of militia, sent word to Winchester that evening, who forwarded the good news on to Harrison by express rider.[14]

The next morning the band of Kentuckians set about the unenviable task of collecting the dead from the frozen battlefield. Many of the bodies were found stripped, and bloody streaks in the snow offered silent testimonies of the enemy wounded and dead that had been dragged into the woods to conceal their losses. When the army turned to inspect the settlement that they had just saved, they found significant quantities of rations, including "apples, cider, sugar, butter, and whiskey," which had been stored up by the recently departed British.[15]

Winchester arrived at the Raisin River on the evening of the nineteenth, with Colonel Wells and three hundred of his regulars from the
17th US Infantry. They were a welcome sight to the men already in town
and it was suggested by Colonel Lewis that they should camp inside the
picketed area near the town. However, military etiquette was not to be
ignored, even in wartime, and Winchester felt the regular infantry
should have the right to camp in the open field just outside of town.
When Winchester arrived he sought out a house from which to establish
his headquarters. It would need to be an appropriate dwelling for a general. Winchester was as sick of the cold unamenable quarters back at the
Rapids as anyone, so not just any house would do. When he finally did
find one that could be deemed acceptable it was a mile and a half from
Frenchtown and the army.[16] Colonel Madison and Colonel Lewis led
their men into the town. The tavern at Frenchtown had a garden area
inside its pickets, which rose six feet high and provided enough space
for the militia to settle down.[17]

Writing to Governor Shelby, General Payne happily reported that
"Since my last, a detachment of 650 men under the command of Lieut
Col WILLIAM LEWIS, 5th regiment Kentucky Volunteers, at the 18th
inst. Obtained a glorious victory over a combination of British & Savages... at the river Raisin."[18] But not everyone was caught up in the euphoria of victory. Without realizing it, Winchester had placed his men
and himself in a dangerous position. They were much deeper into enemy
territory than Harrison had ordered. And, not withstanding its small
picketed area, Frenchtown could hardly be thought of as a fortified position. Not to mention Winchester's advance could not go unanswered.
The British may have been willing to allow the Americans to remain
stationary at the Rapids, but this new sign of advance would certainly
garner some response.

Word of the battle at Frenchtown had travelled quickly, and at four
in the morning a sleeping Harrison was awakened with word of what
had happened. Realizing the precarious situation Winchester had placed
himself in, Harrison immediately ordered reinforcements to the Rapids
to bolster Winchester's force that remained there. Leaving the majority
of his men behind, Harrison galloped ahead to try and save the situation.
Riding into what had been Winchester's camp on the twentieth of January he found it empty. What was so clear to Harrison was hidden from
Winchester. He had taken a third of the Northwest Army and flung it
into a dangerous position without allowing Harrison any chance to pre-

pare reinforcements. To retreat from Frenchtown now to the safety of
the Rapids, even temporarily, might be interpreted as a sign of weakness
and invite retribution from the Indians or, at the very least, cause the
sympathetic inhabitants of the town to lose faith in the Americans and
stop offering their support. The advance may have been unwise, but
there was no going back now. Harrison again sent word ahead, ordering
Winchester to "maintain the position at any rate." Harrison waited until
the militia he had left behind arrived and then immediately sent Payne
with three hundred Kentucky militia forward to bolster Winchester's
force. Whether they would arrive in time to prevent a counterattack (if,
indeed, there was such an attack on the way) remained to be seen.[19]

At Frenchtown, many of the men were beginning to become uneasy
as well. They knew Harrison was on the way but so were those British
reinforcements who had intended to reinforce the men they had evicted
a few days before. Where were they? How close would they be now?
The retreating British defenders of Frenchtown had no doubt warned
them by this point, and they would be eager to recoup what they had
lost. On the evening of the twenty-first, a refugee entering the American
camp warned that a large number of British and Indians were on their
way to retake Frenchtown. Strangely enough, the same commanders
who so willingly accepted the word of the emissaries from Frenchtown
days earlier now scoffed at this new piece of intelligence. But for the average enlisted man, it was not as easy to forget about.[20]

This new rumor of an approaching enemy would certainly have been
of interest to an ensign named Harrow, but on the evening of January
21, he had new orders to keep him busy. Some of the men were breaking
curfew again. Being outside the camp, especially near dark, was dangerous. Harrow was ordered to take a few men and round them up. Leading
his detachment out of Frenchtown, they followed the Raisin River westward in search of their comrades. Not long after the light of camp had
faded into darkness a new light could be seen in the distance. Drawing
nearer it soon became obvious that the light was not a campfire but an
inn. It is hard to think of a more likely place for soldiers with little
knowledge of the area to find refreshment and company than the local
watering hole, so Harrow and his men moved forward to investigate.
The question was, who owned the inn? Or perhaps more importantly,
whose side were they on? Whoever it was, they were obviously home.
Harrow swung the door open and entered cautiously. The first floor was
empty. Turning to the stairs, Harrow climbed to the second floor. There

he came face to face with three individuals. The one in civilian clothing was obviously the landlord. The remaining two were British officers. The three men looked up with some surprise. The landlord immediately regained his senses and, abruptly ending the conversation with the officers, led Harrow downstairs amiably. Turning his charm on Harrow he quickly answered the obvious question. He admitted that, yes, the men were British, but they were too few to be of any danger and Harrow and his men had nothing to worry about. Finding themselves standing outside the inn, Harrow and his men decided the most prudent course of action was to alert the camp. Riding parallel to the dark waters of the Raisin, Harrow reported his findings to Colonel Lewis as soon as he could find him. Lewis listened to this fantastic tale politely but then dismissed it. British officers so few in number and so close to camp? No, the men could not have been officers. Harrow had made a mistake. Either way, it was of no consequence. An undoubtedly discouraged Harrow, having completed his mission, returned to his tent for the night.[21]

The men who had felt uneasy by the recent series of events passed an uneasy night in the frigid Michigan wilderness waiting for the attack they were sure was inevitable. Mercifully, the darkness faded into gray and the colors of the dawn began to peer over the treetops and illuminate the village. Feeling somewhat relieved to hear reveille beat, the men arose and began getting dressed. Sleepily going through the morning routine with the roll of the drum in the background they stopped. Was that a gunshot? Two more followed. It was the sentries. Something was wrong. The troops scrambled into formation to find a large body of British troops advancing on their camp. The rumored troops had arrived. The hail of musket fire was bad enough but the "balls, bombs, and grapeshot" that erupted from the woods shook the town and must have made the men wish for sturdier cover. The militia under Lewis and Madison inside the picket grabbed their muskets and opened fire on the approaching enemy. Through the chaos of battle they could see they were able to stall the advance on their position. Maybe they could hold the British off after all. Looking over the wall to where Wells and his regulars had made camp they found a different story. Without the pickets to buy them time or shelter, the men were easy targets. As the battle commenced they had burst from their tents and valiantly tried to form under the withering fire of the British, but confusion reigned and the men gave way. Falling back the men tried to form their lines again, but there was no time and the closing British wave started to sweep over them. The militia inside the safety of the wooden wall watched in horror. They had to do something or Wells' men would be annihilated. Colonel Lewis led some of the militia in a mad dash from the pickets toward the floundering regulars to try and reinforce them, but once they cleared the safety of the wooden walls they proved easy targets. Most made it only a few steps before British fire brought them down. The rest disappeared into the melee.[22]

The remaining men inside had little time to think about Wells and turned their full attention to their own defense. The British had taken such heavy fire from the picketed tavern that they were forced to retreat to just beyond the range of the militia's guns. But having rallied their troops, the British and their Indian allies rushed the pickets again. The residents of Frenchtown had made "port holes" in the pickets, which allowed the men to steady their rifles before firing. This aided the already deadly accuracy of the militia, which forced the unsuccessful attackers to seek shelter in the nearby woods for a second time. In the distance the men could see a sled undoubtedly loaded with ammunition being pulled by several soldiers toward the British cannon. It had been firing almost constantly since the battle began and had to be low on ammunition. With Wells' men out of the way, the cannon focused its full attention to the trapped militia. Determined not to be picked off like fish in a barrel some of the men took aim at the sled and, before it could reach the cannon, picked off the men pulling it. No one else seemed willing to take up the task. At least that was one threat neutralized.[23]

With the failure of the second attack the constant roll of firing died away with the exception of random shots fired by Indian snipers from the cover of the woods. The Kentucky militia took advantage of the inaction to eat some bread with an ever-watchful eye toward the woods. The men who had tried to rescue the regulars still lay where they fell in the snow not far from the walls, and several men were missing, including Colonel Lewis. No one had seen him die, but in the confusion of battle that did not mean anything. While chomping on their breakfast and surveying enemy lines they saw a single figure emerge with a white flag in his hand—probably some British demand for surrender or a truce to reclaim the dead and wounded. They watched warily as the man approached. As he got close they realized he was not a British officer sent to parley but one of their own men. Entering the safety of the enclosure the man bore a message. He had been captured but then sent with a message from Colonel Procter of the British forces. They were ordered

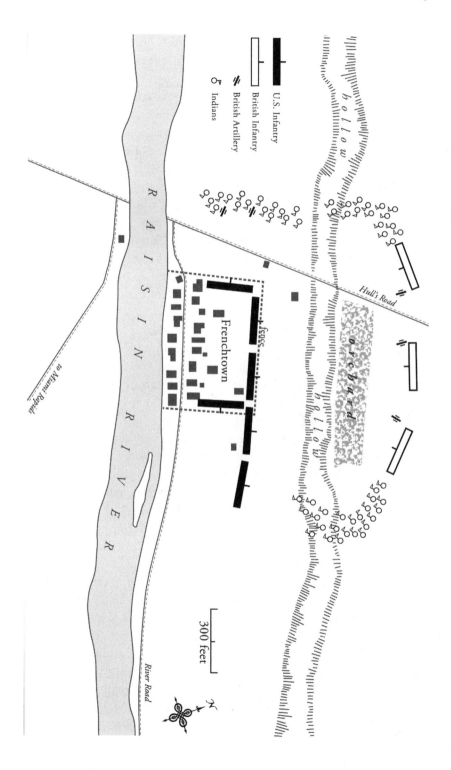

U.S. Infantry
British Infantry
British Artillery
Indians

hollow

Hull's Road

orchard

hollow

RAISIN RIVER

Frenchtown

fence

to Miami Rapids

River Road

300 feet

to surrender at once on order of General Winchester who was now a prisoner of the British. And if that was not motivation enough, Colonel Lewis had also been captured.[24]

Madison and his stunned officers were left to consider the situation. They had repulsed two enemy attacks and, knowing that Harrison was coming as quickly as he could, there was always a chance they could hold out. After all, there was always the possibility that one of Wells' regulars had escaped to tell Harrison what was happening. If so, he would move even faster. Time was on their side. What they had done twice before they could surely do again. On the other hand, who could tell whether a second wave of British regulars, Canadian militia, and native warriors were not marching south at this very moment? A reinforced Procter, especially if he was reinforced with artillery, would not hesitate to overrun the position. On top of that, the battle had eaten up much of their ammunition. All that remained was a single keg of cartridges and it was less than half full.[25]

The British watched attentively until finally Madison emerged. Crossing the open area he met a triumphant Procter. The descriptions of events like the massacre at Pigeon Roost were still fresh in the minds of both sides and Procter knew this provided him with additional leverage since even those willing to die in battle would be less open to being massacred. They would surrender, Madison told him. But only if they were protected. If the British planned to turn them over to the Indian warriors then they would remain where they were until the end. Angered by this continued display of defiance, Procter stamped his foot in the snow and demanded, "Sir, do you mean to dictate to me?"

"I mean to dictate for myself." Madison shot back. "We prefer selling our lives as dearly as possible, rather than be massacred in cold blood."[26] Procter was offended but he was forced to agree to four main points before the Kentuckians would lay down their arms. First, the private property of all soldiers was to be respected. It was common for native warriors to seize the possessions of their captured enemy and the men left inside the picket wanted to be protected from that. Second, sleds were to be sent for the wounded as soon as possible, to convey them to Malden to receive medical treatment. Third, a guard of British soldiers was to be left with the wounded to ensure they were not harmed by the Indians before they could be retrieved. Finally, sidearms, a costly sign of rank, were to be returned to the officers once they reached Malden.[27] All was hastily and dismissively agreed to. As the men marched out the native

warriors rushed forward and began stripping the men of their possessions as Procter looked on. Madison ordered the men to "Stand to their
arms and sell their lives as dearly as possible." Only at this sign of the
battle reigniting did the British step in.[28] Once stripped of their arms,
the healthy portion of the prisoners were prepared to march north immediately. Procter knew that Harrison was approaching, and he did not
want his wounded men to face another battle against fresh troops. To
withdraw was the only option.[29]

Harrison had indeed been marching north, but, hearing that his worst
fears were manifest, he had paused en route and immediately called a
council of war to answer one question. Should they continue or return?
It was decided that the only reason to advance would be to save Winchester by overrunning the British force that had defeated him, and the
likelihood of that with such a small force worn out from marching was
slim. Once the Pennsylvania and Virginia troops promised arrived from
the east, Harrison could strike at the British. Until then, the only thing
to be done was to send out detachments of men along the roads in hopes
of finding and protecting those who had escaped. No more than thirty
men were found alive.[30]

As a dispirited Harrison marched south again, a concerned Procter
withdrew northward. Any wounded Americans who could not travel
without assistance were left at Frenchtown in their agony. The villagers
took the wounded into their homes and, with the help of the militia doctors left behind by Procter, began treating the wounds as best they could.[31]
The wounded who were well enough to apprehend what was happening
around them must have felt an uneasy dread as they watched their fellow
Kentuckians disappear into the woods with their British captors. Perhaps
what was more disturbing than seeing the last Kentucky militiaman disappear was to see the last British soldiers march out of sight. The guard
promised by Procter at Madison's surrender had never materialized.[32]

One party of around forty men had escaped the battlefield and fled
southward before being overtaken by a chief who promised their safety
if they would surrender. They did so, but almost half were massacred
anyway. The newly made prisoners were led back toward Frenchtown,
passing by the bodies of those who had died along the way and had their
clothes stolen and their scalps removed. The solemn march was continued through the town toward Malden.[33]

Early on the morning of January 23, a large war party, possibly two
hundred strong, entered the camp. If any of the wounded Kentuckians

doubted their intentions they were soon made clear by their yelling as well as the war paint they wore on their faces. They dispersed quickly and began entering the houses where they plundered the homes of anything they wanted that could be carried. Next, they turned to the wounded that lay helpless before them. They were stripped of their possessions and many were tomahawked. Two homes that contained particularly high numbers of wounded were set on fire. When those inside realized what was happened they struggled to the door to escape the flames. Those who couldn't make it were burned alive. Those who did make it outside the inferno were tomahawked by waiting warriors and tossed, lifeless or dying, back into the flames.[34]

But not all prisoners who were spared the flames of Frenchtown were destined for a prisoner cage in Canada. Some would remain prisoners of the tribes who had fought alongside the British. Those men had been marched away from the town and were mercifully out of earshot of the screams of their perishing fellow soldiers. They, too, were left to expect the worst but without confirmation. Americans who found themselves prisoners of the Indians were often taken to the village of their captor where they were expected to become a functioning member of the society. One such soldier was Thomas Mallary. As Mallary struggled to march with his fellow prisoners he witnessed a horrible scene unfolding in stages. The long column of prisoners that snaked through the snow was kept in check by the watchful eye of their native captors. When any soldier began to slow or show signs of fatigue he was instantly tomahawked. It soon became clear that the only hope of survival was to march through the pain. Arriving at an Indian village along the river Rouge, Mallary found himself among a considerable number of wigwams that were occupied by women and children, which he estimated to be around two thousand in number.[35]

Soon after arriving in camp, Mallary was stripped of his clothes and given Indian attire. Cooperating for the moment, Mallary changed his clothes and then submitted to having his ears pierced. Following this began the process of having his head shaved with the exception of one lock of hair on top. Approaching again, his captors made it clear they intended to pierce his nose, but here Mallary drew the line and the natives assented.[36]

Now dressed in native attire, Mallary was adopted by a Potawatomi family to replace a son they lost at the Raisin and was given the Indian name of "Ke-wi-ex-kim." With his new clothes, name, haircut, and fam-

"Massacre of the American prisoners, at French-town, on the River Raisin, by the savages under the command of the British Genl. Proctor, January 23d., 1813." This drawing by an unidentified artist was published in 1813 to suggest that British forces condoned frontier atrocities. (*William L. Clements Library, University of Michigan*)

ily, Mallary lacked only one thing to make his new Indian identity complete—a wife. When one prospective bride was brought before him he declined, claiming he needed more time to heal from his wounds. The excuse was grudgingly accepted for the time being and Mallary soon found himself being given a steady supply of tea made from sassafras and cherry tree bark to speed the process.[37]

Gradually Mallary was given a greater role in the village as he gained more trust from his new family. When the warriors left to go hunting it was made clear to Mallary that he was not yet trusted with the privilege. Instead, he was given the job of cook, which, to the Indians, mainly involved making stews. Between cooking and travelling to British-occupied Detroit for supplies life proved fairly routine. The one exception to this was when warriors would return to camp with alcohol. The celebrations during these scenarios would get louder and occasionally violent. During a "drunkin frolic," as he called them, Mallary had to be hidden by the women of the village to prevent any harm coming to him. Such events could last for several days and, at one point, Mallary recalled having gone four days without food because the warriors were too inebriated to trade with the British or hunt.[38]

This communal life allowed little time to escape from his Indian captors and it looked like each day would deviate very little from those before it until a visitor arrived in the village. The Shawnee warrior
Tecumseh himself had come to visit and to plan. The warriors would
soon set out for Fort Wayne again and there was much to do. Tecumseh
spent much of his time rallying warriors for battle. The process finally
climaxed when the men gathered around the fire in a group. A ground
mixture of tobacco and swamp willow was brought out. The first warrior
took some in his hand and inhaled his portion before passing the mixture
on. Before leaving for battle, the warriors gathered around the fire where
each of them took some. After inhaling a sufficient amount the remainder was cast into the fire and the party leapt to their feet with a yell.
With this, the warriors disappeared into the woods with one thing in
mind—the unsuspecting guardians of Fort Wayne.[39]

Mallary knew he would not be afforded a better time to escape. With
the warriors out of the village the number of watchful eyes was reduced
significantly and the women would not pursue him far. But where to
run? He could try to go south, but it was some distance to the nearest
settlement and it was doubtful he knew the way even if one was close
by. But Mallary had been to Detroit to trade and he could make that
short trip more readily. He would still be a prisoner of war but at least it
would be with some of his fellow Americans. Sneaking away from camp
he ran straight toward Detroit. Finding his way to the home of a sympathetic citizen, they let him inside. But there was little time to catch
his breath. The Indians would have long since discovered his absence
and as soon as a group of male warriors returned he would be pursued.
If they found him there would be only one punishment for breaking the
new family covenant he had been initiated into: death. The man led the
way to the house cellar and uncovered a hole large enough to conceal a
man. Mallary descended into the gaping gash in the earth and then
watched as the home owner covered the hole with whatever was available
to conceal its existence. Sitting in the darkness, Mallary could probably
have heard the few native warriors who had stayed behind come in
search for him looking around the cellar before departing. When the
coast was completely clear, Mallary was given to a British officer who
got him safely to Malden where he could be processed with other prisoners of war. On May 16, he was taken to Cleveland and released.[40]

But being a prisoner of the British was far from easy. The original
prisoners from the Raisin who had been marched northward the day of

the battle were taken to Amherstburg where they were divided into two groups to make them easier to manage. The majority of the men would be marched to Fort George just across the border from New York State where they had been paroled. However, the leaders of the army, including Winchester, Colonel Lewis, and Major Madison, were taken to Quebec as prisoners where they would remain for some time.[41]The march east was long and arduous for the prisoners. Several nights were spent in barns with no fires where the men shivered through dark.[42] By the thirty-first of January, the men were reduced to sleeping with their shoes beneath their heads to keep them from freezing.[43]

On February 5, the weary column passed elements of the 41st Regiment on their way to reinforce Detroit. The two armies must have recognized each other for what they were at first glance. The ragged, unarmed column of Kentuckians in homespun clothing stood a stark contrast to King George's men at arms. As the two columns passed each other the British troops called out that they would soon put General Harrison on the run. Colonel James Allen replied that "before that time your Irish hides will be riddled, so that they would not hold hickory nuts."[44]

Allen's same spirited defense of the American cause rose to the surface again the next evening. The men found themselves in the town of Buford that night and the British officer in command of the prisoners, mercifully, gave them permission to seek shelter in the homes of the town's residents, provided they could obtain permission. As the men went door to door many Canadians in the village took the bedraggled men in. Elias Darnell and Colonel Allen found themselves standing at the same front door. The owner of the home was named Boon and, taking pity on the men who had spent so much time in the cold, Boon admitted them with the warning that his father also lived there. The elder Boon had been a "Tory Major in the American revolution" and still harbored strong opinions on the subject.[45]

The shelter from the arctic winds and the glow of a fire in the hearth was a welcomed break from crusted snow that had been their daily lot since leaving Frenchtown. Before long this peaceful respite from the war and weather was broken by the voice of Major Boon, the family patriarch. The United States had no chance of winning the war, he asserted, for the British would loose seventy thousand Indians on them when warm weather returned. They would also deploy seventy thousand British troops from the West Indies and three hundred thousand Turkish troops! If this was not enough, it was also true that God, Himself, was on the side of the British.[46]

At this last comment Colonel Allen found it impossible to hold back any longer. Feigning surprise that God would turn against "his own people," the old man fired again by declaring that the United States had had no right to be in Frenchtown to begin with. Hull's surrender had turned the entire Michigan Territory over to Britain. Allen dismissed the statement by comparing it to Satan's temptation of Christ in which he offered him the world if he would bow to him, but, in reality, he didn't own any of it to begin with. The argument turned to the number killed at Frenchtown, with the Canadian declaring the British loss to be negligible and Allen declaring him incorrect. Allen then accused the British of hiring Indian warriors to attack civilians which, predictably, the Canadian denied vehemently.[47]

Throughout the argument, the anger of both men continued to build, and twice Allen and his fellow prisoners were ordered out of the house, but they refused to budge until morning. The argument reached its peak when the conversation turned to the number of Canadians who had joined the Americans when Hull had crossed the river. The old man acknowledged that this was true. "There are men mean enough to join against their own country," he assented. Allen, in a backhanded agreement, stated, "None but a mean low-lived wretch would fight against his own country." Fully understanding Allen's allusion to his own conduct during the American Revolution, the elderly gentleman erupted in anger. He observed that Allen seemed to know "all crimes England ever committed" and that he must be "one of the greatest enemies the British had." Allen replied that "he had done his best; and if they were ever exchanged he would shoot at them as long as he could crook his finger to draw the trigger."[48]

A young lady who had been present for the scene suggested that the Americans had come north with deeds to Canadian lands, which they had planned to take from the rightful owners. Knowing this to be false, nevertheless Allen chivalrously refused to argue with her and simply replied, "I must believe it because you say so, but if I had seen it myself I would not." This was the olive branch the elderly Canadian needed and the conversation soon turned civil again.[49]

The next morning, the march resumed much as it had before. On February 10, their long nightmare came to an end. The British took their names and regiments and instructed them not to fight again until they had been "legally exchanged." This idea might seem strange to modern ears, but in an era where it was hard enough to supply the troops, neither side had a great desire to house, guard, and feed thousands of POWs. The men would be disarmed and released far from the theatre of war where they had served with the understanding that they would not fight until they had been exchanged on paper for an equivalent number of men on the other side. Such a system might seem naive since it works primarily on the honor system, but in war in which such small armies with limited resources were tasked with protecting vast tracts of land, it was ideal. Not to mention that the penalties for rejoining the fight before the exchange had taken place were severe. With this last warning still ringing in their ears the men were then ferried across to Fort Niagara in New York State and released.[50]

It would take weeks for the men to make it back to Kentucky. They arrived in a trickle to the relief of their families who had been waiting to see them since news of the battle had arrived. The news of the initial victory at the River Raisin had caused celebration throughout the state. However, on the second of January, a second rider entered Frankfort by horseback. It is not possible to know where he went first, but if he went in search of Governor Shelby, he would have found the governor's mansion empty. After a dreary winter day in Frankfort, Shelby had decided to take in a play at the local theatre. In the middle of the play Shelby's attention was drawn from the performance taking place on the lighted stage to the messenger who had made his way through the theatre and was now at his side. Theatergoers must have found it hard to follow the play while a soldier, who no doubt wore the signs of the long ride he had just completed, whispered into the governor's ear. Shelby immediately rose and the two disappeared into the darkness beyond the theatre doors. The news of the defeat spread like wildfire and before long "the fictitious scene of public amusement, was quickly abandoned for the private firesides, to mourn the loss of friends and the misfortunes of the country."[51]

The legislature was preparing to rise in dismissal when dispatches from General Harrison arrived. As the dispatches were opened and read the horror of the situation was realized. The legislature immediately decided to remain an extra day in which they authorized the governor to call up three thousand militia for up to six months. There was one additional detail that made this call up slightly different. In a letter to General Harrison, Shelby confided "The General Assembly by their joint resolution has authorized and requested me to command this force, which I have consented to do should the whole be ordered at once into Service."[52]

On January 24, Harrison wrote to Shelby with details of the loss. "My dear Sir, I send Colonel Wells to you to communicate the particulars (as far as we are acquainted with them) of an event that will overwhelm your mind with grief, and fill your whole state with mourning. The greater part of Colonel Wells' regiment, United States Infantry, and the 1st and 5th regiments Kentucky Infantry, and Allen's rifle regiment, under the immediate orders of General Winchester have been cut to pieces by the enemy, or taken prisoner."[53]

As a prisoner of war, Winchester made the whole thing sound less like his fault than it was. He would later write that the men had sustained a withering fire and were forced to "retire from the lines and submitted." Finally, he ordered the remaining men to surrender to save their lives, as they were promised safety as POWs. He failed to mention his fateful decision in which he elected to leave Wells' regulars out in the open instead of behind the pickets. He finished with "however unfortunate may seem the affair of yesterday, I am flattered by the belief, that no material error is chargeable upon myself and that still less censure is deserved by the troops I had the honor of commanding. He then adds with an N.B. (the postscript of its day) "The Indians have still a few prisoners in their possession which I have reason to hope will be given up to Colonel Procter, at Sandwich."[54]

Meanwhile Procter was offering his own version of what happened at the Raisin. On January 26 he described the action at the Raisin to Major General Sheaffe. The report contained few details other than to give the bare facts. The Americans had driven his force out of Frenchtown on the nineteenth where they retreated eighteen miles to the safety of a Wyandot village named Brownstown. Procter assembled his force here and then marched for Frenchtown. On the twenty-second, they captured the American force there while a supply contingent south of the town was destroyed by Indians. Winchester had been captured by the Wyandot Chief Roundhead and was turned over to Procter. A single admission to having suffered "a considerable loss" was the only dark cloud to interfere with his silver lining. Procter heaped praise on the militia as well as the Indians, whom he described as having "fought with their usual bravery." No mention was made of the massacre in the report.[55]

While most American accounts tend to focus on the brutal deaths during the period, it is hardly surprising that Canadian sources differ. When discussing the role of the British in the massacre, Procter and his subordinates are often exonerated of most or all of the blame. Procter, himself, claimed he never made any agreement with Madison regarding the safety of the Kentucky militia if they willingly surrendered.[56] One eyewitness account cites the frustration of British Indian agent Matthew Elliot when he heard of some of the killings, as he complained that the natives could not be controlled.[57] Regardless of whether the British could have controlled the revenge killing of unarmed prisoners, their failure to do so only fueled American accusations of British-sponsored violence against settlements in the west.

Many native leaders defended the action of their warriors by claiming they were only applying the same practice as the Americans.[58] Even Procter accused Kentuckians of firing on the wounded as they lay on the ground.[59] Such actions seem unlikely considering the source and the fact that there are no American accounts of the same. Despite their many differences both the British and Americans had an appreciation for European rules of engagement, which required the honoring of those who surrendered. For this reason, the shooting of a civilian or combatant attempting to surrender would have been noted and received punishment. The emphasis on this can be seen in Harrison's address to his men before crossing into Canada on the Thames Campaign in 1813 (more on that in chapter seven) in which he reminds his troops of their duty to honor the rules of engagement when it came to surrendering troops. The obvious question that must be answered is, what if the Americans did not want to sully their reputation and simply turned a blind eye to the occasional killing? This sort of casualty is always possible in war but seems unlikely in this scenario, at least on the scale that Procter suggested. Regardless of whether the statement is true or not, historian Sandy Antal suggests that this battle was significant, not only because it shifted the war's momentum to the British but because it initiated a move to more brutal tactics by both sides.[60]

In February the remains of Winchester's army were discharged with the men serving under Colonels Barbee, Pogue, and Jennings being released on the first of March.[61] The last vestiges of the campaign in 1812 had vanished and as spring arrived in 1813 the mood in the United States, but particularly in Kentucky and states and territories west of the Appalachian Mountains, had changed. The citizens of these areas still believed in the justice of their cause and the necessity of the conflict. However, the idea that Canada would fall to the American army was gone. The idea that the sons of liberty could easily trounce the armies of the monarch had been tempered by the reality that shot and ordinance are indiscriminate in battle.

By the time Henry Clay returned home from Congress in the spring of 1813 he found his fellow Kentuckians still very upset over the handling of the war, and it's relatively safe to assume the disaster at Frenchtown was a frequent topic of conversation. Clay had only a few months at home before returning to Washington for a special session and he did his best to remain optimistic, although the coming year seemed every bit as bleak as the previous one. Madison had been reelected, but this was the only victory to be found. In his message to Congress, President Madison pointed out that the nation's coffers were empty. Foreign loans were the only thing keeping the United States afloat. More taxes and more soldiers would be needed if the war was to continue. In short, the young republic's quick and easy war was turning into a protracted conflict that showed no signs of abating, and they had nothing to fight it with.[62]

Perhaps no one was more aware of this than General Harrison and Governor Shelby. The band of Kentuckians that had marched north had impressed all spectators in their path. They had been described by some as being "some of the best stuff in Kentucky."[63] Now, the entire Michigan Territory was lost and the Maumee River in Ohio was the new border between the two countries. Having gobbled up two American armies already at Detroit and Frenchtown, the British with their Canadian and Indian allies were sure to drive farther south. The only thing standing between them and the settlements of central Ohio were a series of forts along the Maumee River: Fort Wayne, Fort Defiance, and Fort Meigs. If these forts fell, the whole Northwest would be in danger and a war that once seemed far from Kentucky was getting closer with each campaign.

Chapter Six

SAVING FORT MEIGS

THE EFFECTS OF THE LOSS at the River Raisin reverberated in Washington. The Madison administration was becoming increasingly dissatisfied with the militia and their undisciplined mishaps. To remedy the problem the War Department issued an order restricting Harrison to using federal troops instead of militia to reinforce the fortification at the Rapids. While defenders of the militia could point to the fact that the militia had been led to their defeats by regular officers in many scenarios, it was obvious that controlling them was not easy. Some units had even refused to cross into Canada, arguing that it was unconstitutional to force them to leave the United States.[1]

All of this convinced the Madison administration that the status quo was no longer acceptable. Congress authorized the raising of twenty regiments of federal infantry at considerably higher wages for twelve months. While the federal government was beginning to relearn the lessons of the Continental Army forty years earlier (especially the value of well-trained soldiers), the trans-Appalachian West would not provide the recruits that the East would need despite being the seat of support for the war. According to Kentucky Militia General McAfee of Mercer County this was primarily due to the agrarian-based economy. Unemployment was low west of the mountains and the developing society meant there were few people willing to sign up for service under unfamiliar, federally appointed officers with the possibility of leaving their

homes behind for a year.[2] The attempt to raise volunteers for federal
service seemed defeated before it began.

In the meantime, Indian attacks on settlements and military detachments continued, and news from beyond the state's borders weighed
heavily on the minds of the public. One officer writing to the governor
from Vincennes estimated that there were six thousand warriors in the
areas of Ohio and the Indiana and Illinois Territories. The Pottawatomie, Miami, and Kickapoo alone could raise a minimum of 1,400
men and "they are within a week or ten days march of us."[3]

There was also trouble closer to home. Intelligence suggested a party
of hostile Indians in the area of the Tennessee River on Kentucky's western border. The local officer, Colonel Theophilus Skinner of Christian
County, immediately ordered a detachment of militia to patrol the area.
A few days later, two natives were killed, suggesting the reports about
Indians in the region were accurate although it did not necessarily verify
their intentions were hostile. Local residents were becoming nervous
again, especially when they considered that the militia on guard could
only be activated for thirty days without special permission from Frank-
fort. Activating what men he could was the logical choice, but Colonel
Skinner was unsure how to proceed after the thirty days had expired.
Was he to just disband the militia and hope for the best? Keeping a force,
even a small one, in the field indefinitely was a costly endeavor. Still,
Skinner believed it worth the effort. Summing his feelings up in a letter
to the governor he stated, "I think our frontiers are in danger . . . and we
Ought to protect them."[4]

Back in Frankfort another attempt to raise an army to attack Indian
settlements along the White and Wabash Rivers in the Indiana Territory
fell through due to a lack of officers. A second attempt found enough
men available, but the supply boats coming upriver to Fort Harrison
were attacked and all were forced to turn back with one lone exception.[5]
The army seemed to be floundering and the plans that had been so carefully concocted just months before now seemed uncertain. The only sure
thing that Harrison could count on was that General Procter would take
advantage of the shrinking Northwest Army to go on the offensive. Evidence of this arrived in camp in the form of residents of Detroit who
had fled south. One fleeing refugee who made his way into the American lines assured them that the British would turn their attention to Fort
Meigs by building defensive works on the north side of the river where
they could shell the fort with cannon in hopes that the troops there

would flee to the south side. They would run straight into the arms of a large contingent of Indians who would ambush and destroy them.[6]

If Procter were successful, this would be as much, if not more, of a disaster than the River Raisin. On the bright side, Harrison's line of forts and blockhouses had progressed despite the disasters in the field. Each finished location strengthened the chain and made it difficult for the British to advance farther south without leaving their flanks exposed to a well-supplied army. But the fall of Fort Meigs would provide enough of a gap in that line to allow men and material to pour into the Indiana and Illinois Territories. If the British could destroy one link in the chain and maintain a sufficient presence in the area it was likely that other forts would fall as well, leaving much of the territory north of the Ohio River open to attack.

But Fort Meigs did have a few points in its favor. Built on top of a nearly forty-foot natural embankment overlooking the Maumee River, it was surrounded by a stockade of thick logs, which enclosed nearly ten acres. Within the post, Harrison's men were kept busy building several storage buildings as well as an underground powder magazine at each end of the fort. Seven two-story log blockhouses were spaced irregularly along the stockade, and five elevated artillery pieces peered over the wooden walls. Fort Meigs also stored more than just muskets and powder. It could boast a bakery, butcher shop, a tannery, and a small dock on the Maumee for loading and unloading.[7] It housed everything needed to equip and sustain an army. If the British were ever to truly secure the Michigan Territory for themselves they would need to capture it.

Harrison, who had arrived at Fort Meigs on April 12, could not have been surprised when word arrived describing an imminent attack, and he acted immediately to prepare for it.[8] It was now spring and the British had been preparing all winter for a new campaign. Harrison had been kept well briefed on his journey north and, having been advised of recent skirmishing around Fort Meigs, must have felt somewhat impatient for the arrival of the next contingent of Kentucky militia, which were supposed to be following him to the fort. When he had requested the troops Shelby had immediately complied, calling up the men and placing them under the command of General Green Clay of Madison County. Clay was one of the most experienced and wealthiest citizens of the state and a respected citizen who could lead. Clay's experience meant he was sure to act carefully instead of rashly. But moving an army took time and Harrison's was running out.[9]

Shelby also issued orders for one month's pay to be issued to each of the officers while the rest of the army received a ten-dollar advance.[10] Unlike the reactionary Winchester, Clay was a methodical and cautious commander who organized every detail. This became particularly evident to the men under his command as they marched forward. Ammunition and supplies were placed in the center with twenty-five men guarding each of the four sides around it. Next, the wagons were circled (or in this case squared) to form an additional perimeter around the supplies. After this came a line of several fires for cooking and warmth and then another square consisting of soldiers' tents. The breastwork protecting the camp lay beyond this and then the sentries who guarded the camp. The final characteristic of the camp was the continual burning of six fires on each side of the square sixty paces in front of the sentinels. If anyone came within range of their muskets, they would be illuminated.[11]

As this latest contingent of Kentucky militia crossed the Ohio on their march north to strengthen Harrison's army, it must have stirred a fatigued feeling of déjà vu in Governor Shelby. Many times before, Kentuckians had rallied to the flag of their country only to be defeated or discharged without a battle. Some progress had been made against Indian villages that Tecumseh's warriors were using as bases of operation, but that success must have seemed small in comparison with their defeats. It was true that the militia tended to be raw and undisciplined, but the government policy of sending small detachments to fight far from friendly settlements that could reinforce them had added to the crisis as detachment after detachment marched north to be swallowed up by superior numbers. Shelby had tried before to induce the federal government to alter its piecemeal strategy but without success. However, the recent defeats caused him to try again. In a letter to the secretary of war, the governor argued that if any serious invasion of Canada was to be envisioned it would require a much larger army.[12]

"Impressions begin to be entertained that the views of the Government are too limitted," Shelby stated candidly. "That it is not disposed to call out an adequate force, and that those who are sent out will of course hazard unnecessary danger. Under such impressions little is to be expected from the people." The fact that the federal government had failed to pay many of the troops who had already served added to this dissatisfaction. Less than half of the wages for troops in earlier campaigns had been paid out despite their having been discharged and sent home months before.[13] Shelby went on to reiterate that the army that is "sent to invade Canada . . . should be *an imposing one.* The best blood and interests of our Country should not be hazarded by an army barely adequate for the object." Any force less than between twelve and fifteen thousand would be too small to conquer and occupy Upper Canada. A large force would also be required to intimidate any native populations in the area from attacking. As to tactics, the militia are very useful, Shelby argued, provided they are used as anchors on the flanks of the regular army.[14]

Having signed, sealed, and sent his dispatch, Shelby shifted his focus to the more immediate danger. If the threats against Fort Meigs were not enough to occupy the thoughts of the governor, intelligence began to arrive in Frankfort that many of the native tribes in the southern states and territories might soon become hostile to the American cause. The area west of the Tennessee River had seen increasing numbers of Indians using this corridor to communicate and travel between the Old Northwest and the areas to the south.[15] If hostile tribes on both sides of the state coordinated their efforts Kentucky's western settlements would truly be in danger.

While Shelby wrestled with the enormity of securing the state's borders, Harrison was still focused on securing Fort Meigs. He could not have known, but five days before his call for additional troops went out Procter and his army of around 3,200 Canadian militia, Indians, and British regulars had marched out of Amherstburg for Fort Meigs.[16] The same day Harrison's messenger departed, reconnaissance parties from Fort Meigs discovered elements of the British force just down the river from the fort. This could only mean one thing; the siege was about to begin. Taking advantage of the open lines of communication while they lasted, Harrison dispatched messengers on April 28 to carry word to Governor Meigs of Ohio. Harrison described the situation and then asked that the letter be passed on to Governor Shelby. The British gunboats had been discovered just two miles away and the woods surrounding the fort were full of enemy warriors. Despite being the target of the siege he was confident about the battle. "Do not my dear Sir doubt the result—the enemy little dream of the bitter Pill I have prepared for them." The letter reached Governor Meigs and a duplicate copy was quickly scribbled out and dispatched to Frankfort by a soldier named William Oliver, who added that the men were in "fine spirits" at the prospect of gaining glory from victory. Though, undoubtedly, they would have been even happier to see the arrival of Clay and the Kentucky militia before the British could make their attack.[17]

Harrison and his men watched the British ferry their native allies across the river, and the sounds of the Indian shouts from beyond the trees and the periodic firing of muskets found their way to the fort's walls. But Harrison was ready and he reminded his men that they were made of the same stuff as Mad Anthony Wayne's men who had secured Ohio two decades before. "To your posts then fellow citizens," Harrison ordered, "and remember that the eyes of your country are upon you." The British soon finished mounting their guns on high ground around three hundred yards away from the fort where their shells could still reach the wooden walls and where the marshy lowlands between them and the American post discouraged the possibility of a contingent of Harrison's soldiers rushing out unexpectedly to capture the guns.[18]

As the Indian presence increased, Harrison separated his army into thirds, leaving one third on duty at all times in three-hour shifts. Outside of firing shots at the emboldened Indians from time to time they could do nothing but wait and stare at the tree line several hundred yards away. The occasional tree trunk that had been left where it fell offered some shelter to the natives as they worked to find safe positions close to the fort where they might pick off any of Harrison's men who became too bold (or curious) and exposed too much of themselves above the log walls of the fort.[19]

In the late morning of May 1, the thunder of cannon erupted as the British unleashed their artillery on the fort. The promised aid from Kentucky had not arrived in time to prevent the siege. Harrison's only hope now was that they would arrive in time to prevent the attack from being successful. The shelling continued into the night but finally fell silent around an hour before midnight. The results of a full day of bombardment were one, possibly two, dead with four wounded. The next day the British tried again with little or no results. Fort Meigs had been carefully planned and constructed and now that battle had begun those preparations showed. At this point the British decided to take some of their guns to the opposite side of the river and shell the fort from both directions. Once everything was in place the battle entered its third day of shelling as projectiles riddled the fort from two directions.[20] The cannonade was so severe that settlers claimed to hear the roar up to fifty miles away.[21]

With each hour that Harrison's army held out, the chance of success increased. Green Clay and his army of Kentuckians were getting closer by the day and, after leaving St. Mary's Blockhouse, the army split in two with Clay leading part of his army down the St. Mary's River while Colonel Dudley took the other half down the Auglaize River. The two forces were to meet at Fort Defiance and reunite for the march to Fort Meigs. While moving his men down the Auglaize, Dudley received word of the siege and the desperate situation of the fort. He instantly dispatched a party of six men to sneak inside, if indeed it was still holding out, and let Harrison know help was nearby. The men left immediately for the fort and traveled through the night. At sunrise, they found themselves around a mile from the walls and, to their immense relief, saw the American flag was still flying. There was still a chance to save it. They dug their oars into the river and continued on. But the early morning stillness was shattered when enemy musket fire from the bank echoed not far away. Paddling hard to reach the other side of the river, the scouts returned to Dudley with news that they had failed to reach Harrison, but at least the fort was still in American hands.[22]

By nightfall the bulk of Clay's reunited army was less than twenty miles from the fort. A second dispatch was sent and this time succeeded in getting into the fort. Sneaking past the native warriors patrolling the woods the men were quickly admitted and, to the relief of everyone inside, informed them that their salvation was not far off. Harrison immediately sent orders on how to proceed. If everything went according to plan the British could be taken by surprise and a complete rout would be possible. The two batteries of cannon would be the first priority. If they could no longer lob their munitions inside the walls of the fort, Procter would be reduced to small arms and a fort like Fort Meigs would be impossible to capture in a drawn-out siege. If eight hundred of Clay's men could disembark around a mile and a half from the fort, they could travel over land and take the cannon that had been such a thorn in Har-

Overleaf: "Plan of Fort Meigs' and its environs : compricing the operations of the American forces, under Genl. W.H. Harrison, and the British Army and their allies, under Genl. Procter and Tecumseh. By an officer of the Kentucky militia." William Sebree, c. 1813. In this idiosyncratic and fascinating sketch of the siege of Fort Meigs, the attack by Col. Dudley and the Kentucky militia against the British artillery and their subsequent annihilation are shown above the fort. To the right of that action, where mounted Native Americans are drawn, Sebree describes Tecumseh's disgust at Procter allowing the prisoners to be massacred by native warriors. Below the fort, Col. Miller's attack on another British battery is described. At the far right, the British camp is shown prior to their abandoning the siege. (*Library of Congress*)

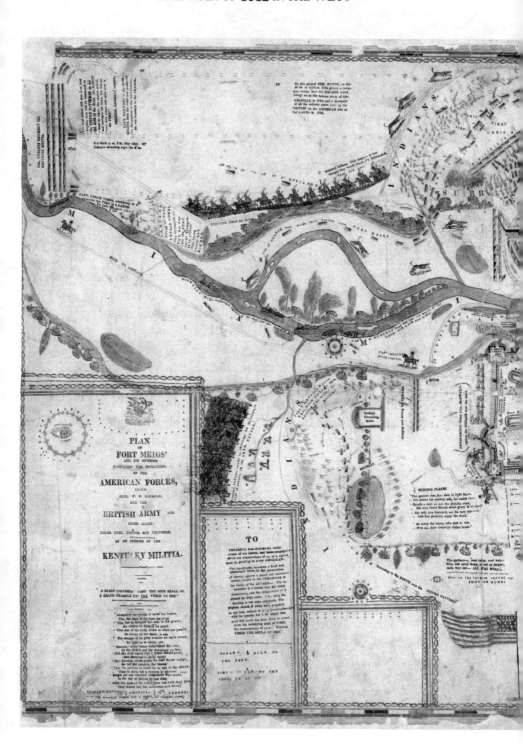

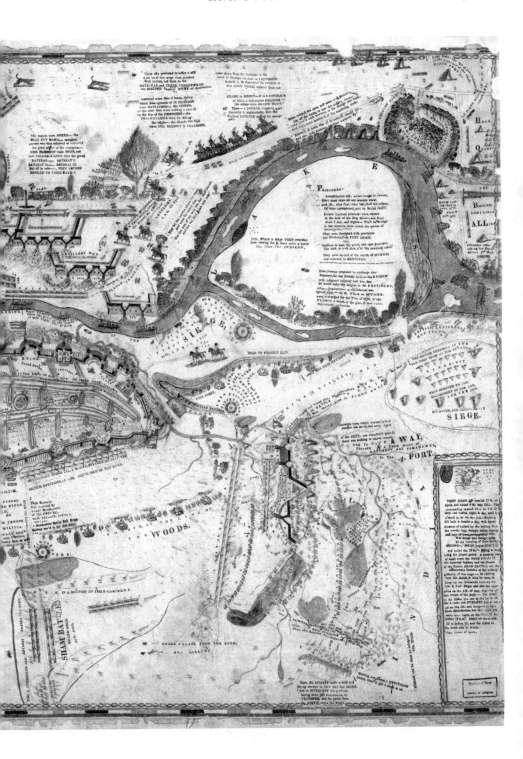

rison's side before the British even knew they were in the area. The force of British troops manning the cannon and their Indian allies nearby would not have to be completely eliminated as long as the cannon were spiked and the carriages for them destroyed. Once that was accomplished the men would cross the river and enter the safety of the fort. While they were disabling the cannon the rest of the army would smash into the Indian forces before the fort and battle their way inside, increasing the number of men inside the fort and eliminating some of the enemy who were surrounding the fort.[23]

Receiving the message, Clay responded immediately and divided his force once more in accordance with Harrison's order. Colonel Dudley was again given command of the second half of the army with the order to capture the guns that Harrison described. As Dudley's men disappeared into the woods, Clay led the rest of the army toward the fort. After four days of shelling, the British artillerymen had reason to feel confident. Despite the stubbornness of the men inside the fort there was little they could do to retaliate. As Dudley's men erupted from the surrounding woods, the British regulars were caught completely off guard and were forced back into the cover of the trees. Immediately, Dudley's men turned their attention to the cannons. Hearing the commotion, Harrison's men watched eagerly from inside the fort, and he along with his whole army erupted in cheers when they saw the British flag that had flown above the batteries torn down. Help had finally arrived. From the other side of the fort more noise signaled the arrival of General Clay and the other half of the army who successfully entered the fort.[24]

As Dudley and his men prepared to enter the boats that would take them to their fellow soldiers inside the fort, muskets belched forth smoke and lead from the woods around them. Some fleeing Indians had re-formed from the safety of the forest and had returned. The surprise of the attack mingled with the adrenaline of victory. Major Shelby (son of the governor) was ordered to stay behind with a contingent of men to protect the area around the guns. Dudley and the rest of the men then sprang toward their attackers.[25] From inside the fort an anxious William Henry Harrison could heave a short sigh of relief as the last of Clay's men entered the fort and the gate was closed. Turning his spyglass to the opposite side of the river he witnessed the scene unfolding with horror. The flashes of light from the woods, the rallying of Dudley's men, and the movement into the tree line all spelled disaster and Harrison knew it. Harrison yelled across the Maumee in a desperate attempt to

"The Siege of Fort Meigs." 1848. (*Anne S. K. Brown Military Collection, Brown University Library*)

turn Dudley's men but to no avail. The general quickly offered a thousand-dollar reward to any man who could cross the river and turn the army back. One small boat ventured into the rapidly flowing river before finding the current was too strong to cross in time. The small craft made its way back to the fort. Harrison and Clay could do nothing but wait.[26]

Chasing the Indians through the woods in a rolling battle, the Kentuckians fought on, ducking behind trees for shelter and taking aim at will as the Indians continued to retreat. Moving from tree to tree, the lines of battle broke down. Forest fighting was popular among the men but it prevented much coherence of command and most soldiers simply acted as they thought best. The constant, if somewhat irregular, firing of muskets let each man know the battle continued, and they moved deeper into the forest. When they finally broke through the spring foliage they gazed in horror at the canvas tents and supplies of a British camp. They had been led into a trap. By the time it became obvious to the men what was happening the natives had been reinforced and the tide had turned.[27]

Having repulsed an attack from some British regulars, the anxious Major Shelby and his detachment waited with the guns as the battle in the woods beyond them raged. The sounds of the battle soon made it clear that something had gone wrong and that Dudley was in trouble. Major Shelby and his guards rushed into the woods to help, but it was too late to change the outcome. Many of the militia now turned to run for their lives and most were overrun by the British and Indians pursuing them. Realizing what was happening to his command Dudley turned to retreat with his men. Darting through the undergrowth and around trees he groped his way toward safety. But, in an instant, a searing pain in his leg brought his flight to an abrupt halt and he crumpled to the ground. A pursuing brave burst through the trees behind him. The last thing Dudley saw was the descending tomahawk that took his life. Of the 800 men sent to take the guns around 170 survived the battle.[28]

The portion of Clay's men who entered the fort hardly had time to catch their breath before they could tell that something had gone wrong. The sounds of battle had moved farther afield and the constant firing and screams of the wounded must have told Clay that his men were in trouble. Immediately he petitioned Harrison for any extra men he had so that he could lead a rescue expedition. Their efforts were in vain, and to make things worse, by taking his reserves to rescue Dudley, Clay prevented Harrison from using them to follow up and overwhelm the surprised Indian force supporting the British flank. Had Harrison been able to launch a counterattack the native warriors would have disintegrated entirely, leaving Procter's force of regulars and militia to deal with the situation alone. "Instead," Harrison later bitterly lamented in a letter to Shelby, "I was forced to recall our men when they were in full pursuit of the enemy, and every moment making prisoners."[29] Clay eventually returned to the fort without rescuing Dudley's men. That night sentries reported screams from the forest beyond the fort as many of the wounded were killed.[30]

Despite the destruction of the force under Dudley, it was clear that Procter no longer had the upper hand. His cannons were useless and Fort Meigs now had more defenders than ever. Taking a page from Brock's book, Procter sent a messenger to the fort on the morning of the fifth. Reading the note from Procter, Harrison saw that it was demanding the surrender of the fort. But Harrison was no Hull and he immediately refused. This continual resistance coupled with news of American victories on the other side of the lakes at Fort George proved to be too much for the British. By the ninth, the British forces were withdrawing, aided by gunboats and a sloop to help evacuate the remaining cannon and baggage.[31]

Meanwhile, those Americans who had remained at a distance from the fort were left to guess as to the result of the battle. There was nothing they could do but wait. Militia colonel John Campbell wrote to Shelby on the seventh, informing him that nothing had been heard from the fort or from the men under General Clay. This could be a sign of the fort's capitulation. "To save him [Harrison] and his army is all important," he unnecessarily reminded the governor. What if the British had found out about Clay's approach and split their force to intercept him while the other half kept Harrison in check? "Will Kentucky bleed afresh?" he asked rhetorically. Despite the survival of the fort, Campbell would soon find out how prophetic his words had been.[32]

A sense of relief may have descended on the American forces in Fort Meigs but not necessarily victory. The loss of the men under Dudley was a particularly bitter pill to swallow after the defeat at Frenchtown. These feelings were heightened by the fact that the loss was completely unnecessary. An embittered Harrison later wrote in his official report that "It rarely occurs that a general has to complain of the excessive ardor of his men—yet such appears to be the case whenever the Kentucky militia are engaged."[33]

In a more informal letter to Shelby, Harrison lamented, "my orders were clearly delivered to him [General Clay], and I have no doubt were well understood by Colonel Dudley; and nothing could be more easy of execution. . . . Never was there an opportunity more favorable to strike a brilliant stroke, than was presented on this occasion, if the plan had been properly pursued." Harrison went on to speculate that if he had only had Dudley's men he could have pursued Procter and, perhaps, overtaken his whole force. Instead, they were now safely on their way back to Canada.[34]

For the small portion of Dudley's men captured alive, the nightmare was just beginning. Those who survived and were later released told tales of wounded men being shot during the retreat and of Indians clothed in American army jackets and other memorabilia taken from the living and dead. The most disturbing statements included American skins stretched to dry like cow or deer hides and even some indication that bodies were boiled in kettles. When the Shawnee leader Tecumseh arrived in camp he was aghast and immediately demanded why Procter had allowed this to happen. "Your Indians cannot be commanded," Procter responded. "Begone," retorted the Shawnee chief, "you are not fit to command, go and put on petticoats."[35] This story, whether true or not, garnered respect for Tecumseh as a more worthy and chivalrous adversary than Procter, who was either afraid or ambivalent about preventing atrocities at the hands of the tribes under his command.

Regardless of the high cost, the fort had been saved and, at least for the time being, the British had been checked in their advance, though their return was inevitable. Harrison returned to Lower Sandusky (the modern-day town of Fremont, Ohio), leaving General Green Clay in command of Fort Meigs and sending word to Kentucky to cancel the order for additional troops. These men, who had already rendezvoused at Frankfort, were dismissed but were exempted from any future drafts as payment for their troubles.[36]

Shelby received Harrison's communications, especially in relation to Dudley's men, with some anger and prepared to pass the details on to Congressman Henry Clay. Letting his despair and anger flash, he penned, "a more careless in considerate waste of Human blood cannot be found upon the Annals of North America."[37] Having read Harrison's report Shelby dismissed its conclusions, which blamed Dudley entirely for the defeat. "It cannot be supposed by any rational mind that Colonel Dudley would have rushed his handful of men into the midst of several thousand British and Indians, had he been aware of their force, or had he received orders to retreat upon spiking the Enemys Cannon." Harrison's report also suggested that, after the cannons were rendered ineffective, calls across the river to Dudley's men could not induce them to come back. This suggestion drew Shelby's ire more than most others. Was Harrison really suggesting that men in the midst of battle would hear shouts "at least half a mile distant"?[38] It was more likely, thought Shelby, that Harrison's original verbal orders were misunderstood after passing through multiple messengers. If this was the case, a boat should have been sent from the fort to Dudley telling him of the danger he was in. Shelby's anger was on a personal level as well as a professional one, as one soldier who escaped to St. Mary's carried erroneous word that Shelby's son had been killed in the action.[39]

"This mournfull Event has I assure you deadened the feelings of many of our best patriots, and abated their Confidence in the Commanding General[.] It will have an unhappy effect upon future calls on Kentucky for men."[40] Surely all of this could have been avoided if those in Washington were only willing to listen. "When I consented last year to Serve as the chief magistrate of this state, it was under a belief I should be able to render services to my country in the event of a war with the savages, having had a long and an intimate knowledge of Indian affairs, and under that impression, have taken the liberty, both last year an[d] this, to make various lengthy communications to the War Department. In very few instances have I been answered except by a bare acknowledgment of the receipt of my letter."[41] Now, to make things worse, rumors spread that the men who served from Kentucky in the recent relief of the siege of Fort Meigs might not be paid for their services. It may be true that, as governor, Shelby had legal obligations to carry out for the federal government, but "I am free to declare to you that as an individual, my Confidence in the Administration especially as it relates to War Measures in the western Country *has greatly abated*."[42] Shelby recoiled slightly in closing as his anger gave way to grief. He admitted that he had already written more than he had intended and some of the sentiments in the letter were a result of "the perturbed state of my feelings." He ended with "I pray God that my forebodings as to future events in the western Country may not be reallised."[43]

"Dudley's Defeat," as the disaster came to be called, soured quickly in the minds of the public. The defeat at the River Raisin had come as a result of an attempt to protect the citizens of Frenchtown, and the wisdom of advancing there could at least be debated. However, this loss of life seemed utterly unnecessary. Always the ardent defender of his fellow Kentuckians, Shelby's critique of the battle in his letter to Henry Clay probably reflected Shelby's true feelings on the matter, but it can hardly be accepted as a true account of the facts. The zeal of the militia and officers like Dudley had been the cause of the defeat—not Harrison.

Dudley's defeat also did little to bolster Kentucky's reputation outside the state. The *Kentucky Gazette* reprinted an article that had appeared in the *Pennsylvania Gazette* and condemned its sentiment, though it's words probably struck home with some readers. The article was entitled "KENTUCKY IN ARMS!" and began with the hard-hitting phrase, "The pompous phrase was the pride and boast of our western warriors. . . . Their rage for war was such, that their fury could not be confined to the hostile tribes who were actually annoying our frontiers, but vengeance and destruction must be extended to the peaceable and unoffending inhabitants of Canada." The article went on to state that Kentucky had wielded their authority in Congress with impressive success. The author suggested that the citizens of the commonwealth kept kindling, tar, and feathers on hand to deal with anyone who dared question the war effort. It went on to indict "Hull, Hopkins, and Winchester" for their failure to achieve anything at all. "Instead of the conquest of Canada, have they even *retaken* an inch of the ground, or a shilling's worth of the property which Canada has taken from us?"[44]

The *Gazette* itself admitted that "the fate of war indeed falls heavily with its afflictions on KENTUCKY!" The article concluded in more conciliatory tones that the state "has cause to mourn—but not to despair. If her sons, taken from the occupations of civil life, and hurried into battle, are unfortunate as they are deficient in polished discipline, yet they display a faring intrepidity and courageous ardor when encountering the enemy. . . . Kentucky and the 'Backwoodsmen' will be recorded by the historian as an example of patriotism for future generations."[45]

But the poetic ending of the editorial did little to soften the sting of reality. An exasperated Governor Shelby remained in his office in Frankfort pondered the string of defeats at the hands of a misguided War Department and overzealous, underdisciplined officers. The invitation to personally take command extended by the legislature simmered in the back of his mind. Doubtless flashes from battles of the Revolution, especially King's Mountain, materialized in his memory in vivid detail. Of course, he was only thirty at the time of the battle. He was sixty-three now and a journey of well over three hundred miles on horseback was quite the undertaking. But if Shelby harbored any self-doubts they were not shared by most of his fellow Kentuckians. As early as March 1, Shelby began receiving letters from Kentuckians eager to join him if he marched north. The aged Joshua Bartlett, who claimed he was known to his neighbors as "Old 76," wrote to the governor to say:

> I was just a lad at the battle of the point [Point Pleasant] with my old Countryman Col. Fields where I first had the pleasure of seeing you and was also at the Battle of Kingmountain [Kings Mountain] with you. my heart glows with pleasure to see you again our Chief magistrate But a double glow to find you heading our troops again. I wish Very much to come with you.[46]

Other letters would continue to arrive throughout the spring and summer as the Northwest Army struggled to regain its feet and take the offensive. However, the government's order to Harrison following the River Raisin disaster prevented any significant force of militia from being raised. This stubborn obstacle was finally removed on July 20 when Harrison received a dispatch from Washington. The raising of federal troops had, apparently, not gone well, and Harrison was again permitted to take the number of troops he felt he needed from the surrounding state militias. Not long after this, a rider was making his way to Kentucky with a letter for the governor. Acknowledging that it was late in the year to organize an army from scratch and admitting that he was aware of the "indisposition" of Kentuckians to join an army that struggled to win as well as pay them, he believed that Shelby could cause them to rally to the cause.[47]

It was then that Harrison gave Shelby the opening he had been waiting for. Not wanting to commit too many details to paper that could possibly fall into the wrong hands, Harrison wrote dismissively, "send me as many good men as you can conveniently collect or as you may deem proper to call out [,] not less than *four hundred* nor more than *two thousand*." [48]

Since the outbreak of war, Governor Shelby had warned against the practice of recruiting smaller armies one at a time that would only be pounded by well-trained British regulars or enveloped by Indian ambushes. Any measure that would lead to success would require a large, well-armed force, and Shelby sprang into action to make sure he had one.

However, before any campaigns against Canada could be carried out, General Procter would try to invade once more. By the twentieth of July, General Green Clay and the men under his command, who were still at Fort Meigs, noticed increased levels of Indian activity in the woods just beyond the fort. Oxen and other animals had gone missing and that evening several British boats could be seen making their way down the river toward the fort. Alarmed at this development, Clay dispatched an express to Harrison who immediately moved his headquarters to Seneca to prepare for another siege. Procter was back. [49]

On the twenty-sixth of July, the silence of the forest was broken by Indian war whoops and the firing of muskets, but the tree line concealed everything from view. Scanning the horizon from behind the picket walls Clay and his men pondered the situation. The sounds suggested the Indians had attacked a possible relief column on its way to break the siege. Based on this intelligence, General Clay had two options. He could send most of his men out in an attempt to surround the Indians and relieve the men, if indeed there were any, from the attack. The other option was to assume the whole thing was a trap and wait to see what happened next. If a relief expedition was just a mile or so away, arriving in time might be critical. On the other hand, marching his men from

the protection of the fort into the arms of the waiting warriors would
be a disaster. Perhaps thinking back to his own arrival at the fort just a
few months earlier to break Procter's first attempt to squeeze the fort
into submission, Clay would have remembered that he sent messengers
ahead to the fort, alerting the besieged garrison of his presence. He had
received no such messengers or even seen any evidence that an American
force was in the area. Something just did not seem right. Clay opted to
wait. Surprisingly, two days later the British evacuated the area once
more and returned to their boats. The siege was over as abruptly as it
had begun. Despite the fact that Clay had received no reinforcements
and had fought no battles, the British and Indians had just left. Both
Clay and Harrison (who was away from Fort Meigs at the time) were
suspicious. Why would Procter take the trouble to gather supplies and
transportation for a siege if he meant to give up so easily? There was
only one logical answer. They were aiming for somewhere else. The target soon became obvious, as several Indians had been seen marching in
the direction of the tiny, undermanned Fort Stephenson at Lower Sandusky. As suspected, Procter was not leaving; he was only pounding on
a weaker link in Harrison's chain.[50]

Harrison, having realized Procter's goal, had no intention of letting
his men be captured and deemed it better to evacuate the fort. Late on
the morning of June 29 the few defenders of Fort Stephenson squinted
into the rays of the early morning sun to see a rider approaching. Once
inside the fort he delivered his message from General Harrison to the
fort's commander, Major Croghan of Jefferson County, Kentucky. The
message was short and to the point. "Sir, Immediately on receiving this
letter, you will abandon fort Stephenson, set fire to it, and repair with
your command this night to headquarters," it began. "Cross the river
and come up on the opposite side. If you should deem and find it im-
practical to make good your march to this place, take the road to Huron
and pursue it with the utmost circumspection and dispatch."[51]

After reading the brief note, Croghan realized he had been meant to
receive it on the previous night and return under cover of darkness, but
the message had not arrived in time. The delay in getting the orders
meant it was now nearly noon and the enemy was in the vicinity. Would
Harrison still want him to retreat? A council of officers was called and
it was hastily decided to remain in place until additional word could be
received from Harrison. As he prepared to write his response to Harrison, a thought occurred to Croghan. If the British and their native allies

were already in the area in great numbers there was the possibility that the messenger might be intercepted. In that case, any note that seemed uncertain or indecisive might be misinterpreted by the enemy as a sign of weakness, which could prove fatal. With that in mind, Croghan formed his response to sound confident. Unfortunately, as he later recalled, it also sounded defiant. When Harrison received the reply he angrily ordered Croghan to his headquarters immediately. Threading his way through the enemy-occupied forest Croghan complied with the general's demand and soon found himself stammering to explain his refusal to follow orders. Surprised and apologetic, Croghan explained his intent, and his sincerity proved sufficient to convince Harrison that he had acted justly and he was allowed to return to Fort Stephenson.[52]

Having successfully escaped one rather precarious situation Croghan returned to the fort to find himself in the midst of another one. Within hours of the wooden gates closing behind him, his men could see enemy warriors in the surrounding woods. The men attempted to make a show of force by firing the only cannon they had (a mere six pounder) at the enemy. The shots did the trick temporarily and the Indian warriors sought the cover of the forest, although both sides knew it would be short lived. The native warriors were waiting for their British allies to arrive with their artillery before commencing the real assault. Half an hour later, gunboats appeared on the river, and shortly after that men and supplies were being unloaded. With the arrival of the British, the Indian warriors returned in full force and once again surrounded the fort. This would have been a familiar sight at Fort Meigs, and the men there, with their significant number of artillery and large army, could expect to survive another siege if they remained vigilant, but the men at Fort Stephenson had no such luxury. The small, untested fort with its single cannon and youthful commander appeared to be in dire straits. However, the die had been cast and Croghan was determined to see it through.[53]

Never one to fight where an easy victory could be obtained, General Procter dispatched a major and a civilian representative to the American post. Croghan's men watched over the wall as they approached with a white flag raised. An ensign by the name of Edmund Shipp of the 17th US Infantry was sent to meet the delegation outside the walls of the fort. The major began with the statement that Procter had sent him because "he was anxious to spare the effusion of human blood," which would be inevitable if his men attacked the fort. Shipp calmly replied that the Americans had already determined to "maintain their post, or to bury themselves in its ruins." The major then turned to a familiar fear tactic. He explained that the Indians could not be controlled once the battle was won, and who knew what they might do? A massacre would certainly be the result. Shipp again replied that there would be no massacre, because if the British and Indians gained access to the fort that would mean the men inside were already dead. At this a nearby native warrior who had followed the British representatives lurched forward and attempted to seize the sword that hung on Shipp's side. The British representatives intervened and separated the two, probably fearing the armed men watching the discussion from inside the fort, and both sides returned to their positions knowing that battle was inevitable.[54]

Not long after the encounter the guns on the waiting gunboat came to life as it began to pour shells into the little fort. The British forces on land also opened up and the barrage lasted through the night. Some estimates placed the British force at five hundred regulars and eight hundred Indians participating in the siege. If Harrison had entertained any notion of coming to Fort Stephenson's rescue he would have met a very prepared Tecumseh and two thousand warriors on the road to the fort. Any relief force was sure to be swallowed up. There would be no help for Croghan and his men. They would live or die based on their own actions.[55]

Despite its unimpressive appearance, the fort survived the artillery barrage that lasted for a good portion of the night with little damage, and a brief respite allowed the men to assess their situation. Croghan studied the movements of the British. They were obviously preparing for an assault. But where would it come from? The weak light of dawn soon turned the shadows into nothing more that silhouettes, and the British guns opened up once more. There was nothing Croghan and his men could do except hunker down and wait for something to develop. Around 4 p.m. Croghan noticed a pattern. The British had begun concentrating their fire on the northwest angle of the fort. This was the clue Croghan had been waiting for. Without knowing it, the British had revealed the place they intended to attack. Immediately, Croghan ordered bags of sugar and sand packed against the walls in the northwest corner in hopes this would help absorb the blows of the cannons. Late that night, the British infantry rushed the fort from the south. They were quickly repulsed, but more attacks were sure to come. This was the opposite of where the Americans had expected an attack. Croghan had to decide: should he move his men to focus on this southern angle or assume that this was just a diversion and trust his instinct? Trusting the telltale signs of earlier in the day Croghan had the majority of his men focused on the northwest. A second assault emerged from the darkness in the direction of the southern corner, and again it was repulsed by the tiny American force. [56]

But as some of Croghan's force sent the British and Indians scurrying for cover on one end of the fort, an eagle-eyed guard in the northwest corner shouted the alarm. The British were sneaking toward the fort and were just "twenty paces" from the walls. The waiting soldiers all opened fire, lighting up the night sky and filling the air with even more acrid smoke. Immediately following this show of force with small arms the lone waiting cannon unleashed a volley that struck down several in the approaching British line. Confused and wounded, the force under British colonel Short fell back before being rallied by their colonel and charging again. The men leapt into a ditch that led to the fort hoping to find cover from the American muskets that were reaching over the wall searching for targets. When they were just thirty feet from the walls, Croghan sprang his trap. In front of the British column, a "masked port hole" was uncovered by the Americans, exposing the gaping mouth of Croghan's only cannon. The single shot that erupted caused havoc on the neatly queued up British lines. As the second feint on the southern angle and the actual assault on the northwestern angle failed, both columns retreated. The entire assault had lasted around half an hour.[57]

As the smoke cleared, a significant portion of the attacking force, including Colonel Short, lay dead in the trench. The screams of anguish from the wounded wafted over the walls and the Americans dug a hole under the wall to allow the wounded British who could crawl to enter the fort where they could have their wounds treated. Buckets of water were passed over the wall in an effort to ease the suffering of those who lay immobilized in the ditch. Some Kentucky sources originally estimated the losses at 150 British dead while the Americans had lost one man and had seven wounded.[58] Later totals were revealed to be a little less dramatic and British losses were readjusted to a much more believable twenty-six troops dead and twenty-eight wounded or captured. American losses remained at one dead and seven injured.[59] Despite the correction of casualties the victory was undoubtedly a success.

On August 3 around three in the morning the British marched away from Fort Stephenson leaving the Americans victorious. When

Croghan's men ventured out they found around seventy stands of arms and a good number of other supplies. The British had left in a hurry, no doubt expecting a renewed Harrison to follow up the victory. Harrison later mused that "It will not be among the least of general Procter's mortifications, to find that he has been baffled by a youth [Croghan], who has just passed his twenty-first year."[60]

In his report to his superiors, Procter was unable to avoid admitting "the attack has not answered fully the purpose I intended," which was something of an understatement. However, he then pointed out that the campaign had not been a total loss, as he had almost entirely wiped out the men under Dudley only a short time before. Procter even went so far as to suggest that if all of the men under Clay had successfully reached Harrison's besieged army, "I should have had at this critical juncture to contend with him for Detroit, or perhaps on this shore." But the victory was bittersweet for the British. Harrison had been resupplied by Clay, despite Dudley's defeat, and the native warriors were making preparations to return to their villages with their dead and wounded. Procter would have to fall back to Canada yet again. To add insult to injury, many warriors left before the cannon could be moved, leaving a handful of Indians and Procter's men to load their ships while under intense American fire.[61] In dispatches to his superiors on the failure to capture Lower Sandusky, Procter was less charitable toward his native allies than he had been in the past, claiming a lack of "sufficient cooperation" from them was one reason for his failure.[62]

Chapter Seven

VICTORY AT THE THAMES

T HE VICTORIES AT Fort Meigs and Fort Stephenson had given the
American public something to cheer about, but they were defensive
victories and hardly erased the losses of the previous year. A counterattack was needed and had to be launched as soon as possible or the British
would regroup. On July 31, Shelby dispatched a handcrafted call for volunteers. These dispatches were destined for the regimental commanders
of the state militia with instructions that the call be passed on to their
men. As the colonel of each regiment opened the letter they found that
the moment so many had anticipated had arrived. There would be another army marching to meet the British, but this one would be led by
Shelby himself! The time had come to end the war in the West.[1]

The call was meant to rally public sentiment and was written not in
a matter-of-fact military tone but in an emotional appeal to the general
public. Less than three hundred words in length, the proclamation
summed up Shelby's intentions.

> Fellow Soldiers, Your government has taken measures to act ef-
> fectually against the enemy in upper Canada. General Harrison
> under the authority of the President of the United States has
> called upon me for a strong body of troops to assist in effecting
> the grand object of the campaign—the enemy in hopes to find us
> unprepared has again inverted Fort Meigs—But he will be driven
> from that post.

To comply with the requisition of Genl Harrison a draft aught have been enforced; but believing as I do that the ardour and patriotism of my countrymen has not abated—and that they have waited with impatience as an opportunity of avenging the blood of their brethren and friends. I have appointed the 31st day of August next at Newport for a General Rendezvous of Kentucky Volunteers.

I will meet you there in person[.] I will lead you to the field of battle—and share with you the dangers and honours of the Campaign. Our services will not be required more than sixty days after we reach headquarters.

I invite all officers, and others possessing influence to come forward with what mounted men they can raise—Each shall command the men he may bring into the field—the Superior officers will be appointed by myself at the place of Genl rendezvous and I shall take pleasure in acknowledgeing to my country the merits & public Spirit of those who may be usefull in collecting a force for the present emergency[.]

Those who have good rifles and know how to use them will bring them along—Those who have not will be furnished with muskets at Newport. Fellow citizens, now is the time to act—and by one decisive blow [an] end to the contest in that quarter.[2]

In the call to arms Shelby utilized his greatest asset—his own reputation. Unlike the march to the Raisin under General Winchester, this time the Kentucky militia would march north under a commander they all knew and respected. His promises to share in the dangers of the campaign with his "fellow soldiers" would have resonated with the men under his command and his presence would have aided their confidence. He was not a federal appointee or some recent arrival. He had been in Kentucky from its earliest days and had poured his years and strength into its soil. Shelby's success was tied to the commonwealth's success and everyone knew it.

Learning from the mistakes of past campaigns, Shelby had explicitly pointed out that the men would serve under the officer that had organized them for service. This decision solved three problems before the campaign even began its march. For one, it prevented arguments over who should lead the men at the regimental and company level by removing the often-cited disputes about seniority among the officers. It also allowed the men to be on their way to the rendezvous more quickly. In addition, it served as an incentive for officers to raise men in their areas. Those who wished to gain the accolades of command would have to do the legwork involved in raising a force to serve under them. The more men an officer raised the greater the role they would likely play in the coming battle. Shelby's promise of a campaign lasting no longer than sixty days also quashed the fear that the men would end up in a drawn-out campaign similar to some of the Indian campaigns of 1812 or that they would be left to languish in substandard winter quarters as had happened on the fateful Raisin expedition under Winchester. Whether this venture was a success or a failure, it would be over quickly. Finally, the governor appealed to the "ardour and patriotism" of his fellow citizens to avenge the fallen family, friends, and neighbors who had gone before them. While the phrase applied to anyone who had paid the ultimate sacrifice during the war, the memory of the River Raisin was certainly invoked.

But how many men would actually volunteer from a state that was starting to show the fatigue of war and whose citizens had the events of the Raisin and Dudley's defeat still fresh in their minds? Initially, Shelby seemed optimistic and expected the response around the state to be so great that he would have his pick of five thousand volunteers. However, when responses from the counties began to arrive in Frankfort, it was clear the number would be smaller than previously thought. Not everyone who had so ardently supported the idea of the hero of King's Mountain taking the field were eager to show their support by marching with him. Mingled with the affirmative replies of many came a barrage of questions. Will forage be provided for the horses? Will the troops be reimbursed for horses that are killed in battle? What about mounts that die on the march? What will the pay be? The federal government's delay on paying for earlier campaigns had not gone unnoticed. The men were patriotic enough, but most had families and something was needed to help compensate for their absence from their fields for weeks and months at a time.[3]

Of course, there was also the matter of timing. By the time the expedition marched it would be fairly late in the year for a campaign of this magnitude. It was one thing to man established forts or fight small-scale battles in Ohio or the Indiana Territory in the fall of the year where a week's march would land most of the men back in their homes. But to march to Canada, endure the first stages of winter on the Great Lakes, engage the entire British force stationed in western Ontario, and then return safely? That was something else entirely. There was also the harvest to bring in, and the winter frosts would not wait for the end of the campaign before coating the fields of crops with its silvery kiss of death. One local officer wrote that he had delivered Shelby's address as ordered, but he only expected around one hundred men would volunteer from his Mercer County.[4] By the tenth of August, only nineteen men had volunteered from Jessamine County.[5] Other similar answers poured in from farther afield in the state. Only thirty to forty men could be expected from Mount Vernon and the counties of Caldwell and Livingston were again under threat of Indian attack, which would mean many in the local militia would want to remain at home to protect their families so little help could be expected from that quarter.[6]

The slow massing of recruits embarrassed and somewhat surprised the governor. Patriotism always trumped personal needs in the mind of Isaac Shelby and he expected the same of those around him. Despite the hardships the state had endured, the fact that his countrymen would not volunteer en masse left him "mortified." Writing to Harrison, Shelby admitted, "I never have been so far disappointed in the patriotism of my countrymen before, I am at a loss to what cause to attribute their backwardness all at once." The arrival of the postman caused Shelby to end his bewildered lament prematurely and seal the letter for delivery.[7]

The problem was not that *no* troops would volunteer. As the governor pondered the mounting pile of letters arriving, it would have been clear to Shelby that he would have no trouble raising the four hundred minimum that Harrison had requested. But to take such a small number would be to lose an opportunity. The federal government had finally come to its senses concerning the use of militia, and Harrison, though somewhat unintentionally, had given Shelby a free hand in raising this force. Detroit, the Raisin, and Dudley's Defeat were glaring examples of the "too little, too late" policy that seemed to be the norm so far. This time could be different. Using the authority delegated to him by the legislature earlier that year new orders were drawn up and dispersed to the corners of the state. In addition to the volunteers raised, there would be a draft of 1,500 militia that would meet at Georgetown before proceeding to meet the volunteers at Newport. If only enough troops would turn out, they could seize the momentum from the British.

With the draft under way Shelby turned his attention to other needs. Writing to the quartermaster general of the 8th Military District to make sure enough provisions were laid back for the horses was one key concern. Harrison had not called specifically for mounted men, but that was what he would get. Shelby intended to move fast and it simply could not be done without a mounted force. The governor sent word that he needed enough forage for four thousand horses to be prepared. Before long a messenger placed the reply to his somewhat ambitious request in his hands. Supplies would be no problem. Stations were being set up between Cincinnati and Urbana that would allow the men to march north in good order with no shortages. Almost as an afterthought, the quartermaster mentioned that Perry had sailed on August 2, to engage the British fleet on Lake Erie.[8]

The Americans had no way of knowing, but the British fleet at Lake Erie was desperate for a victory for two reasons. The first was Perry's growing presence on Lake Erie had kept British admiral Barclay and his fleet bottled up in port on the Canadian side of the lake. As the weeks rolled by their supply levels were growing dangerously low. Unless they were able to break through and get resupplied they would not be able to continue.[9] The other motivator to move came from Barclay's Indian allies who were becoming increasingly alarmed at the American approach and increasingly irritated that their British allies had not acted to stop them. As relations between allies deteriorated many British sailors feared that, if they did not act soon, they would be massacred by the angry warriors.[10] The outcome of the battle would be more significant than either Shelby or the quartermaster writing the letter could have realized at the time.

Meanwhile, Shelby continued his preparations with so much zeal that even Harrison appeared to be getting tired of the constant flow of letters coming out of Frankfort as Shelby worked to arrange for arms and supplies for his men. In an uncharacteristic move, Harrison had his aide reply to Shelby's inquiries (as opposed to writing himself) to assure the anxious governor-turned-field-commander that the supplies needed would be ready when they arrived. As for the soldier's salaries, they would be paid what they deserved, despite any statements to the contrary. The letter closed with a paternal admonition for Kentucky to do her duty.[11]

With the troops gathering Shelby now turned to preparing himself for what would be an arduous march. It had been several years since he had been on campaign. It was true he had faced the British and Indians before, but he was a younger man then. Now he would do so one last time. Reaching for his quill he began a letter to his son. It was likely that between four and five thousand men would travel with him, he confided, returning to his original estimate. For himself, he would need "at least three hundred Dollars" to address any expenditures that arose on the trip. The money was to be advanced to him at once. In a sign of how troubled the economy truly was he reminded his son to be careful and make sure any funds he got from the bank were legitimate. The state of things meant counterfeits were being circulated.[12] As for his son Stephen, who would be accompanying him, he should be sent to Danville where he could buy heavy cloth for a "round about coat" and two pairs of overalls: one lined with deer skin and one without. He would need a good pair of shoes and would need to prepare the horses for the Spartan trip by letting them eat plenty while they could. "If the little gray don't fatten well perhaps I had better take the young Dallana mare."[13]

But there was more to prepare for than just physical necessities and logistical support. There was the oft-unspoken possibility that he, as with any other soldier, might not return from the campaign. As Shelby's mind began wandering to his family he transformed from commander to father long enough to encourage Isaac Jr. to see Doctor McDowell in Danville to "ward off any approaching illness." Then there was his other son Evan. He need not come on the expedition. His family would need him at home and, lest he be concerned for his aging father, Shelby added, "I have my health. I am as able to shift as he is and I hope that Providence in whom I always trusted will shield me in the hour of battle and crown me with victory." This momentary flicker of passion soon passed. The mail had come, he wrote. It contained no official word from Fort Meigs, but the rider reported that the British had withdrawn.[14] In a few weeks, Shelby would assess the situation for himself.

As spring faded into summer, there was little to do but wait and speculate before the busy autumn arrived. The plans had been made, supplies were being gathered, and men were preparing for the march. By mid-June, the heat of a Kentucky summer had set in and First Lady Susannah Shelby and their daughter Letitia had departed to visit friends. Despite the presence of his sons Isaac and Alfred the governor's thoughts turned to home. Writing to his son on the seventeenth he stated, "If nothing prevents me I will be up early in the harvest & spend two or three weeks at home. I cannot at present foresee anything that will require my attention here—the heat in this place has made it quite intolerable[,] it almost melts me."[15]

With the legislature out of session, Frankfort returned to its sleepy demeanor. But with the passing weeks the date of the rendezvous came closer and closer. A few at a time, men from across the state began filtering into the city. When not being advised of the arrival of new volunteers the governor was busy reading letters promising that more were on the way. The pessimism that had seemed to haunt the expedition in its planning stages a few months earlier was beginning to fade. It was true that the state had not risen en masse to the governor's call, but the men were beginning to add up. Harrison's reply concerning pay had helped clear up some of the misgivings as well. By August 30, Shelby, undoubtedly feeling justified, found that enough volunteers had been raised to allow him to cancel the draft. Whether they had left their homes to defend the cause of freedom or to avenge the death of a relative, or to seek personal glory, the men would march with knowledge that everyone in the army was there because they chose to be.[16]

Shelby now moved on to organizing the clumps of arriving soldiers into a single, functioning regiment. George Walker was ordered to act as a brigadier general and quartermaster. As such, he would be responsible for keeping up with the various returns from the hundreds of small groups descending on the rendezvous point and to see how many troops had brought their own arms. Every private weapon and horse was to be assigned a value and a list delivered to each commander. This would make it easier to replace the inevitable losses that would occur during a battle. Those who did not have arms with them when they arrived would have them issued. In addition, all the men would be given enough ammunition to practice their aim on the march north. Unlike the attempted silent march of General Winchester's army the year before, Shelby's men would be firing constantly to alleviate boredom and blow off steam as much as to practice marksmanship.[17]

When the day of the rendezvous arrived, the governor was not disappointed; he had his army. With a renewed confidence the army marched out of Frankfort on the road north. By eight in the evening on the first of September, Shelby found a few minutes to write to Harrison. The men had been crossing the Ohio River for three days. Despite his attempts at preparation there seemed to be a shortage of everything from blankets to corn to guns. The advance pay was not all there either. Still, enough supplies had been amassed to allow the men to continue their march north. If everything proceeded smoothly, the army would unite with Harrison and the men already under his command in just ten days' time.[18]

By September 10 Shelby sat in the midst of a bustling military camp at McNary's Blockhouse. He had received word from Harrison telling him that he awaited his arrival and the governor was eager to comply. The news that some of the Ohio troops had gone home displeased him, but he had two hundred Indian allies who promised to fight with him in his ranks.[19] Like many who had come before him, Shelby found the territory to be "the most beautifull Country I ever beheld" (high praise from a man who had tilled the virgin soils of Kentucky), although he was disappointed that many locals refused to join the expedition. Speaking of the local residents Shelby noted with asperity that "they have fleeced us of every cent in their power, their ordinary wild hay at 50 cents a hundred & Green sheaf oats (which they are only now cutting) at the same price pr dozen, if a single roasting ear is taken they follow up mowing and whining until they get paid, such sordid avarice I never saw before. . . . I do not mean to expose publickly the Citizens of a sister state," he fumed, "but hereafter so far as I may have any influence they shall fight their own Battles."[20] The men under his command were confident despite the fact that many were young and a little careless. Sounding like the grandfather he was Shelby sighed that he was "perpetually trying to ecite their appreciations of the scenes that are before us to induce them to keep their arms in order." The duties of commanding the force kept the governor busy and often tired. He dreamt of returning home to Susannah as soon as possible.[21]

As the Kentuckians rode their way through the Ohio countryside, Perry's fleet was making its way across Lake Erie and an anxious Harrison was as eager to hear the results of that battle as he was for Shelby and his militia to arrive. On August 31, he had provided Perry with one hundred volunteers from the 28th US Infantry and some of the Kentucky militia, which were already under his command, to serve as sharpshooters on board ship during the upcoming battle.[22] There had been no word since. Finally, on the tenth of August, Harrison received Perry's immortal message: "DEAR GENERAL—We have met the enemy and they are ours—two ships, two brigs, one schooner and a sloop. Yours with great respect and esteem OLIVER HAZARD PERRY."[23]

While there is no dispute that the Battle of Lake Erie is one of America's most enduring engagements, modern historians struggle to fully grasp the decisions made by those involved: both Barclay on the British side and Jesse Duncan Elliott (one of Perry's subordinates) on the American side. Elliott had proven slow to engage the enemy, though

The Battle of Lake Erie drawn by Thomas Sully and engraved by Murray, Draper, Fairman & Co., 1815. Commander Perry is shown tranferring his flag from the disabled *Lawrence* to the *Niagara*. Despite the damage to both fleets, rather than retreat, Perry pressed the battle until the British were forced to surrender. (*Library of Congress*)

he claimed he had been following orders by Perry to hold the position he currently occupied.[24] While the role of Harrison's men is not clearly described the Kentucky sharpshooters must have had some effect, as British admiral Barclay claimed the loss was partially due "to the unpresented fall of every Commander, and second in Command" on the ships in his fleet.[25] Such a description seems to suggest the individual targeting of officers with small arms rather than the arbitrary casualities that were a signature of cannon fire. This provided some long-awaited good news. With Lake Erie now in American hands, the men could march forward hugging the shoreline to protect their flank without fear of some large force landing behind them without warning. On the fifteenth, the Kentucky militia under Shelby arrived at Portage (modern-day Port Clinton). Their long ride was over. Here, they would trade their horses for the decks of Perry's ships, which could carry them across the lake and land them in Canadian territory.[26] This would be quicker than marching around the lake and give them the element of surprise.

The most obvious question now was, what was to be done with the horses? It would be a logistical nightmare to try and transport them as well as the troops and there would be no forage readily available on the Canadian side. On the other hand, building a corral large enough to keep them all would take too long. They needed a place where they could be kept and fed until the army returned. The answer was in the terrain. Sandusky Bay and the Portage River met to create a small peninsula nearby. This field of grass hemmed in on three sides by water provided the perfect corral for three thousand horses. The army only needed to fence the forth side. The troops were ordered to lay aside their rifles and muskets and to pick up their axes. Trees and brush were cut and dragged to the narrow point of the peninsula where they were piled high in a makeshift fence. It may not have been pretty to look at, but it was quick, easy, and did the trick. Once the fence was completed, the horses were turned loose to graze in the wide expanse. Then one out of every twenty men were left under the command of Colonel Chris Rife to guard the horses until the army returned.[27]

As the men prepared to embark for Canada, a small disagreement arose in camp. Harrison also had some Pennsylvania militia on hand who were to be part of the invasion force. When the time came to board the ships, many of the men expressed what McAfee sardonically referred to as "constitutional scruples" about actually leaving the United States. It was perfectly legal for the federal troops to do so but as militia, called up to defend their country, many protested the idea of landing on Canadian soil. Harrison was a little annoyed but was not much delayed by this question of legality. "Thank God, I have Kentuckians enough to go without you," he told them.[28] That ended the discussion, and as some men went home, Harrison prepared to march forward.

Troops under Shelby marched from Urbana to Portage Bay in six days. At Upper Sandusky, an express from Harrison arrived to Governor Shelby telling him of the capture of the British fleet on Lake Erie by Perry. From Portage Bay the Kentucky troops watched the unloading of many prisoners from Perry's victory. The area was "sand banks and nothing but water as far as we can see in front and for six miles back a leval pararie."[29] How much of the plans were made known to the officers, or even how much was known ahead of time, is not clear. Certainly Harrison and probably Shelby had goals in mind though. According to James Simrall in a letter to his wife, the army expected to find Fort Malden deserted and "there was no intention of the Kty troops doing anything more than [sic] go to Malden and return back in the fleet to this place. I have great hopes of being in Kty by the 20th October."[30]

The destruction of the British fleet on Lake Erie combined with the fast approaching army under Harrison and Shelby forced Procter to call a council with local allied chiefs to decide his next move. Procter described the dire situation to the chiefs and then suggested they fall back, destroying the forts at Detroit and Amherstburg. Some favored the idea, but Tecumseh vehemently opposed it. He reminded Procter how during the American Revolution the British placed the hatchet of war in the hands of their fathers but betrayed them after they were "thrown on his back by the Americans," making peace with them without even considering the tribes that had supported them.[31]

Now a new conflict had arisen and again the Indians were called on for help and cajoled with promises of getting their lands back. They were told they could bring their families to Canada where they would be safe. "When we last went to the Rapids, it is true," Tecumseh admitted, "we gave you little assistance. It is hard to fight people who live like groundhogs." He fumed in reference to the American practice of digging in.[32] But now Procter wanted to retreat and thus renege on the British promise of protection without confiding what his next objectives would be. The Americans may have won by water but they had not yet won on land. To retreat without seeing the first American was akin to being a "fat animal" (presumably he meant a dog), who can quickly drop its tail and run whenever startled.[33] The reaction from the chiefs to this speech was to draw their tomahawks and yell in agreement. The answer was clear. If Procter wanted native support he would have to engage the Americans sooner rather than later.[34]

As Procter planned, Harrison and Shelby moved. September 20 proved a busy day for the Americans who stood on the shores of Lake Erie as camp was struck and Harrison's army boarded Perry's waiting ships. No mention of any hesitations on the part of the soldiers survive, although they certainly would have been understandable. For most of the Kentuckians present, this was the first time they had seen a body of water so large that the opposite shore was not in sight. Now they would have to cross it. Harrison's army was too large to be ferried all at once to the Canadian shore and it would have been too great a gamble to try to leave a few hundred men alone on the Canadian shore while the ships went back for the rest. With this in mind, it was determined to ferry the men from island to island until they could reach the Canadian shore. From the twentieth to the twenty-second, Harrison's army was ferried to Bass Island in Lake Erie. With its wooded 1,500 acres it provided a waypoint for Harrison's troops who had to be transported in shifts due to limited space on Perry's fleet. From there, Perry would take them to Middle Sister Island. With only five to six acres, Harrison's 4,500 men would find it a little crowded and even more uncomfortable.[35]

As might be expected, the conditions on Bass Island deteriorated quickly. One officer stated that the water was poor, the meat they had was two days old and spoiling, and many had fallen sick and would have to be returned to Portage on the mainland to recover. Among them was Shelby's son. The sickness that wracked the troops was not named but was almost certainly dysentery. The cramped conditions and poor water made it almost inevitable. Shelby was forced to leave his son behind but was kept informed by letter of his progress. In an effort to comfort the governor, the author of the letter assured him, "I will pay every attention in my power to your boy and take him with me [back to Portage] he Cant walk without help."[36]

It was here that the Kentuckians were forced to leave behind their last four-legged recruit. A group of troops from the central portion of the state found that, on their way to the rendezvous in Newport, they had picked up an extra soldier. A hog with free time on its hands decided to join the expedition and fell in behind the men as they marched toward the rendezvous. It followed them to Newport and, much to the amuse-ment of the army, made the crossing into Ohio and continued the march north. Before long, the animal had become an unofficial mascot and was highly prized by the men. The hog even boarded one of Perry's ships at Portage and made the trip partially across Lake Erie. However, Bass Is-land proved to be all the patriotic swine could handle and, perhaps fear-ing worse conditions at the next port of call, refused to go farther and was eventually returned to the American mainland.[37]

On September 27, having survived the uncomfortable island hop-ping, the men were landed on the Canadian shore just four miles below Malden. For some, it was the first time their feet had touched the main-land in a week.[38] Harrison felt that an attack by the British was inevitable and issued extremely detailed instructions on the order in which the men were to march and what to do if they were attacked. Shelby would as-sume the role of a major general and the Kentucky militia under his command would make up the right wing of the army. The left wing would be made up of the regulars under Generals Cass and McArthur as well as Colonel Ball's Light Corps led by Harrison. Drums were dis-tributed to order the march and the men prepared to advance.[39]

Before the army marched in the direction of Malden, Harrison addressed the issue on the mind of the Kentuckians. "Remember the Raisin," he urged, "but remember it only, whilst victory is suspended. The revenge of a soldier cannot be gratified on a fallen enemy." There would be no atrocities made by this army, regardless of what Procter's policy was. Within two hours of this final order the advanced elements of Harrison's army disembarked from their boats and splashed onto Canadian soil. The advanced guards were met with silence. As the main body of the army rapidly disembarked with guns at the ready they found the scene just as empty. A somewhat surprised Harrison directed his troops in the direction of Malden, which had served as the British base of operations over the last year, but they met no resistance. Were the British waiting inside the town? Was it an ambush? With arms at the ready the men marched until the town of Malden came into view. What greeted them was as surprising as any waiting army. There was nothing but smoldering ruins. Procter had ordered the fort and navy yard burnt as he and his British regulars retreated. [40]

Securing Malden, Harrison's army continued their march northward to Sandwich. Many in the army felt this must be the place Procter had chosen to resist the invasion, but they were pleasantly surprised once again. Arriving on the twenty-ninth, there was no one to meet them but the few villagers who had remained when the army retreated. The only resistance they met came from a nonexistent bridge that had been destroyed before Procter's retreat. Otherwise, their march had continued unabated. Now they stood on the banks of the Detroit River looking across at Fort Detroit. General McArthur and his regulars who had marched with Harrison quickly crossed the river and retook the fort and town. Hull's cowardly surrender had been avenged. Harrison immediately ordered the original civilian government restored. The next day word reached Shelby of some of the Kentucky militia violating the personal property of people in the town. Orders were issued to halt any such activity immediately. Harrison had meant what he said about acting like an army and not an avenging mob. [41]

On September 30, Richard Johnson and his mounted men arrived at Detroit to further bolster Harrison's force. [42] Johnson had been ordered by Harrison to bring his cavalry northward weeks before and he eagerly complied. En route they had to pass through the now-infamous Frenchtown, which they reached on the twenty-seventh. The significance of an American force reaching this town would not have been lost on the command made up entirely of Kentuckians. Their arrival and Winchester's ill-fated attempt that January could not have been more different. Far from being the frozen and desolate landscape bristling with armed soldiers and cannon it was now quiet and virtually empty. As the men rode into town a few residents who had remained with their homes despite the war came out to greet them. The fruit trees that must have been a source of pride in previous years were heavy with fruit, testifying of a once-bustling town that now housed too few hands to pick them all. But it was not the green foliage or the brightly colored fruit that caught Johnson's attention. Instead it was the splinters of white that dotted the fields. They were the bones of men who had been left in the elements—the only testimony of the Kentuckians who fell at the River Raisin seven months before. The sight of the unburied skeletons was seared on the memory of the men who rode into town. One soldier later recalled that the bones "still appealed to heaven, and called on Kentucky to avenge this outrage on humanity. . . . The feelings they excited cannot be described by me—but they will never be forgotten—not while there is a recording angel in heaven, or a historian upon earth, will the tragedy of the river Raisin be suffered to sink into oblivion."[43]

While most of the Kentucky militia who had gathered at Malden may not have put it quite so eloquently, their passions were no less elevated. As they rode into Detroit to meet Harrison's army they carried these memories with them. The number of troops gathered now numbered 5,500 and Shelby, mindful of his promise of a quick campaign, urged Harrison to pursue Procter as soon as possible. With General McArthur and his men left to guard Detroit, Harrison and the rest of the army struck camp at sunrise on October 2 in pursuit of Procter who, it was now obvious, was fleeing east.[44]

General Procter was well aware that he was being pursued and that the number of American troops was growing. The only option that seemed viable was to fall back, shortening the British supply lines and buying time in hopes that Harrison would overextend himself and use up the last precious weeks of autumn. But Tecumseh and his warriors continued to voice their concern, as Procter's actions seemed less like a strategy and more like a disguised retreat. Each mile that Harrison advanced meant one mile less of safe hunting grounds for the Shawnee and Britain's other allied tribes. Tecumseh began to ratchet up the pressure on his British allies even more and his open comparison of the British commander to a frightened dog still hung palpably in the memory of everyone in camp.[45] For Procter, this unwelcomed moniker was only the latest sign of how quickly his plans were coming apart at the seams.

As the American army continued its march east, anticipation and the spirits of the men continued to mount. They were no longer retaking lost territory but were adding new ground to their conquest. The sight of an eagle soaring overhead was taken as a good omen.[46] On the fourth of October, the army received a more tangible reason to be confident. A schooner and nearby house were found engulfed in flames. Despite the flames, Harrison and his men could see they were full of military supplies and weapons. The loss of something so valuable could only mean one thing: Procter did not have time to retrieve them before the Americans arrived. He wasn't just withdrawing; he was running. The fact that both were still alight when the Americans arrived proved that Procter was not far ahead. Intelligence later came in to verify that the British army were camped just a short distance ahead on the other side of the river. As evening came, the army made camp and Harrison and Shelby stayed awake much of the night overseeing a breastwork being dug by their men in case of a predawn attack by the British. There would be no repeat of the early morning surprise that led to the slaughter at the Raisin. If the British did attack they would find the Americans dug in and ready. Finally, in the early hours of the morning, the exhausted Shelby decided to retire for a few hours' sleep. Seeking out the part of the line nearest the enemy he found a tent with a vacancy. Crawling inside, he shared a blanket with one of his men and waited for the battle that would surely take place in a matter of hours.[47]

The army rose early the next morning and began preparing for the inevitable. By nine o'clock two gunboats and a handful of prisoners had been captured on the river Thames, but this was not the battle they were looking for. That was still to come. Johnson's mounted men each carried an extra soldier on their back and they crossed the river to the side where the British were camped. Not long after setting foot on the opposite bank Harrison's men captured a wagoner who confessed the British were just three hundred yards away in battle formation waiting for the Americans. Harrison's spies soon returned and excitedly confirmed it.[48]

The reports from spies and prisoners proved that while Procter might be retreating he had not lost his head entirely. The place he had chosen to stand and fight was a narrow strip of land flanked by the Thames River on one side and a large swamp with plenty of shielding trees on the other. In the center of the field lay a second, smaller, marshy wooded area that would force the attackers to divide their force between the two clearings or funnel them into the narrow confines of the open area and directly into the arms of Procter's waiting regulars. As Harrison and Shelby scanned the field of waiting soldiers there was something peculiar. Tecumseh was nowhere to be found and neither were his warriors. They had to be waiting somewhere in the shaded marshes where they could pick off the advancing Americans a few at a time. Regardless of which route the army took their flanks would be exposed. The road lay on the south side of the little marsh and it was here that Procter lined up the majority of his regulars and artillery.[49]

Harrison prepared for the attack and ordered Johnson's men to clear the swamp of Indians. Meanwhile, the infantry would attack the British regulars lined up in the clearing. As the attack prepared to move forward, an American major rushed up to Harrison. He claimed to have gotten close enough to the enemy lines to see the British were lined up in "open order." In other words, they had spaced their soldiers several feet apart rather than standing shoulder to shoulder as they normally would. This was probably meant to prevent the British lines from being such an easy target for Harrison's backwoods sharpshooters but may have also been used to spread the troops out to look like there were more of them. Regardless of the reason, if this intelligence were true it presented an interesting opportunity, and Colonel Richard M. Johnson offered to take advantage of it. Instead of marching the now-dismounted militia forward, his horsemen could rush through the gaps in the lines and reform behind the enemy infantry.[50]

It was a little unconventional and extremely risky to charge well-prepared and heavily armed lines of infantry from horseback. At close range, the cavalry's horses would provide excellent targets. But Johnson felt his men were ready and it would be worth the risk. They had been practicing for charges through heavily wooded areas to assail their enemy. The generously spaced British lines would be no different. They could slip through the gaps and be in the British rear before they could react. Harrison agreed and Col. Johnson then sent his brother, James Johnson, with half his force to carry out this change in plans while he and his men prepared for the illusive Tecumseh and his warriors who lay ensconced in the swamp. Word of the change quickly spread and Johnson's officers rode up and down the line encouraging their troops.[51] The infantry lined up behind Johnson's men and prepared to advance immediately so that

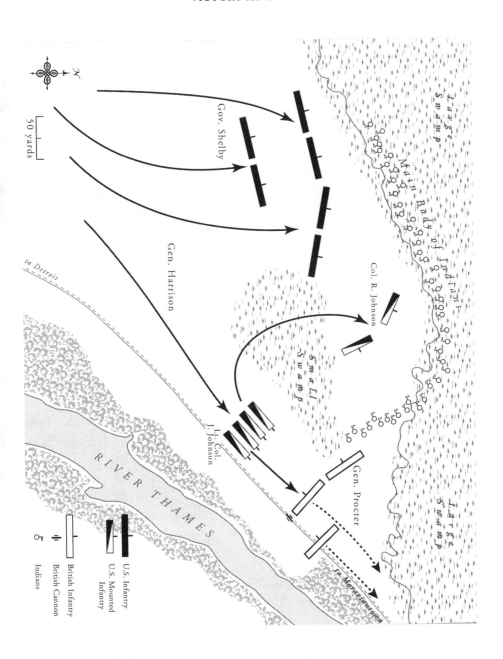

"Remember the Raisin!" Kentucky mounted riflemen led by militia col. Richard M. Johnson attack British foot soldiers. (*Ken Riley/USACMH*)

the broken British lines could not reform without being overrun.[52] The orders were given and the line of horses and riders lurched forward. Shouting "Remember the Raisin!" the soldiers quickly shifted the horses from trot to cantor to gallop and the thunder of hooves stormed toward the British lines.[53] The two lines of British regulars opened fire, temporarily spooking the horses in front, but the columns soon recovered and burst through the British lines. One soldier recalled that "No sooner had our horsemen charged through their lines and gained their rear, than they began to surrender as fast as they could throw down their arms."[54]

While this was transpiring, Richard Johnson and his men moved toward the swamp. It had been decided that the only effective way to fight the warriors hidden in the foliage was to find out where they were concentrated. This meant exposing a part of his force to draw their fire. The direction of the muzzle flashes would tell the Americans where to focus their charge. Twenty men volunteered to act as bait and urged their horses forward toward the tree line in what was obviously a suicide mission. As they drew closer the plan worked and the shadows were illuminated by a series of musket flashes as trails of smoke rose through the

Top, "A view of Col. Johnson's engagement with the savages (commanded by Tecumseh) near Moravian Town, October 5th 1812 [1813]." Bottom, "Battle of the Thames and the death of Tecumseh, by the Kentucky mounted volunteers led by Colonel Richard M. Johnson, 5th Oct. 1813." Johnson and his troops dismounted before engaging Tecumseh; it is also not clear who killed Tecumseh in the melee. (*Library of Congress*)

tree branches. Nineteen of the twenty men were hit and many were mortally wounded.[55] In the years that followed the small band of men were given the name the "Forlorn Hope" to honor their sacrifice, although the phrase was not unique to this group of men and had been used before. Most paintings and engravings of the battle show Johnson and his men on horseback charging through the swamp. However, McAfee points out that horses would be of little use in the swamp and, as a result, with the exception of the Forlorn Hope, the portion of Johnson's men charging the swamp dismounted. The battle raged ruthlessly as the remaining Kentuckians in reserve watched anxiously from a distance, ready to attack as the battle unfolded. It was becoming obvious that the battle in the swamp would not be easily won. Shelby ordered the first portion of the infantry to support them. The waiting lines of militia rushed into the trees. It took less than ten minutes to eject the body of Indians from the swamp through a rolling battle that took around half an hour as the Kentuckians pursued the retreating warriors, with each pausing at times to fire at the other.[56] When the smoke cleared, the battle had been a complete rout. Almost the entire British force had been taken prisoner. The Shawnee chief, Tecumseh, had also been killed in the melee, some suspect by Richard Johnson, who was forced to bow out of the battle after receiving a shot in the hip as well as a shot in the left hand. All told seventeen of Johnson's men lay dead and thirty were wounded. The British had eighteen dead and twenty-six wounded with around six hundred prisoners of war.[57]

The one man, however, who was not to be found was General Procter. Having observed the battle from a distance he had witnessed his lines collapse. Without waiting for the outcome, Procter fled. When it was realized that the British commander had escaped, sixty of Johnson's men led by Major Duvall Payne charged after him in pursuit, but he was nowhere to be found. However, Procter and the men fleeing with him did leave a trail of items in their wake. The Kentuckians captured his sword and personal papers as well as three brass cannons. Upon inspection it was revealed that one of the cannons was the Saratoga cannon that Hull had surrendered at Detroit.[58] While capturing the Saratoga cannon may have been of psychological value, the three thousand stands of arms and six other artillery pieces were not bad either.[59]

On the seventh, Harrison returned to Detroit, leaving Shelby to tend to his Kentuckians and plan for the trip home. The cold winds of late autumn were already blowing when the men began their march south.[60] There would be no fleet of ships to take them home this time. Perry had sailed on to new endeavors. They would have to march around the lakes. Despite the weather and the need to get home as quickly as possible, Shelby's men had one final stop to make before they returned to Kentucky. Marching through Detroit the men moved south to Frenchtown. Johnson's men had buried some of the dead from the River Raisin on their way north from Fort Meigs, but there had been no time to collect and bury them all. Now that the battle was over, the job could be finished. The army under Shelby was able to collect sixty-five skeletons of their fellow Kentuckians and give them a decent burial.[61] Now the men could resume their march toward home in a race against winter. There had been snow before they had even crossed into Michigan Territory and any further delay would be dangerous. The men reclaimed their horses at Portage and headed south.[62]

On November 4, the men mustered for the last time and were discharged from the army. In a little over two months, they had accomplished their goal.[63] The army of Kentucky volunteers was discharged at Limestone (modern Maysville). As the men dispersed throughout the state, word of the victory spread, and crowds formed to cheer and welcome their soldiers home. A defeat of Procter's men would have advanced the American cause, but the complete destruction of it had turned the tables entirely. Many Indian tribes including the Ottawa and Chippewa sued for peace immediately, which Harrison accepted. These offers were soon followed up by the Miami and the Potawatomie who returned the prisoners of war in their possession.[64] Not only had Procter's army been defeated but his native alliances were crumbling.

Procter's actions at the Thames have been the subject of much debate among historians of the war. On the one hand, American accounts make it sound like Harrison's army was gaining on Procter each day they marched and it suggests that Procter was forced to select a field of battle and meet his enemy head on. The number of native women and children on the march would certainly support the idea that the British column was lumbering forward while the lightly armed and equipped American army (especially the mounted component's like Richard Johnson's regiment) covered more ground than the British. If this is true, he did a good job of choosing a defensive terrain which suggests that, despite being pursued, he still had enough options and time to select a battlefield that would be to his advantage even if he did not have the choice of avoiding battle altogether.

The second factor that has to be considered when analyzing Procter's decision to fight was the role his native allies played in forcing a battle. American sources tend to emphasize Tecumseh's role in pressuring Procter to engage the Americans. Such a decision would be logical since each mile the British army left behind them was one more mile of native territory ceded to the Americans. On the other hand, each mile that Harrison and Shelby marched into Ontario was an additional mile added to the American supply lines. Major fortifications had to have detachments assigned to them to keep lines of communication open, which meant Harrison's army was slowly being strung out along his route, which meant each day he had fewer troops to engage Procter with once he finally caught him. With this in mind it could be argued that, if Tecumseh was truly the deciding factor in forcing Procter to turn and engage the Americans when he did instead of continuing to draw Harrison into the interior, he was the cause of the defeat.

But Canadian sources tend to place the decision more firmly in Procter's hands. The Indians were a factor in Procter's choosing to fight at the Thames, but Procter was motivated by compassion rather than intimidation. According to Antal, Procter still "stubbornly adhered to native considerations in planning future movements."[65] Procter does seem to have been an advocate of the needs of the native population, and it is possible that this concern bore some influence on his decisions. However, the fact that Procter tried to make this idea of native homeland manifest through the cessation of American territory alone leaves some room for concern about his true motives. Procter's decisions following the capture of Hull's army, such as moving the Indian Department to Detroit, suggest the British government would not have been willing to grant similar concession from Canada, making this an arrangement the United States could never adhere to.[66]

Regardless of Procter's motivations, there can be little doubt of the significance of the battle. Historians such as Donald Hickey view the Thames as a turning point in American and British history but also of the native people of the region.[67] The defeat at the Thames severely damaged Britain's ability to strike the United States from western Ontario for a very valuable length of time and, thus, the war transferred to the eastern theatres around the New York border. Hickey suggests it was this victory that would later defeat the British efforts to secure a native homeland with the Americans (something that Antal would agree with). However, Hickey also says, "Never again would Indians seriously threaten the United States and never again would a foreign nation tamper with American Indians."[68] Truly, it can be argued that the War of 1812 was the last realistic hope for the indigenous peoples of North America to secure a permanent territory against American expansion. Once the Thames had collapsed the native alliance, this threat never reemerged.

Chapter Eight

FIRE AND FEDERALISTS

As the dust settled on the Battle of the Thames, American dominance in the Indiana, Illinois, and Michigan Territories was assured and a large portion of western Ontario lay in American hands. Although the campaign had not been without casualties (and substantial expense with the feeding of thousands of soldiers and horses) a remarkable victory had been achieved quickly and with relatively few casualties. In a letter to the War Department, the governor estimated that 3,500 Kentuckians had volunteered for military service during the campaign.[1] As the New Year began the legislature reported back to work with renewed optimism. Robert McAfee, of Mercer County declared "The Legislature in close session all day—time rolls along, the opening year is Big with great events, many hard battles." It was true that these would come with casualties but, with any luck, one last concerted effort against Canada could finally wrest the country from British hands once and for all. "He went on to boast that he was entirely "convinced that with the Blessings of Divine Providence we will carry a victorious army to the walls of Quebec."[2]

Kentucky's members of Congress also shared this rosy point of view. Kentucky representative William Duval boasted that when he returned to his seat in Washington he "never will consent to restore to England [Upper Canada] on any terms." Rather it must be used as a springboard for invading Lower Canada and pushing the British into the Atlantic.[3] Duval's confidence was unbounded and he greeted the offer of the Russ-

ian tsar to negotiate a peace treaty as a promising sign. "It is highly prob-
able we shall have peace in six (?) Months."[4]

With the campaign at an end, the governor had also returned to
Frankfort and his more mundane duties. A little more than a month
after his arrival home, a letter from Secretary of State Monroe arrived.
Monroe explained that, in a departure from the standard practice, the
British had taken twenty-three Americans to Britain to be tried for trea-
son as British subjects. Whether they had formerly been subjects of the
Crown or not was not mentioned in Monroe's letter and, in all likelihood, was irrelevant in the eyes of both the secretary and Governor
Shelby. What mattered was how the United States would respond. For
the Madison administration, the matter was very simple—an eye for an
eye. If the British were going to hold Americans in British prisons then
the United States would have to reciprocate. Twice that number would
be marched to Frankfort and interred in the state penitentiary there.[5]

Shelby complied with the request to prepare quarters for the prisoners
and ordered the keeper of the penitentiary in Frankfort to have rooms
prepared for the arrival of the prisoners. By December 12, the first nineteen prisoners had arrived. They were given rooms on the second floor
of the penitentiary where they were separated from the other prisoners
and were afforded "every comfort compatible with a state of close con-
finement."[6] Despite such an amiable order, a prison was still a prison
and the uncertainty of the whole affair left many British POWs with
doubts on how their captivity would end. Lieutenant Benjamin Geale
was one of the British regulars taken at the Thames. He had survived
the march southward with the triumphant returning militia but now
found himself locked inside a prison. Taking his pen in hand he wrote
to his brother Piers in Dublin, Ireland, to let him know that he was
safe—at least for now. "Its from within the walls of a prison your unfortunate Brother addresses you," he scratched gloomily. "This perhaps is
the last letter you will ever receive from me, if the men in England are
executed my days will shortly after conclude." He commended the care
of his wife and child to his brother and promised to send a copy of his
will before adding with some asperity, "What a war this is likely to be.
. . . However thank God I die with honor to myself and country."[7]

The arrival of British prisoners was certainly an event of note in
Frankfort, but any feelings of curiosity their arrival may have excited
would have been tempered by another event that had transpired just over
two weeks before. The night of November 27 had descended on Frank-

fort like most others. Of those brave enough to venture into the cold autumnal darkness none seemed to notice the light burning in the window of the capitol building. The single flame glowed from the adjutant general's office window in the middle room on the second floor. The next day passed like any other and the citizens of the town returned to their homes. One by one the windows of the different homes went dark as people braced for another November night in Kentucky. At some point in the middle of the night they were jolted awake by the cry of "fire." The town's citizens came scrambling and stumbling into the streets. It was the capitol, and by the time any real help could arrive the building was engulfed in flames. One brave resident burst inside the building to attack the source of the fire and made it to the door of the adjutant general's office where the fire was centered. Trying the knob he discovered the door was locked and the key was nowhere to be found. There was nothing left for the citizens of Frankfort to do but salvage what they could. Rushing into the surrounding rooms people began carrying out stacks of papers and books. When dawn rose on the smoking rubble it was clear that the building was a total loss. However, most of the papers had been rescued with the exception of the secretary of the senate's documents and, of course, anything in the adjutant general's office.[8] The state seal and the secretary of state's official seal were only a few of the casualties.[9]

Despite the loss, the government had to continue. The first order of business would be finding a place to work. Governor Shelby instructed the secretary of state to rent room enough for the legislature to meet when they returned to Frankfort.[10] The governor then asked the court of appeals to investigate and provide him a report of their findings on the cause of the fire. They reached the conclusion that the fire had to come from the middle room where witnesses now recalled having seen a light the night before, because the two rooms on either side had not had a fire in their grates for a week. The official hypothesis put forth is that slaves may have been using the building for gambling at night (which was against the law in Kentucky at the time) and their light led to the fire. However, the court had no real proof of the fire's cause, but no other possible alternatives were put forward.[11]

The rest of the year would pass in relative quiet as the state worked to pick up the pieces. On January 25 Shelby wrote to General Harrison to congratulate him on his retirement. Having retaken Detroit and a portion of Canada, Harrison felt he could finally end his military career, having done his duty and restored his nation's honor. Perhaps feeling a little envious of the tranquility Harrison could now look forward to, Shelby expressed his hope that he might enjoy his own home soon.[12] But that would not be for a few years yet. Until that time, the aging governor would have to push on. The war was beginning to take its toll not only on Shelby but on the commonwealth. A significant portion of Kentucky's militia had seen action by the start of 1814 and many were not anxious to do so again. To make matters worse, the state's coffers were running dangerously low. While the federal government was responsible for paying back any expenses incurred by the state in defense of the nation, reimbursements took some time. In order to fund future campaigns, the legislature was forced to ask the Bank of Kentucky for a loan of $100,000.[13] The legislature passed a resolution that it forwarded to Kentucky's members of Congress urging them to pay the men who had fought the previous fall.[14]

The peace signed with the Indians in the North did not result in peace with those tribes west of the Tennessee River and south of the Kentucky border. This fact was driven home to the residents of Livingston County in July when one member of a volunteer guard was shot. His son was later found tomahawked.[15] A few weeks later, a party of seven to ten (presumably hostile) Indians was spotted in the area, again sending shockwaves of fear into the hearts of settlers. Not long after, another resident was fired on from the shadows as he stepped outside his home into dawn one morning.[16]

Additional calls for troops continued to pour in as the federal government requested the state raise an infantry corps of 5,500 men "for immediate service." This was larger than the number of militia Shelby had raised for the Battle of the Thames, and that venture had taken months to organize. And now the state was expected to find the men and materials to repeat it on an even larger scale. Dutifully, Shelby again complied with the request, though he pointed out in a letter to the secretary of war that he could not name a place of rendezvous since he did not know where the troops were even going to be sent.[17] After a night of considering the actions of the federal government and remembering how inadequately it had worked to pay the men who had marched with him the previous year, a fuming Shelby rose the next morning to write a second note to the secretary of war. His tone was less than cordial and his impatience began to show. Dispensing with any formalities except a very short "Sir," he began:

In the month of February last I forwarded to the war Department complete muster Rolls of the forces which served under me last fall in the Service of the United States against Upper Canada. I had flattered myself that as soon as the Rolls were received the subject would have been taken up and the necessary arrangements made for the immediate payment of these troops and that I should have been informed of the measures taken[.] Hitherto I have received no information whatever on the subject, I must therefore be permitted to call the attention of the President of the United States to it and to request to be informed when these men will be paid[.] They left their homes at a very short warning, equiped at their own expence prompted by a zeal to avenge the disasters and disgrace our Country had previously suffered in that quarter.[18]

There were some participants, Shelby conceded, who were wealthy and the cost of the trip was no problem. However, this was the exception rather than the rule. Most of the men had to go into debt to buy the equipment they needed, not to mention the cost of feeding themselves and their horses on the way to the rendezvous. Some of the men from the western part of the state had travelled around three hundred miles to reach Newport. "What the North Western Army did with the aid of this force I need not repeat—the world knows it—That it could not effect what it did without this force is demonstrable to any man of Common sense," he wrote.[19]

But the disgruntled mumbles of a western governor like Shelby were overshadowed by those of the Northeast, which advocated even more drastic action. The war had never been popular in New England, whose economy relied so much on British commerce and whose population lay dangerously sandwiched between British Canada and an Atlantic that was becoming more and more populated by British ships. By October 1814, the General Court of Massachusetts issued a call for a new constitutional convention. While the proposal was far from unanimous it seemed to suggest, for the first time during the conflict, that the union itself might be in danger if the war continued. By the time the group gathered in Hartford, Connecticut, representatives from Rhode Island, Massachusetts, New Hampshire, Connecticut, and Vermont had gathered to participate. The Hartford Convention, as it would come to be called, proposed a drastic reduction in the power of the federal government by limiting the number of days it could enact an embargo, limiting the presidency to one term, and calling for a two-thirds vote before Congress could declare war rather than just a simple majority. These and other demands were sent off to Washington.[20]

Meanwhile, more and more troops were going unpaid. Despite the constant promises of compensation and back pay, the real answer was becoming clear. The United States was in dire straits and only peace would allow the government's coffers to refill, troops to be paid, and supplies and munitions to be restocked. The offer by the tsarist government in Russia to mediate a peace conference earlier in the war was eagerly accepted by the Americans but rejected by the British who, at the time, thought they might come out with substantial gains in territory if they pressed the Americans. However, as the war dragged on, it became clear that neither side could easily deliver a knockout blow to the other and, with no end in sight, both sides finally agreed to meet in Gothenburg, Sweden, to discuss peace. The Americans put together a sterling team of negotiators that would include, among others, future president and current minister to Russia John Quincy Adams, Secretary of the Treasury Albert Gallatin, and Speaker of the House Henry Clay.[21]

Despite the quagmire the war was becoming, Clay had remained popular in Congress. While his cousin Green Clay was marching to save Fort Meigs, Henry Clay had remained in Congress and continued to be an ardent supporter of the war. Throughout 1813 Clay had worked to get benefits for those who were killed in battle. He had succeeded in getting a pension pushed through Congress for the widow of Colonel John Allen, who had died at Frenchtown, and was working to get relief for others.[22] But the invitation to be part of the peace delegation was too good to pass up and Clay began making plans to travel for Europe. The loss of Clay as speaker must have been a bitter blow to his political allies, but there was no denying that his oratorical skills would come in handy when facing off against the tough British negotiators. He would also serve as a representative of the West and would serve as a counterbalance to fellow committee members like Adams of Massachusetts and Gallatin of Pennsylvania. When he resigned his seat, the House voted a show of support to the former speaker, which passed by a vote of 144 to 9.[23]

Clay's ship successfully made its way across the choppy North Atlantic to Gothenburg, where he remained for some time waiting for the other attendees to arrive. Eventually the location of the negotiations was moved to Ghent in modern-day Belgium and the travel-weary Americans convened there instead. Nearer to the heart of Europe, Ghent was a picturesque city for the negotiations. Divided by a number of canals, the city boasted a population of just over fifty-five thousand with large streets and open market places. It also boasted a statue of favorite son and one of Europe's greatest emperors, Charles V. It was Charles who had checked the Ottoman threat to his central European empire during the sixteenth century and a likeness in memorial of him must have served as a subtle reminder to the American delegation if they happened to pass by. This was a continent that gloried in strong monarchs. Those who crushed their enemies were celebrated more than those who negotiated with them.[24]

But while the United States readied herself for another year of war, the American delegation in Europe was spending more of its time fighting one another rather than fighting the British. Adams and Clay represented polar opposites on the political scale, which would be one of the central obstacles for fruitful negotiations. But the first challenge was making sure negotiations would take place at all. James Bayard (another member of the peace delegation) and Gallatin had arrived in Europe before the others and made their way to London by April 9. To their horror they found that, ten days before, Britain and her allies had marched into Paris. The day after their arrival word of Napoleon's official abdication reached London. This meant Britain could now turn her full attention to the war in America. Perhaps more disturbing, Bayard and Gallatin discovered, to their horror, that the average British subject, swept up in the patriotic euphoria of victory in Europe, was in favor of continuing the war in America.[25]

If there was any lingering doubt that the tables had turned the truth soon became obvious when the Americans inquired about the details for the commission. They found that the British had not yet appointed commissioners to represent them at all, nor would they until the entire American delegation arrived. Once this was done, discussions about where to hold the negotiations could begin. The two dispirited diplomats returned to their rented rooms to await their colleagues and any further developments.[26] They knew the delays signaled a change in British policy. Napoleon's defeat had erased some of the leverage the Americans felt after the capture of Procter's army on the Thames. If the Royal Navy was able to cross the Atlantic the American Seaboard would be at its mercy. But the crossing would take time. And time was exactly what the British were buying.

Back on the other side of the Atlantic the American public could at least take hope in the thought that the two sides were preparing to negotiate. But not everyone was confident the British wanted the war to end. One person who was particularly skeptical of Britain's intentions was Governor Shelby himself. When the legislature reconvened in Frankfort in January 1814, Shelby delivered his report on the state of affairs since the legislature had met last. "The time of your annual meeting having arrived," it began, "I have great pleasure in stating to you that no public occurrence of any unfavorable kind, has taken place in this state since the last session of the general assembly." The crops from the previous season had done well and the citizens of the commonwealth had "great reason to express the warmest sentiments of gratitude to the benign Author of all good and to congratulate each other on the plentiful appearance which our country exhibits." However, the war was another matter.[27]

Tempering expectations on the negotiations in Ghent, Shelby reminded the legislature that there had been ample negotiations before the war and they had all ended in failure. That Americans wanted peace was proven by their acceptance of Russia's offer to mediate months before, but the British had refused. Shelby acknowledged that the Napoleonic Wars in Europe had "terminated highly favorable to the British nation." This meant they could turn their full might on America. All of this seemed to suggest that Britain did not want a quick end to the war. On the contrary, "they dispatched the most powerful armaments ever sent out by Great Britain against us, for the avowed purpose as announced in the public prints, of teaching us *unconditional submission.*" Great Britain waited until their fleet was within striking distance of the United States to allow negotiations to begin and now wanted three things. The first was to be able to regulate American policy and interactions with Indian peoples inside the borders of the United States. The second was to demand the ceding of portions of American territory, and the third would require the United States to surrender control of the Great Lakes. Once these concessions were obtained the British promised the negotiations could start in earnest! "Thanks to an overruling Providence—thanks to our brave soldiers and sailors, we have men in arms who have proved themselves equal to the occasion." Shelby stated. "The proud legions of the enemy, flushed with their conquests in Europe, have gained no laurels in America—unless they choose to dignify with that name, the burning of houses; the plundering of negroes; and the viola-

tions of the sanctuaries of the church & of the *grave yards!*" It was time
for the federal government to act. If that meant raising taxes and insti-
tuting conscription so be it.[28]

Despite the hawkish words of the governor there was actually very
little for Kentuckians to do at the moment. With no immediate military
threats in the West, those who were not enrolled in federal units were
forced into the role of spectators in large part as things began to heat up
in the East. The recent end of war with Napoleon's France meant Great
Britain could now turn her navy on the extremely vulnerable American
coastline. The British government had selected a reliable veteran for the
job. Vice-Admiral Alexander Cochrane (sometimes spelled Cochran)
was the younger son of a British earl. Cochrane had joined the Royal
Navy as a boy and seen action in the American Revolution. He rose
through the ranks and had been engaged in the Napoleonic Wars from
the very beginning. Now he was being sent to Bermuda, which he would
use as a base to inflict damage on the United States.[29]

In a letter to Secretary of State Monroe, Admiral Cochrane wrote
that he had been called upon by the governor general of Canada to assist
in striking back against the United States for their actions in Upper
Canada. And by striking back Cochrane meant burning and destroying
towns along the coast. "I had hoped," lamented Cochrane, with mock
regret, "that this contest would have terminated without my being
obliged to resort to severities, which are contrary to the usage of civilized
warfare," but the actions of the Americans warranted it. If the American
government would pay for the wanton damage they had caused on
Canadian soil then this retribution could be avoided. Otherwise, the
promised destruction was inevitable.[30]

Within weeks of writing his letter, Cochrane proved to be a man of
his word by striking a blow that would shake the young republic to its
core. Having dispatched Rear Admiral Cockburn to wreak havoc elsewhere, Cochrane unloaded the rest of his British troops on the Maryland
shore on August 19 under the command of General Robert Ross. The
army quickly marched toward Washington. General William Winder,
who was tasked with defending Washington and the surrounding area,
had only 1,700 men to face 4,500 well-disciplined British regulars. The
tiny navy of gunboats that were supposed to protect the area were now
of no use and were blown up to keep them out of enemy hands. Americans scrambled to burn bridges and provide any possible impediment
to the British advance, but it had little effect.[31]

When the two sides finally met it was at Bladensburg, Maryland, on August 24. Three lines of American troops formed in good order and, for the first time since landing, the British army had an obstacle in its path that it had to deal with. Winder's urgent calls for help had swelled his army to more than six thousand men at this point, though they were mostly poorly trained militia.[32] The now-outnumbered British attacked while their arsenal of Congreve rockets screamed overhead. Despite moments of promise, the American lines broke remarkably quickly and the British army advanced like a well-oiled machine, scattering their American counterparts in all directions as they went. Now nothing stood in the way of the capitol, and as the Americans were blowing up the Washington Naval Yard to keep it out of British hands, the British were marching into the White House itself. Once inside the executive mansion they found Madison's dinner, which had been laid out ready to eat. The president had obviously left in a hurry. The mansion and the majority of the federal buildings in the city were burned.[33]

After winning this symbolic victory, General Ross eventually evacuated Washington and moved north toward Baltimore, Maryland, in search of a more strategic target. In one of the better-known episodes from the war, the American force at Baltimore fought a small skirmish with Ross's army, in which the general himself was killed, before falling back to Fort McHenry. Once inside the fort, the men readied themselves for the real assault, which would come from the air in the form of a naval bombardment by the British fleet. A manmade reef of sunken ships prevented Cockburn from getting too close but, on September 13, he was still able to lob thousands of shells at the fort. The bombardment lasted through the day and night, filling the citizens nearby with trepidation. The descending darkness turned the glow of evening into unperceivable blackness, which was only alleviated by the midair explosions of the British ordinance as it rained down on the fort.[34]

Is was these momentary illuminations that offered the only clues as to the progress of the battle and it was these flashes that captured the attention of a young American lawyer named Francis Scott Key, who sat as a temporary prisoner on the deck of a British ship. His gazing into the abyss to catch a glimpse of the large American flag that flew over the fort led him to write a poem known as the "Defense of Fort McHenry." The poem had four verses, but most Americans only know the first:

The burned-out shell of the White House painted by George Munger, c. 1814–15. The odd s-shaped feature at the top might be a remnant of a lightning protection system. (*White House Historical Association*)

> O say can you see by the dawn's early light,
> What so proudly we hailed at the twilight's last gleaming,
> Whose broad stripes and bright stars through the perilous fight,
> O'er the ramparts we watched, were so gallantly streaming?
> And the rockets' red glare, the bombs bursting in air,
> Gave proof through the night that our flag was still there;
> O say does that star-spangled banner yet wave,
> O'er the land of the free and the home of the brave?

This poem was later set to music and, of course, became better known as the "Star-Spangled Banner."[35]

But it would take several years for the familiar words to reach national fame. It was the events of Bladensburg, Washington, and Baltimore that were foremost on the minds of Americans at the time. The details of each soon made their way across the mountains to the West. "The Fate of War Has befallen the City of Washington," bemoaned the *Kentucky Gazette* as it recounted the burning of the capitol, executive mansion, and other public buildings.[36] But the dark events of the British invasion soon gave way to relief as later editions brought news of Fort McHenry, reading "Huzzah for Baltimore" and providing copies of dispatches from commanders in the field who asserted victory.[37]

Had Americans known what was transpiring in Europe they may have heaved an even greater sigh of relief. In Ghent, negotiations between the two delegations had finally commenced on August 8. But Britain's opening proposal had astounded the Americans. To begin with they would not, under any circumstances, discuss the issue of impressment. This must have been surprising to the Americans since the subject had long since ceased to be a factor in the war and it would have been easy enough for the British to state in writing that they would never resume the policy. Second, the settling of the Canadian-American border must result in territorial gains for Britain, and third, the American border with the Indians must return to where it was when the Treaty of Greenville was signed following the Battle of Fallen Timbers. This meant, of course, that complete control of the Great Lakes would have to be given up.[38]

Such proposals were rejected out of hand by the American commissioners. Stretching the truth somewhat, the American delegation declared that the only reason for the creation of a permanent Indian territory was to allow it to serve as a buffer state between Canada and the United States, which was obviously unnecessary since the United States had never declared the conquering of Canada to be her intention. If the war could be ended without gaining any territory then so be it. The Americans cited their past efforts to jump-start peace negotiations as early as October 1812 as proof of their desire for peace. After all, to launch an unwarranted, impromptu attack to conquer Canada would leave the East Coast of the United States open to the might of the British navy and their commerce on the high seas would be the sacrifice for such an action and it alone was worth more than Canada. "The best security for the possessions of both countries will, however, be found in an equal and solid peace," they argued.[39]

As to surrendering the Great Lakes to Britain, the Americans pointed out that, with the exception of two forts, all American territory in the region was in American hands, while the Battle of the Thames had placed a significant portion of Upper Canada under the control of the United States. This hardly seemed to place the British in a position to ask for the lake country. In response to a sovereign Indian state, it was interesting that the British should now declare the Indians to be owners of the land they lived on.[40] Negotiations seemed to be grinding to a halt before they could even get off the ground. The commissioners on both sides returned to the drawing board. Time, or news from the Americas, would have to break the stalemate.

It would have been logical to focus on the Atlantic Seaboard to provide such an action. However, the western border between the United
States and Ontario, a region which had spent much of 1814 more quietly
than it had the previous year, was about to become the scene of yet another campaign. On July 30 another request for troops arrived in Kentucky from the Michigan Territory. General Duncan McArthur had
received permissions from the federal government to request one thousand militia to maintain the defenses around Detroit.[41] Shelby ordered
the men to be called up as requested but could not help but ask why the
Ohio militia (which was closer to Detroit to begin with) could not have
been called up instead.[42] The response in Kentucky was as might be expected. Few men were willing to sign up and those that did wanted to
be sure they would be exempted from future drafts.[43] In a letter to Shelby,
James Allen of Nelson County summed up what most Kentuckians were
thinking when he expressed his belief that Kentucky's quota had already
been filled. Regardless of whether that was the case or not, it would be
difficult to get volunteers if there was no guarantee that they would receive full credit for service and whether they would be permitted to go as
mounted men or if they would be required to march as infantry.[44]

Despite the expected grumbling of some, seven companies were eventually raised, and by September 20 they had reached Urbana on their
march north, where almost 250 Ohio militia also joined their ranks. The
ultimate goal of McArthur's raid was to eliminate a Potawatomi threat
around Lake Michigan. Seventy-five loyal Shawnee, Wyandot, and
Delaware warriors also joined the Americans as they continued north.
When they reached their destination on October 9, there was no enemy
to be found. Any resistance that had existed in the area had evaporated.
McArthur now had the problem of deciding what to do with his army.
He had more than seven hundred well-armed, well-equipped men ready
to march. Deciding the opportunity was too good to pass up, McArthur
told his men they would be crossing into Canada. Pressures in the East
were mounting and, with trouble brewing on the Eastern Seaboard,
something had to be done to relieve them. If he and his men were to
march into Canada they could draw some of these forces west, offering
their American counterparts in New York a chance to catch their
breath.[45]

Marching his men deeper into Michigan Territory, McArthur suddenly veered across the Saint Clair River and plunged into Canada on
October 26. The isolated Canadian villages were caught off guard and,

despite some halfhearted attempts to entrench, were quickly overrun. At Malcolm's Mills, more than 170 miles into Canada, McArthur's men met their first sizeable enemy army comprising native warriors, Canadian militia, and British regulars. Along the way McArthur's men destroyed a number of mills in the area as they went. At Dover, McArthur finally brought his incursion to a halt. He had accomplished his purpose and each day he remained across the border grew more dangerous than the one before. The retreat took a week, but on November 17, the men reached Fort Detroit where they were discharged.[46] Whether McArthur's raid actually affected the battle plans of British commanders to the east is unlikely. However, his policy of burning mills would earn him a blacker reputation among Canadian and British historians than other American generals. These actions did serve a military purpose in that they destroyed stores of provisions that could have been used to sustain troops on the peninsula, but they also destroyed a major source of sustenance for the surrounding civilian population.[47]

But despite small victories such as McArthur's raid, little had changed. After hanging on for over two years the United States' fortunes looked gloomier than ever. The British had lost portions of Canada to the Americans, but with Napoleon out of the way for good they could finally bring the might of the Royal Navy to bear on the almost defenseless American coastline with devastating effectiveness, which was more than evident in the smoldering ashes that once comprised Washington. With no end in sight, Kentucky's role was limited to protecting what they had achieved in Canada, but even this would drain the spirits of her militia.

A contingent of the 16th Kentucky Militia was one of the many units that made the trek north to protect the Northwest and Canada from British efforts to recapture what they had lost. The unit crossed the Ohio River on the eighteenth of September and marched north as the Kentucky countryside, which contained their families and homes, slowly disappeared over their shoulders.[48] Like so many expeditions that went before it, the men were in high spirits. Sergeant Ennis Duncan of Maysville, one of the latest to make the trip north, was no exception. He used his spare time to draw up additional blank forms for the unit's future use and did his best to remain busy and useful. But even before they reached Canada his spirits had begun to sink. The monotonous march was plagued by bad weather, and with only three or four tents in the whole army the men were soon saturated. The roads went from muddy to a quagmire until the men were marching in ankle-deep mud. Then there was the fact that the musicians kept playing the song "The Girl I left Behind Me," which did not help attitudes much either.[49]

In a letter to his wife Hester on the twenty-fifth, Duncan lamented (with some exaggeration) that the roads were actually thigh-deep in mud and the ankle-deep mud that he had lamented in previous letters was now considered to be evidence of a good road. The march had been so difficult he had lost sixteen pounds on the trip and could now tighten his belt an extra four notches. By mid-October the men had reached Malden and were settling in and Duncan claimed his duties kept him so busy, "I hardly expect to close my eyes this night. . . . Nearly the whole regiment is busy writing letters home."[50]

By the time autumn gave way to winter he was even more distraught. The nearest post office was in Detroit and the slow pace of the mail meant long absences between letters aided the onset of depression. Letter writing remained the best pastime for soldiers seeking refuge from the Canadian winter. While he continued to write, his letters now reflected a drastically different tone. "My Very Dear & Beloved Wife," he began. "I think it appears that you have almost forgotten that you have a Husband in the Army in U Canada."[51] Life at home in Maysville was just as difficult. Hester confided that she often dreamed he was home in such detail that she would wake and expect to find him beside her only to realize his was still in Canada.[52]

Drawing on his faith, Duncan wrote to his wife that "I am much exposed to trials & temptations but I find a friend that sticketh closer than a Brother," he reminded her, quoting Proverbs 18. Military life had not been the exciting adventure nineteenth-century writers often portrayed it as. For Duncan, it had been lonely and difficult. He added "I expect to return to Ky without the fun of seeing or changing shot with a red coat."[53] Although the fact that he would soon be returning home seemed to soften this blow a bit.[54]

Chapter Nine

NEW ORLEANS

Before McArthur requested his detachment of one thousand men for the raid into Canada, the Kentucky militia was strapped for supplies and arms. After the raid, supplies, even at the federal arsenal at Newport, were reaching critical levels. The drain on the state's finances by the almost three-year-old conflict was beginning to tell on the economy as well, and in 1814 the Bank of Kentucky made the decision to stop issuing coins as currency and were forcing those making a withdrawal to take paper notes instead. The bank itself was still making a profit on paper but, thanks to the war, many southern states had stopped issuing coinage, forcing Kentucky to follow suit or risk having a run on the bank by wary investors who sought the security of cold-hard cash.[1]

National unity was also reaching a crisis by the end of 1814. Many of the New England states had suffered from the lack of commerce and the debate had shifted from limiting the power of the federal government to talk of outright secession. Almost fifty years before the American Civil War, several states were debating whether to shatter the fragile union. The United States needed to end the war soon or risk seeing the nation torn apart. Despite some of the flagging zeal for the war, the idea of secession was still abhorrent to many, especially in Kentucky. In a resolution that was passed on to Governor Shelby, the legislature asked the governor to notify the state's representatives in the House and Senate as well as the leaders of Congress of their opinion that they "consider the

Constitution of the United States, as the most perfect and stupendous work of human wisdom and virtue" and that they would give "the last cent of our treasure, and drop of our blood" to defend it against "Internal enemies, instigated by the demon of discord."[2]

While watching the nation teeter on the brink of dissolution, Kentuckians soon learned their services had been requested yet again as autumn brought yet another call for troops. But this time they would not be marching north. General Andrew Jackson had been immersed in the Indian wars that had plagued the southern states and territories. Jackson had proven an able leader against this kind of foe, but now the British were preparing to strike the heretofore-unmolested southern coast. The target of choice along the sparsely populated Gulf shores was obvious: New Orleans. The city sat at the mouth of the Mississippi River like a sentinel. If the British could successfully take the city, their representatives in Ghent would be in a much stronger position to negotiate a settlement to the war. After all, controlling the river meant having the ability to strangle American trade on the Mississippi and limit American expansion. The significance of this possibility was far from lost on Kentucky's many farmers and tradesmen. In a state whose population was spread out across a countryside with few roads, rivers were a lifeline. Excess crops, raw materials, and other goods could float to the larger markets farther down the river, which fueled the inland economy. Major rivers like the Kentucky, the Sandy, the Green, the Salt, the Tennessee, the Cumberland, and others eventually found their way to the Ohio, which, in turn, flowed to the Mississippi. Losing the right to trade at New Orleans would be a death knell to Kentucky's economy. The only other options for trade would be polling rafts up the Ohio River into western Pennsylvania or traveling overland through the Cumberland Gap. Neither were efficient, safe, or cost effective.

As he had done several times before, Shelby took his pen in hand to acknowledge to the secretary of war that he had ordered men to rendezvous on the tenth of November to reinforce the city of New Orleans. "I still have very great fears respecting arms & ammunition," he added. The quartermaster had reported that only 254 stands of arms were available at Newport. Of course, he had asked the men that had arms to bring them along, but the force being compiled was very different than some of its predecessors. The regiments that would be traveling to New Orleans were mostly draftees or substitutes for those who had been drafted. They were poor and most likely would not be able to equip themselves.[3]

In reality, there were still four or five hundred arms at Newport, but they were in need of repair before they could be of any use. Even if the parts had been available, restoring so many guns to working order would take time—something the Americans and the city of New Orleans, in particular, did not have. Shelby ordered them to be fixed immediately but with the knowledge that this would not satisfy the current need. Perhaps the more urgent issue was how to get the men to New Orleans in time to be useful at all. The more than three-hundred-mile march to Detroit had taken weeks. To march more than seven hundred miles to New Orleans would take even longer. The only obvious answer was the Mississippi River itself, but this would mean acquiring enough boats to move hundreds of men simultaneously. Richard Taylor,[4] who would serve as quartermaster for the militia going to New Orleans, had been scouring the towns along the Ohio in search of private boats that could be purchased. Not every boat owner was excited at the idea of selling their only means of transportation across the river. Those who would sell would only do so if they had cash in hand.[5]

Despite his experience in stretching supplies to make ends meet, Taylor found it almost impossible to raise the amount he needed in such a short time. Vessels large enough to transport troops were also large enough to transport goods to market, and few businessmen along the Ohio River were willing to part with something so valuable without being fairly compensated for it. The federal government's reputation for being slow to pay troops and the well-known state of the commonwealth's coffers meant Taylor would have little luck unless he could pay up front. With no other options open to him, Taylor turned to the Bank of Kentucky, but even they refused to issue the loan. These were shaky times financially and their policies dictated that some form of security be mortgaged before they would loan the money, no matter how dire the situation was. Taylor was stuck. Thousands of men were marching to the Ohio River and he had no way of getting most of them to Jackson. Using the only option left to him, Taylor put his own sizeable estate up as collateral and obtained a six-thousand-dollar loan from the bank. If the government dragged its feet in reimbursing him, he would lose everything.[6]

On paper the army looked much more formidable than it actually was. Three regiments of around one thousand men each would be sent to Jackson, though by the time desertions, removals, and the inevitable deaths brought on by camp life were factored in, Jackson should receive, it was estimated, around 2,500 men from the commonwealth.[7] Time was continuing to tick away as efforts were made to gather men and supplies. To make the process even quicker, several points of rendezvous were established on the Ohio River in order to allow men to march to whichever was closest to them. This was easier on the soldiers as well since many would not have to spend the majority of their resources in just reaching the starting point of the expedition.[8]

The impossible seemed to be happening as Kentuckians mobilized yet again to fill boats that had seemed impossible to acquire. Still, the rush led to some confusion, and despite the governor's effort, vital details were often lost along the way. When Jefferson County's portion of troops departed they were still unsure whether they were supposed to bring their own guns or not. The question remained unanswered and many marched to war in hopes that the government would figure it out before they arrived. Some had heard that General Jackson had ordered the Tennesseans coming to his aid to bring their own weapons since he had none to give. On the other hand, it was the army's job to supply arms. The fact that weapons were so limited was no secret, but was such a rumor true? Were there really more men than guns? If so, what was the point of sending men who could not arm themselves and who could not be armed by Jackson once they arrived? The question would hang palpably in the air as the expedition moved forward. Despite these shortcomings, the fact that the war-weary state was able to move a significant number of men at all is surprising. The first rumbling of the Thames campaign in the previous year had been uttered that spring but had taken until the late summer to materialize. This campaign, which also involved a large force of militia, was being outfitted in a matter of weeks.[9] As Shelby had indicated, the tireless efforts of dedicated militia officers throughout the state had borne some fruit. There was plenty of powder, several boats, and the 254 stands of arms that Shelby had mentioned in his letter to the secretary of war as well as ammunition. The men could also count on having axes, buckets, and other equipment necessary for erecting a military camp. They were short on saws, which would be helpful in setting up camp in the dense Louisiana terrain, and a shortage of kettles for preparing supper around the campfire provided an additional annoyance, but these problems were not insurmountable.[10] But it was becoming clear that many of the men who were preparing to march to New Orleans had left their homes before the order to arm themselves had arrived, if it arrived at all. What's more, many had reached the rendezvous points and could not be ordered home again. Shelby handed out the few arms that had been rounded up and then sent word to the governor of the Indiana Territory to request any spare guns kept at Vincennes.[11]

By late November, every possible exertion had been made and there was nothing left to do but wait and hope that the men would reach Jackson in New Orleans before the British attacked. Every spare boat that could be bought off the wharfs of the Ohio River around Cincinnati had been purchased, and they were now floating west on their way to the mighty Mississippi that would take them south. The arsenal at Newport that had once held thousands of stands of muskets stood empty with the exception of seventy-five guns that were beyond repair. Kentucky had emptied her coffers, her storehouses, and her counties of men, supplies, boats, and arms. There were no more reserves to tap. Word of a shipment of up to two thousand guns going down the Ohio to New Orleans did offer some encouragement. Perhaps the secretary of war had heeded the governor's letters after all and these rifles were meant for the militia that had left just before them.[12]

While little additional action could be taken in Kentucky, New Orleans was becoming a hive of activity. Andrew Jackson had arrived on the second of December and had instantly gone to work preparing the city's defenses.[13] On the sixteenth, the no-nonsense Jackson declared martial law. From that point forward, every person entering the city would report to his adjutant general or risk arrest and interrogation. Once in the city, no one—whether they were solider or civilian—was allowed to leave without written authorization. At nine in the evening, all street lamps were snuffed out and anyone found out after that time without written permission would be arrested and treated as a spy.[14]

Jackson was turning the whole city into one giant encampment. These actions kept order in the city while delivering the message that Jackson was in control, lest any citizens should consider chaffing under his leadership. But for all of his decisiveness and endless preparations Jackson was worried. Christmas had come and gone and still the muddy Mississippi River offered little more to aid him than the seasonal glut of branches, miscellaneous debris, and the odd traveler. Where were the troops he had requested? The British had landed and were obviously preparing their assault. Jackson estimated their strength to be around seven thousand men. At present, he had less than three thousand. In the middle of the digging, building, and drilling inside the city Jackson took a moment to write to the secretary of war, James Monroe, in Washington. An attack could come at any time, but unless the troops from Kentucky arrived his hands were tied.[15]

New Year's came and went, just as Christmas had, without a single word on the reinforcements, which supposedly were coming to his aid. Finally, on January 4, the long-awaited flotilla of Kentucky troops came into view. The hurried and unprepared state in which they left their homes had succeeded in getting them to Louisiana before the British could attack, but it had also left the men in rather rough condition. So rough in fact that the Louisiana legislature voted six thousand dollars to the militia to purchase necessities, and private citizens raised around ten thousand more to purchase necessary supplies.[16] The bedraggled force that was only partially armed was not exactly what Jackson had imagined when he requested reinforcements, but they were better than nothing and even an unarmed man could wield a shovel to help entrench and insulate the city against attack. Jackson could now breathe a little easier.

The British, who had been edging their way forward, had finally made their way to the threshold of New Orleans in the first week of the New Year. The city was officially under siege. January 6 dawned but remained eerily quiet. Deserters reported that the British troops had been busy building scaling ladders for the impending invasion that would be used to more easily cross the fortifications Jackson's men had erected. This was a sure sign the attack would soon commence, but when exactly remained a mystery. Night fell once again and Jackson's men went to sleep knowing that the peace could be shattered at any moment. At six o'clock in the afternoon on the seventh word ran through the lines that the British had attacked the far left, but it was soon discovered that the attack was a false alarm. The camp settled down again to await the real attack.

At four o'clock the next morning, Jackson's army was already stirring. Troops threaded their way between campfires, tents, and supplies as they prepared for the day ahead. Some, no doubt, acted under orders while others, with nothing better to do, fed their horses to be ready for the battle when it finally commenced. Heavy clouds loomed low in the sky and any light that might have been offered by the moon and stars had been stifled. Anxious men peered over the dirt and wood ramparts in the direction of the British camp, but their efforts were rewarded with nothing but darkness. Then, from the gloom, two sparks of light streaked across the sky: rockets. Before their light faded back into the shadows a British cannon roared to life. Men braced themselves for an attack and those on the front line rested their muskets and rifles on the cool earthen wall in front of them. Then they waited. Seconds ticked by in silence without any indication of what would follow.[17]

It was obvious that the rockets had been a signal to the British lines from their commanders. The Congreve rockets themselves did not particularly impress the Americans, as they were wildly inaccurate and caused very little damage. Jackson himself had called them "harmless weapons." At one point, the British would launch around a thousand of them into the American lines, killing only five men and wounding five more. The Kentuckians referred to them as "Kentucky Boats" because they had a long handle that remained attached as the rocket launched into the air. Its appearance from the sky resembled a boat being poled upriver.[18] But even if the rockets had been known for their accuracy or effectiveness, firing only two was pointless unless they were used for signaling the British lines that must lay stretched out and waiting just out of sight of the American defenders.

Almost a full minute passed in what must have seemed more like an eternity. Then, without fanfare, something began to take shape in the gloom. As Jackson's men began to recognize the approaching dusky red coats individual soldiers up and down the line began to take aim at their targets as they waited for the order to fire. Three advancing columns could be seen closing in on the American lines in a rhythmic almost mechanical manner. [19]

Adair's Kentuckians remained ready, although even now not all of them were armed. In fact, only 550 or so Kentuckians arrived at New Orleans with their own weapons. As their commander, Adair had scoured the city for weapons to supply those who were left. The answer was soon clear. A number of men had been exempted for one reason or another from militia service. Their arms would lay unused. Adair quickly borrowed these with promises to return them when the battle was over. Arming his men, he must have sighed in relief. He now had one thousand militia armed and ready to serve where they could. At first, these men were placed in reserve to aid whichever part of the line needed them the most.[20] As the center of the British attack became clear, Adair and his men were ordered into the line. "We may in a great degree attribute the unparalleled destruction that took place in the column on that day."[21]

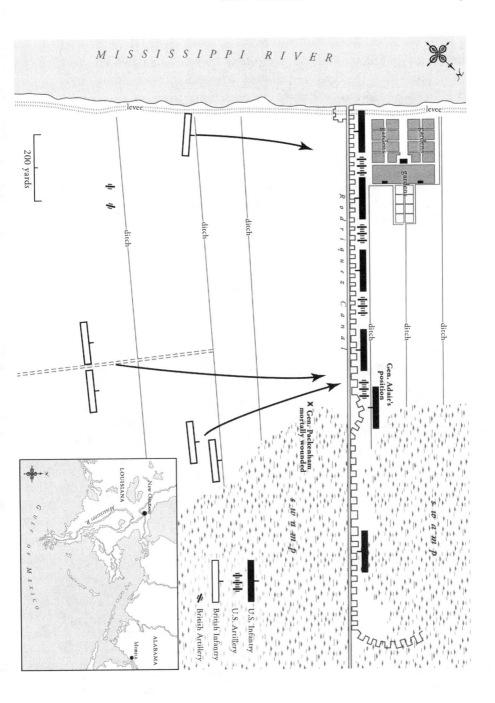

The advancing British columns made their way toward the American lines with grim determination. Despite the fire raining down on them by Jackson's men the British continued their attack, smashing first into the American right flank. But the Americans had made good use of the preceding weeks in preparing their defenses. The skirmish finally broke off with the British attack shattered and forced into retreat. The attack that had ground to a stop found itself at the mercy of Jackson's sharp-shooting backwoodsmen and British casualties began mounting rapidly. The column led by General Packenham himself, with the center column nearby, marched toward the American left flank. They were permitted to advance to the very edge of the breastwork before the Americans opened fire. Small arms and cannon both roared into action, and a cloud of smoke and the bitter acrid smell of gunfire rolled over the battlefield, forcing the British to fall back. The first wave had been subdued but Packenham's battle-hardened men were far from defeated. Watching from behind their earthen defenses, Jackson's men could see the British regrouping rapidly beyond the range of the American guns. Before long the columns of red were reformed and advancing again in the same de-termined manner. The Americans knew the British would not give up easily and were expecting several waves. The militia along the front line calmly took aim again. Their cautious and careful aim paid off as Jack-son's men began to thin the British lines with deadly accuracy. Again the British slowed and then broke as the men were forced to fall back beyond the range of the Americans' small arms. More orders were issued and again the lines reformed and again they advanced. Their battle-hardened reputation was well deserved. The field of battle was now filled not only with the sounds of muskets, rifles, rockets, and cannons but also with the cries of the wounded. The thick smoke would have made it impossible to tell what was happening on other parts of the battlefield.[22] But there was enough in front of the men to keep their at-tention. On the second and third attempts to charge the Americans lines a number of the British troops had actually made it to the ditch in front of the American earthworks, compelling a number of the Tennessee and Kentucky troops to leap on top of the narrow makeshift walls and fight the enemy there face to face.[23]

It was later asserted by some that the British had directed their attack against parts of the line held by militia based on their ragtag appearance. In the minds of the well-ordered and identically uniformed British army, discipline manifested itself in the dress and bearing of the officers. The

A mid-nineteenth century engraving of the Battle of New Orleans showing the desperate charge of British troops against the American breastwork. (*Library of Congress*)

mix of townsmen and various state militias, with their homespun uniforms or hunting shirts, seemed to suggest this was the weakest part of the lines.[24] Whether this is true or pure conjecture is irrelevant. What mattered was the British had rushed the American lines with everything they had and had been repulsed on three separate occasions.

After the last attack broke and trickled away from the American lines there was a lull in the fighting. Not unlike the men at Fort Stephenson, the Americans seized on this break to try and help the wounded British troops who lay near their position, but the sign of any Americans stirring beyond the safety of their defenses instantly drew the fire of the remaining British who had fallen back beyond range of the American guns. Hours passed and the weakened rays of the winter Louisiana sun rose higher in the sky. It soon became clear that, if the British intended to attack again, it would not be the same day. The battlefield testified to the high number of casualties Packenham's force had received. One prisoner of war who had seen action in the Napoleonic Wars in Spain, France, as well as in the capture of Washington stated he had "never witnessed such destructive a fire" as he had at New Orleans.[25] This certainly gave Jackson's men reason to hope. His men had stood their ground all along the lines. All, that is, except the portion that lay on the opposite riverbank.

Here Jackson had placed a small force that was meant to prevent the British sweeping past his position on the opposite bank of the Mississippi and exposing his flank to hostile fire. There had not been much firepower to spare but Jackson still expected any attempts at a British landing on that side of the river to be repulsed. As many as 500 Kentuckians had been sent to reinforce the 450 Louisiana militia. As with the other side of the river, only a portion of Lt. Col. John Davis' men were armed and when the British attacked both the Louisiana and Kentucky militia collapsed, allowing the position to be overrun.[26]

But this small British victory was too little too late, and as the last of the British columns from the main force retreated beyond the tree line it was clear that the Americans had won a victory. But it was only after a collective sigh of relief and a survey of the battlefield that they revealed just how much of a victory it was. Jackson's army had lost thirteen killed and thirty-two wounded or captured. The British had 191 killed, more than 1,200 wounded, and 484 captured or missing. All told, the Americans had less than one hundred casualties while the British had endured over two thousand.[27]

New Orleans was perfectly situated to delay the delivery of news. A messenger returning to Kentucky had two options. He could venture through the dangerous, trackless territory of Louisiana and Mississippi, or he could pole his way up the Mississippi River against the current until he reached the Ohio River, where he would be faced with a similar choice to reach Frankfort. Due to this challenge, it was the twenty-fifth of January before a letter from Louisiana governor William Claiborne was placed into Shelby's hands. Reading the letter, Shelby issued a note to the legislature. "Gentlemen of the Senate And of the House of Representatives, By letters received a few days since from Governor Claiborne, I am officialy advised that the enemy have invaded the state of Louisiana, and are within a few miles of New-Orleans." It was obvious that the British had planned to take Louisiana and strangle trade on the Mississippi. The note went on to state that the governor had faith in Jackson and was confident that New Orleans would remain in American hands.[28]

Despite these assertions of confidence, it would be wise if Kentucky prepared a future force that might be needed. The way in which the haphazard detachment that had left for New Orleans had left a bad taste in his mouth. There should be a force of ten thousand Kentucky militia organized that would serve for six months after they rendezvoused. This would allow plenty of boats for transportation and equipment like kettles (the very kinds of items that had been in such short supply for the scramble to New Orleans) to be prepared ahead of time. The legislature concurred, and the next day the House of Representatives passed a bill authorizing Shelby to obtain everything he had asked for. The bill was given some teeth when a clause was inserted that allowed him to spend the staggering sum of one hundred thousand dollars and to negotiate with the Bank of Kentucky for additional loans as needed. [29]

The strategy of striking a knockout blow early with a sizeable force, which Shelby had advocated for two years, still had not been adopted entirely by the federal government. However, if they would not take the actions needed, Kentucky would. But all of this had come too late for New Orleans. The men were already in the theatre of war. There was nothing else to do for them but wait for word to arrive of their victory or their defeat.

When word of the battle did make its way through the virgin terrain of the Mississippi Valley to reach cities around the country, Americans were ecstatic. No place partook of the celebrations more readily than Kentucky. The victory seemed a vindication of what Shelby had maintained since the war began. Militia could be used as an effective defense against invasion if they were well supplied and concentrated in significant numbers. If there were any lingering doubts on that score they would have been dispelled by Louisiana governor Claiborne's glowing assessment of the militia's role in the battle. In a letter to Governor Shelby that was written on the ninth but which would not arrive until weeks later, Claiborne remarked, "the fire of the Kentucky and Tennessee forces on the left was particularly fatal to the enemy." As for the battle itself, "it is a matter of equal joy and wonder that in a conflict so long, so glorious to us, and so fatal to the enemy, our loss is astonishingly small." In the middle of penning this letter, word arrived from the front. One of the dead had been identified—it was General Packenham himself, commander of the British forces.[30]

Despite this reversal of fortunes, it looked like the British might try again somewhere else along the Gulf Coast, and the shelling of Fort St. Phillips sixty miles down the river seemed to confirm that theory. But soon even this bombardment fell quiet and the Royal Navy disappeared. Intelligence soon began flooding into Jackson's headquarters suggesting that the British might be pulling out entirely, but this seemed too optimistic to most. The battle had certainly been in favor of the Americans,

but the British maintained a significant enough force to be a major threat
if they could catch Jackson unawares. While waiting to see the enemy's
next move, John Adair wrote to the governor with his view not only of
the battle but of the Kentuckians who had been on the opposite side of
the river. The whole force had arrived on January 5, he confirmed, but
the lack of arms remained a problem.[31] The ammunition that had been
hastily gathered and that was brought from private homes around New
Orleans had only been enough to arm a portion of the militia. Adair
was ordered to station his men behind General Carroll's Tennesseans in
the center of the lines. From here, he had seen the battle unfold. The
bravery of the British lines "commanded our respect," Adair admitted.[32]

"The detachment under my command both officers and men have
done their duty faithfully, and honorably sustained the character of the
state to which they belong," Adair proudly stated. "The detachment on
the other side of the river under Lieut. Col. Davis were obliged to retreat
before a superior force—they have been calumniated by those who ought
to have fought with them but did not—some of them perhaps have be-
haved improperly; but I have no doubt Col. Davis did his duty as far as
was in his power. An investigation is about to take place, when I trust
the blame will fall where it ought."[33]

The thinly veiled reference to those who were supposed to be fighting
alongside the Kentuckians is obvious. Adair had been extremely unhappy
with the statements made about his men following the battle, and no
one had been more vocal in their criticism than General Jackson himself.
As to rumors that the British might attempt to take New Orleans a second time, his mind was at ease. "Unless they are mad men, they will not
again attempt our works."[34] General Jackson, however, was somewhat
less confident. In a letter to his superiors in Washington, he confessed
that he was unsure whether the British would cut their losses or try
again. One thing was clear; if the British decided to make a second attempt on New Orleans' well-prepared defenses they would need to have
reinforcements. With the losses they had sustained since landing, to try
another attempt without filling the gaps in the ranks would be unwise.[35]

When battle did resume it would take place several months later and
would be between Jackson and Adair instead of the British and the
Americans. Adair never forgave Jackson for his portrayal of the Kentucky troops on the opposite bank of the Mississippi who had not succeeded in holding the line. In an open letter published to Jackson, Adair
fumed, "SIR:—A Sense of duty to my country, and to the corps with

which I am immediately served, during the late perilous campaign, under your command, has induced me to lay before you the following statement of facts which cannot be controverted." Adair explained to Jackson that on the night of January 7, he was ordered to send four hundred men from camp to the city, where they would be armed and put under Louisiana Militia general David Morgan's command on the opposite banks of the Mississippi. Around seven in the evening the troops marched to town but received surprising news. Half of them could be provided with what Adair called "indifferent arms" while the other two hundred would not be armed at all.[36]

According to Adair, the last of the partially armed force set foot on the opposite bank at four in the morning on the day of the battle. Davis and his troops were ordered to march down and engage the enemy as soon as they found him and slow his advance. This, according to Adair, is exactly what they did. Edging forward through the darkness the detachment had bumped into the British less than a mile from the breastwork. The Louisiana troops with Davis under the command of a Major Arno retreated soon afterward, leaving him to face the enemy alone. Davis formed his men anyway and prepared to open fire.[37]

The 170 Kentucky militia that were left to fight were now placed on the line to the right of the 500 Louisiana militia in a ditch about 300 yards long.[38] The entrenchments offered some protection, but when the British did rush forward it became clear that the brunt of their assault was being concentrated on the beleaguered Kentuckians. Despite having already met the enemy and sustained a small skirmish and orderly retreat, Adair pointed out that the men were able to fire three to seven shots from their trench. The Kentuckians had again done what was required of them. At least "all those whose guns could fire," he added with some asperity.[39]

The fire offered by the Kentuckians slowed the red line advancing toward them but did not stop it. The British continued to close in and soon were able to breach the defenses. As Packenham's redcoats began pouring into the gap the line had collapsed and the men were forced to fall back. Davis' men who were further down the line and unaware of the breach continued to fire on anyone they could find but soon found themselves receiving fire from behind. Wheeling around to see what was going on it was abundantly clear that they were being encircled. As this point, they had two options: be enveloped and cut down or fall back.[40] Taking the only viable option the army fell back in good order and those who had guns fired as they retreated. Finally they made it back to the breastwork. In short, the men had done their duty despite being poorly equipped and only fell back when ordered to do so. What more could be asked of a force that was not even fully armed?[41]

And yet, Adair continued, "to the retreat of that small corps has been attributed the disgrace of that day." Adair scoffed bitterly, "More sir; it has been represented by letters from this place, published in Tennessee, and throughout the Union, as the shameful, cowardly, flight of a strong detachment of Kentuckians without firing a gun." According to Jackson's account, the collapse of that portion of the line held by the Kentucky militia had prompted the retreat in other areas and had caused others within view to fall back, causing a chain reaction that led the entire line to give way.[42] It was true that Adair was challenging the official version provided by the commander of the army in New Orleans, and this report had been based on the accounts of officers who were nearby, but such reports often contain inaccuracies and the confusion of battle can certainly make it difficult to get good information.[43]

In the open letter to Jackson, Adair argued the cause of the men under his command, suggesting to Jackson that "I thus bring to your recollection facts and circumstances, which although they took place under your own orders, may in the hurry and confusion of the moment have escaped your notice"[44] And if there was any doubt about the accuracy of his description of the events, Adair confidently stated that there were a number of officers who would testify to their exactness. In short, "no blame, no censure could possibly be attached to the Kentuckians in this affair."[45]

On the nineteenth of February, a military board of inquiry delivered its own verdict on the collapse of the left bank's defenses. "The court, after mature deliberation, is of opinion, that the conduct of the gentlemen in the action aforesaid, and retreat of the 8th of January, on the western bank of the river Mississippi, is not reprehensible." Major Arno was given full blame for causing the retreat. "The retreat of the Kentucky militia, which, considering their position, the deficiency of their arms, and other causes, may be excusable." The verdict also states that the Kentucky militia under Davis were only 170 strong but "occupied more than 300 yards" of the line.[46]

Despite the fact the report seemed to back up Adair's assumptions, Jackson was unmoved and suggested that Adair's continual objections to his report on the left bank were motivated less by his desire for truth and more by his desire to be elected governor or senator.[47] Jackson also argued that there were not almost one thousand Kentuckians in the lines on the right side but the actual number was less than the 550 Adair had said brought their own weapons. The four to five hundred arms garnered by Adair from those exempt were not gathered until after the battle, citing Major Thomas Butler (a Kentuckian himself) as proof of this. If Adair had borrowed the guns from those exempted from service, why not give them to the men crossing the river instead of those safely behind the lines on the right side? And no permission for borrowing such arms was given by Jackson nor was he notified of it. Even if Adair was telling the truth, would this not tarnish his reputation for breaking military protocol?[48]

Adair replied in another letter that it was Jackson who was seeking to propel himself into office, not he. Adair claimed that not only had he drawn the arms from the exempts before the battle but that he had done so at Jackson's request and had even borrowed Jackson's horse to aid him in his actions.[49] Beyond this, Adair points out that if he were able to obtain the additional arms without Jackson's request, such an action would suggest that the citizens of New Orleans had "more confidence in this small band of Kentuckians" than the general himself.[50]

The Kentucky legislature eventually waded into the fight and passed a resolution commending Adair for his role in the American Revolution as well as the War of 1812. And now "His subsequent conduct in vindicating a respectable portion of his countrymen, from the unappropriate imputation of cowardice (accidently it is hoped, but certainly most unjustly) thrown upon them, has both in matter and manner, the profound approbation, gratitude and thanks of his country, and of this legislature."[51] The feud soon faded from print without being resolved. Many Kentuckians would have trouble forgiving what they saw as a slander by Jackson, but regardless of what they thought of his report there was no denying he had led the Americans to victory. Not only had it been proven that Americans could stand before the best that Britain could throw against them, but the defenders of New Orleans could also congratulate themselves on giving their negotiators in Ghent an additional tool to use as leverage on their British counterparts. Or at least they would have if negotiations had not already concluded.

Chapter Ten

PEACE AT LAST

W ORD OF THE ALMOST inconceivable American victory at New Orleans resurrected feelings of pride in Kentucky and offered one of the few silver linings to a mostly depressing year. But it was hardly an answer to the persistent problems that weighed on the nation. The war continued with a bruised but still very dangerous British fleet lurking in the Atlantic, whispers of secession in New England, and a looming crisis of men, materials, and funds in every state. The governor's latest call for more men to be organized for future battles had not gone over particularly well with the war-weary state. Any anticipated relief offered by Jackson's victory was soon dispelled as a request for five thousand more Kentucky militia landed on the governor's desk.[1] When too few volunteers signed up some officers suggested a draft to raise the number needed.[2] When the government tried to order nearby regiments to help fill the gaps confusion ensued with meager results. Militia general Trotter wrote to Shelby in surprise when he learned that he was supposed to be raising men in place of the nearby 17th Regiment, which could not furnish enough for the most recent call. Was this rumor even true? If so, why had he never received any orders from Frankfort? Were the men to be drafted or was this just a call for volunteers? Are the men to obey the old militia law or has the new one taken effect?[3]

The breakdown in communications was accompanied by increasingly deteriorating discipline within the militia. As the condition worsened, the governor was forced to order officers in the militia to court martial anyone who failed to serve regardless of rank.[4] The *Kentucky Gazette*, which had been full of patriotic sayings, songs, and poems, now began to feature complaints in its editorial pages. One disgruntled contributor evoked the time-honored American tradition of blaming Congress. Describing himself as one of the "millions" who had "become disgusted and sickened at the long and windy speeches..." he declared himself, "most seriously fatigued with your [Congress'] patriotic sayings and belligerent boastings, but conciliating and dubious doings." The long tirade closed with a clear and dire assessment. "Now as we have a powerful army in the North as well as the South to contend with—and as the internal enemy is becoming bolder and more respectable, because of your imbecility." The article ended with the anonymous moniker "An Old Soldier."[5] Others suspected that America's struggles in the war were the direct result of their moral failings. One Mercer County resident confessed that "I am really afraid that the United Stat[e]s have not yet been Punished So much as to bring them to a Proper Sence of their Wickedness and humble them before that God whome they have So awfully Insulted."[6]

But despite the spreading dismay, by early February there were signs that the British were intending to abandon the Gulf Coast altogether. This would at least offer some consolation. Word finally arrived in Frankfort from General John Thomas, then in Camp Dupre two miles south of New Orleans. The camp was the current headquarters to the 7th Military District, and Dupre could happily report that he had seen the enemy abandon their position on the nineteenth and withdraw to Ship Island, leaving their wounded in American hands.[7] This good fortune meant that additional troops may not be needed in the south after all. The secretary of war ordered two thousand men called up instead of the original five, and to be held in readiness but not to march.[8] Even this number would have been difficult to gather, though it did offer some relief. Something drastic needed to happen soon. Fortunately, for the American cause, it did.

February 14 dawned like most other days in Philadelphia. Peter Voorhies was up and completing the daily routine of district paymaster. Far from a glamorous position it was at least a safe and popular one (when pay could actually be divvied out, that is). But this day his routine would be interrupted by word that was spreading like wildfire. News had just arrived from Ghent. A peace treaty had been signed. In a jubilant letter to Shelby, Voorhies wrote that "the City [of Philadelphia] was intoxicated with the news of peace." Prices on goods were already down

50 to 100 percent in anticipation of the resumption of trade. The whole city was "illuminated" after receiving the news. He would hasten to Kentucky as soon as he could get the treasury notes signed. It was finally over.[9] The path to peace had not been an easy one and just months before even the negotiators themselves would have been surprised to learn that peace was so near. As late as the sixth of August the uncompromising attitude and the unrealistic demands by the British had given the Americans little choice but to reject these terms out of hand. The other major hurdle to progress had been the American delegation's trouble getting along with each other. Not only did their backgrounds lead to varying ideas on what was most important but their personal habits were not always conducive either. The often-repeated example of John Quincy Adams' puritanical habit of rising extremely early in the morning to find that Clay had played cards through the night and was only then preparing for bed is an accurate one.[10]

However, by early September, Clay and Adams had reached a ceasefire and the British had also indicated they were willing to make small concessions so that sincere work on the treaty could actually progress. The British representatives gave up their insistence of control of the Great Lakes and the American delegation gave up their insistence that the treaty include language banning any future resumption of impressment.[11] The two sides had argued over several issues with one of the most contentious being control of the Mississippi River. If Britain could secure rights over this vital artery of American commerce they could prevent American expansion westward and cut the nation off from the recently acquired territories they had received from the Louisiana Purchase. Such a diplomatic coup could also stifle the economic foundations of states west of the Appalachian Mountains who got their crops and goods to market via rivers, the majority of which fed into the Mississippi.[12] The loudest opposition to this stipulation came from Clay, who was the only representative to live west of the mountains and whose personal fortunes could be directly affected by the issue. The British eventually acquiesced on this point in exchange for the Americans giving up their demand to fishing rights off Newfoundland and, on Christmas Eve, the treaty had been signed.[13]

By February 16, Congress unanimously ratified the Treaty of Ghent. Travelers carried the word in all directions and local newspapers began printing the story with relish. Celebrations broke out across the country. Few people seemed to notice how remarkably short the treaty really was.

The fact that it did very little to address the grievances that had caused the war in the first place was barely mentioned. Nowhere in the treaty's eleven articles was the impressment of American sailors mentioned. The first eight articles appointed various commissions to settle border disputes between the United States and Canada that had existed since the Treaty of Paris had ended the Revolution. In respect to Native American tribes, both sides agreed to cease hostilities between their peoples and reinstate "all the possessions, rights, and privileges" the tribes had enjoyed before the war—an ambiguous statement to say the least.[14]

With the addition of a general declaration from both sides to work to end slave trafficking, the treaty abruptly ended.[15] Looking at the map, little appeared to have been accomplished by the two-and-a-half-year conflict. The Treaty of Ghent had returned the borders of the United States and Canada to where they had been before the war began. This had to have been a bitter pill to swallow for the men who had fought Procter on the Thames and captured such a significant portion of western Ontario. But this ceding of territory was a necessary sacrifice for the greater good. However, from every other perspective, the Americans had achieved their goals. Impressment of American sailors had ended (albeit before the conflict had actually started), and the rising Indian confederacy under Tecumseh had been crushed and Tecumseh killed. The conflict had also proved, at least in the minds of the Americans, that the Revolution had not been a fluke. While Napoleon had served as a distraction to the British early in the war, his capture in 1812 ended that. America had fought toe to toe with the world's only superpower without the kind of help from Spain, France, or the Netherlands that they had received during the American Revolution. They had emerged from the conflict with their honor intact, but they had paid a high price in return.

All that was left was for the two sides to pick up the pieces. Those who had lost loved ones in the conflict could not bring them back, but there was hope that some things could be returned. In mid-December 1815, the Kentucky legislature took up the cause of compensation for lost horses in the service of the war and submitted a "Memorial" to remind Congress of the suffering of those who had fought in the war. The very nature of the conflict in the Northwest required mounted riflemen more than other areas. Those that had suffered the loss of a horse had "relied upon the justice of their country, which they believed would never be withheld from the soldier, who had risked his life in defense of his country's rights." True, the federal government had created a process through which men could apply to recover money for their horses, but this was terribly inadequate for the Kentuckians who lost their mounts. Being so far from the front meant that Kentuckians had to cover significant ground to arrive on the battlefield where they were needed, and many calls on them were deemed urgent which ensured they would come by horseback to arrive as quickly as possible.[16]

Because of their sacrifices "the remaining forts were saved, the frontier protected, a savage enemy checked in his bloody career, and destruction and retribution carried back into his own country. . . . We therefore most seriously request, that the cases of lost horses alluded to in this memorial, be attended to, and that our citizens be fully compensated."[17] As proof of how congested and slow the process had become one of the applicants still waiting to be reimbursed for the loss of his horse was none other than Isaac Shelby.[18]

Shelby was becoming increasingly dismayed by the inaction of the War Department and their constant call to prove the losses being reported. He had taken the time to have every horse that had made the trip to Canada appraised at Newport before the army crossed into Ohio. When the returning army reached Limestone (Maysville) notations were added detailing which horses were lost. Those rolls had been sent to Washington in March 1814. What more compelling proof could the federal government require? To require additional documentation to be sent three years after the battle would be a "complete denial of justice," he argued.[19] The response was a very bureaucratic and ambiguous answer. The rolls had been received and were enough proof that the troops had indeed served under Shelby at the Battle of the Thames and no other proof would be needed. Except, of course, the claimants would need to hire attorneys in Washington to keep the process moving, and of course, they would need to swear oaths that they had not been compensated already. The appearance of more red tape must have only angered Shelby further. He had pointed out that many lost horses belonged to war widows whose husbands had died defending the United States.[20] Was it really necessary to make them spend the extra funds to hire an attorney for what should be a simple process?

In January 1816 the legislature again sent word to Kentucky's senators in Washington reminding them that the widows and orphans of many men were suffering. "It has been thought sound policy in all, and it had been the practice in most nations, to pay well their soldiers, and to provide liberally for the widows and orphans of such as fell in their country's battles." In America this should be applied to civilians since they made up the militia. The resolution then asks for "liberal allowance" in caring for those affected.[21] Despite these efforts, many soldiers would not be recompensed for their expenses during the campaign.

While economic aid seemed to stall for those who served, their personal prestige flourished as time passed. As the horrors of war were whitewashed from the public consciousness with each succeeding year, those who served were elevated from brave members of the local community to symbols of American freedom. For decades to follow a gracious commonwealth and nation showed their appreciation. In 1835, Congress had a medal struck for George Croghan for his role in the Battle of Fort Stephenson and seven swords were struck for the other American officers at the fort. Croghan's reputation would propel him on to become the army's inspector general.[22]

For many years to come, the massacre at the River Raisin was kept alive as a symbol of American sacrifice and British treachery. Of the many lives lost at Frenchtown all but a company of the 19th Infantry who died that day were Kentuckians. The bodies of the men buried by the men under Shelby and Richard Johnson on their return from the Battle of the Thames were later reinterred in the Frankfort Cemetery.[23] Allen, Ballard, Edmondson, Graves, Hart, Hickman, McCracken, McLean, Meade, and Simpson Counties were all named after men who lost their lives at the Battle of Frenchtown. Major Madison might have received a county as well had their not already been a Madison County named for the president and founding father James Madison.[24] The effort to remember the sacrifices at the River Raisin have continued into the twenty-first century. In October 2010, the Battlefield at the River Raisin became a part of the National Park System and will be maintained for future generations.[25]

As the Battle at Frenchtown would come to signify patriotic sacrifice, the Thames would remain alive in the imaginations of the men of the commonwealth as the supreme example of liberty's triumph over tyranny. Few Americans casualties had resulted from the Thames, but one man, William Whitley, was honored by having a county named after him as well. He had been among the men who charged the swampy area where Tecumseh and his warriors had lain concealed.[26]

But it was the Battle of New Orleans that would be the most celebrated. After news of the battle became known, a songwriter by the name of Samuel Woodworth scratched a few verses on paper to celebrate the victory, and the song, entitled "The Hunters of Kentucky," was an instant hit and remained popular for several years after the war. While far from a solemn ode to sacrifice like "The Star-Spangled Banner," the words truly captured the celebratory mood in Kentucky after the war ended. But more than that, it captured how Kentuckians viewed their own identity and their role in national affairs. Woodworth boasts:

> We are a hardy free-born race,
> each man to fear a stranger;
> Whate'er the game, we join in chase,
> Despising toil and danger;

In the fourth verse, Woodworth carries the theme even further with the following words:

> But Jackson, he was wide awake,
> And wasn't scared of trifles;
> He knew what deadly aim we take
> With our Kentucky rifles.
> He led us down to Cypress Swamp,
> The ground was low and mucky;
> There stood John Bull in martial pomp,
> But here stood Old Kentucky[27]

The battle proved symbolic of how nineteenth-century Kentuckians felt the clashes between monarchy and republicanism should unfold. An army of citizen-soldiers would meet the imperialist "John Bull" face-to-face in a contest of honor. Woodworth does not bother with descriptions of the fortified lines and only mentions the ramparts that Americans fought behind in passing. Nor does he address the retreat of the men on the opposite bank of the Mississippi. His verses are meant to convey sentiment instead of history. They concentrate the essence of the whole conflict into just a few lines. To the burgeoning generation of Americans, especially in the West, the War of 1812 was meant to avenge the United States for the insults it had sustained from Great Britain since the Revolution. It was not a battle fought by bureaucratic paper pushers who sought to accommodate rather than address the problem. It was a duel between liberty and tyranny, and unless the advocates of monarchy were met in open contest, the nation's integrity would remain unrestored.

But the end of the war affected more of the Union than just Kentucky and it proved to be either the beginning or the ending for the public careers of many of its participants. The war proved to be a "turning point" in the mind of the majority of Americans. It had proved the United States could hold its own on the world stage but, according to historian David Hickey, it also punctuated the end of a long string of abuses, of which impressment was only the latest, in Anglo-American relations. British disdain for American prestige had only worsened in the years following the Revolution and Americans had endured any number of slights as a result.[28] But now the United States had ended all of that. Many Federalists would point to the lack of material gain as proof of the war's lack of relevance, but this argument would gain few supporters.[29] William Henry Harrison's retirement as head of the army did not mean the end of his public life. After the War of 1812 he helped negotiate a number of treaties with native tribes. Serving in the Ohio legislature, as a US representative, and then US senator, Harrison was poised to reach new heights. He was elected president with John Tyler as his vice president in 1840 with the memorable slogan "Tippecanoe and Tyler too!" However, after refusing the shelter of a carriage or overcoat on inauguration day, Harrison mounted his favorite horse for his ride to the swearing in where he delivered his lengthy inaugural address. Not long afterward Harrison fell ill. Many attended the president as his symptoms became worse but to no avail. After just thirty days in office, Harrison died. One of the last friends to visit his bedside was Colonel George Croghan, the young officer he had almost relieved of command at Fort Stephenson.[30]

General Hull's military career ended less impressively. He was courtmartialed in January 1814 and found guilty of cowardice for his actions at Detroit. His actions earned him the death penalty, but in consideration of his role in the Revolution he was issued a pardon and the verdict was approved by President Madison. This must have been a relief for Hull but it left him with the unfortunate distinction of being the only general officer in the history of the United States army to be sentenced to death.[31] After the war, Richard M. Johnson returned to Congress and eventually offered part of his Scott County property to serve as the site of an academy for Choctaw Indian children. His fame as the man who killed Tecumseh landed him the vice presidency under President Van Buren in 1836. Afterward, he went on to hold public office in one form or another for much of the remainder of his life. Johnson passed away in 1850 at the age of sixty-nine and was buried in the Frankfort Cemetery.[32]

Henry Clay returned to Congress, where his influence continued to grow, after ending his mission in Ghent. In 1818, Henry Clay asked Congress to strike a medal for the then-retired Governor Shelby and William Henry Harrison and to have a sword struck for Richard M. Johnson to express the thanks of a grateful nation for their services.[33] The unity that brought so many factions and personalities together during the war would not continue in times of peace. Once back in the Senate, Clay would oppose much of the agenda of Andrew Jackson's administration and would unsuccessfully oppose the later Mexican War, in which he would lose a son. Clay's role in the war would eventually take a back seat to his efforts as a compromiser. Clay was able to push through several compromises that prevented the Civil War during his lifetime. His legacy during the War of 1812 had been to avenge the union, but he would be better known for his efforts to preserve it. Several unsuccessful attempts at the presidency marred an otherwise successful career in government that included serving as secretary of state under John Quincy Adams.[34]

Other Kentuckians who had served in the war went on to prominence as well. George Madison, who had helped lead the men at the River Raisin, had returned home a hero in 1814 after being a prisoner of war in Quebec. Despite the disaster of the battle his reputation reached celebrity status and in 1816 he ran for governor. His only opponent dropped out to support him and he won the election with no opposition. But Madison's health had been broken during his time as a prisoner, and within a year of taking office he was dead.[35] Service in the war would continue to aid its participants politically. Six of the eight governors to follow Madison were veterans of the war and a significant number of county and state positions also went to those who had served in some capacity during the war.

One Kentuckian who had not lived to see the end of the war was former governor Charles Scott. He had died on October 22, 1813, just seventeen days after the battle on the river Thames had broken Britain's strength in the West. Word of the victory had been announced through the *Kentucky Gazette* three days before his death, meaning that, in all likelihood, he had lived long enough to know that Detroit was in American hands again and America's future in the trans-Mississippi West was assured.[36]

The war would not be as kind to British general Henry Procter. When the adjutant general's report on the Battle of the Thames was submitted, his actions were a primary focus. Not only had he inflated the number of enemies he faced on the field at the Thames to make his situation seem more desperate than it was, he had also stated that the native warriors had retreated when in fact they fought with zeal and even harassed the Americans on their retreat. To make things worse the army was apparently burdened with nonmilitary baggage while the transporting of military stores like ammunition was "totally neglected." As a result, the Americans had overrun these supplies for the whole division on October 4 and then captured the force itself the next day.[37] He was allowed to remain in the army, but he was suspended for six months without pay and his sentence was read to the whole British army. This would eventually be reduced to a reprimand by the prince regent, but it was enough to destroy Procter's lengthy military career. He returned to Britain where he would not see battle again, and by 1816 he had left the army entirely. He would die just seven years later at his home in Bath.[38]

Surprisingly, Tecumseh's brother, Tenskwatawa the Prophet, had survived the war and lived a relatively quiet life. Having fled the defeat at the River Thames, he made a new home west of the Mississippi where he would be beyond the reach of American settlers. Moving to what is modern-day Kansas, the Prophet would receive relatively little publicity, either good or bad, and would die an uneventful death at his home in November 1836.[39]

Even after his retirement, Isaac Shelby's popularity never abated and his reputation garnered attention in some unlikely places. In 1817 he received a letter from Great Britain. The outside of the letter was simply addressed to "James Shelby Esq, Governor of Ky, North America." Whoever the author of the letter was it was obvious they were not too acquainted with Shelby if they could not even supply the correct first name and could ignore the fact he had been out of office for two years. Opening the note Shelby found it to be from a "Sir Philppart," an amateur historian who was writing a history of notable leaders in different nations. He had completed his work on the British generals of the day and now wished to have Shelby submit an account of his life for the book. Reaching the letter's end, the signature would have probably caused a smile on the retired governor's face. Philppart was in the employment of His Royal Highness the Duke of Kent, fourth son of King George III.[40] There is no word on whether his employer approved of the subject matter of his work.

Shelby's became so renowned that James Monroe, who succeeded Madison in the presidency, offered him a seat in his cabinet in the prestigious position of secretary of war. It seemed Shelby's military experience and wisdom had finally been realized. But the aging and tired governor declined the offer.[41] He was tired of being at the center of political life and looked forward to returning to his farm and family. But he did accept one last public duty before he could permanently retire from public life completely. He was appointed to act as one of the commissioners, alongside Andrew Jackson, to the Chickasaw nation that inhabited what is now far western Kentucky and Tennessee. Their goal was to negotiate the sale of Chickasaw lands east of the Mississippi. If successful, the sale would not only add territory to Kentucky and Tennessee, extending their western boundaries to the Mississippi River, but would also sever the southern tribes from their northern counterparts, forever closing the path that connected them and severing the last communication route between them that had featured so prominently in Tecumseh's plans for a united Indian confederacy.[42] But by now the aging Shelby was tired, and in a letter to Andrew Jackson, he confided that he was not entirely sure he could reach the rendezvous point with the Chickasaw chiefs.[43]

Despite these limitations, negotiations went forward. Calling the Chickasaw "Friends and Brothers," Shelby and Jackson proclaimed their aim to be the strengthening of their friendship. They pointed out that the lands now inhabited by the Chickasaw were sold to the United States after the Revolution but that the president had kept settlers from it to promote peace and allow the Chickasaw to hunt. But times were different now. The game had been hunted out and the rivers that formed its boundaries would be full of "steam ships," which will want the trees on the land for fuel.[44] A copy of the treaty that had sold the land to the American government was presented to the tribe. However, the American government would pay for the land a second time if the Chickasaw would cross the Mississippi River and resettle. There were also lands reserved for the Chickasaw in Georgia, according to the treaty.[45] These efforts were successful and the Chickasaw sold their land in what is now western Tennessee and Kentucky to the United States. The transition happened peacefully and the states' borders expanded once more to take the form they have today. Having committed his final public act, Shelby returned to Traveler's Rest where he would spent the majority of his remaining years.

In July 1826, the United States of America learned that two of their founding fathers, John Adams and Thomas Jefferson, had died on the fiftieth anniversary of the signing of the Declaration of Independence. Around the nation, events were planned to honor the two men who had done so much to secure American independence and to give the young nation a start in the world. In Lexington, a committee was formed to suggest ways of honoring the two former presidents as well. However, a third name was also added to the list: former governor Isaac Shelby.[46] Eight days after the deaths of Adams and Jefferson, Isaac Shelby had eaten his afternoon meal with his family. Rising from the table and taking a short walk in the July sun, he returned to the house and seated himself in a chair to relax. Moments later he quietly passed away.[47]

The news of Shelby's death spread rapidly and the state grieved for the passing of its elder statesmen. "All Hearts are sorrowful; and the state is like a family of little ones, weeping over the shrouded remains of a beloved father!" lamented the *Kentucky Gazette*. "He was indeed a father to Kentucky—his services are interwoven with the history, and his fame blended with the glory of the state."[48] In January of the following year the state legislature voted to erect a tombstone for Shelby at the state's expense.[49]

The memory of Isaac Shelby was not just sustained in Kentucky but in several surrounding states that have counties and cities named in his honor. Shelby's death represented the end of a chapter in Kentucky history as well. There would be no more raids by Indian warriors into Kentucky territory, and the communities that were springing up in the state continued to flourish. Within twenty-five years of Shelby's death Kentuckians were riding in trains on newly laid track and sending messages by telegraph, and many were preparing to fight in another war—this one with Mexico. The War of 1812 slowly faded in the shadows of other, more deadly conflicts of the nineteenth century, but it had achieved its goals and forever altered a nation. The cost of the war had been high in both blood and treasure and the United States had no territorial or monetary gains to show for it. But the ultimate, underlying goal had been achieved. The United States had stood toe to toe with Britain and had responded to what Americans viewed as unwarranted aggression. They had restored their national honor.

NOTES

INTRODUCTION

1. Bennett H. Young, *The Battle of the Thames: In Which Kentuckians Defeated the British, French, and Indiana, October 5, 1813* (Louisville: John P. Morton and Co, 1903), 210.

2. Walter R. Borneman, *1812: The War that Forged a Nation* (New York: HarperCollins, 2004), 1–3.

3. Donald R. Hickey, *The War of 1812: A Forgotten Conflict* (Champaign: University of Illinois Press, 2012), 1.

4. Alan Taylor, *The Civil War of 1812: American Citizens, British Subjects, Irish Rebels & Indian* Allies (New York: Vintage Books, 2010), 12.

5. Hickey, xii.

6. Sandy Antal, *A Wampum Denied: Procter's War of 1812* (Montreal: Mcgill-Queens University Press, 1997), xiii.

7. Taylor, 6.

8. Arthur Quisenberry, "Kentucky 'Regulars' in the War of 1812," *Register of the Kentucky Historical Society* 34 (1914): 15–17.

CHAPTER ONE: HURTLING TOWARD WAR

1. Carl Kramer, *Capital on the Kentucky: A Two Hundred Year History of Frankfort and Franklin County* (Frankfort: Historic Frankfort, 1986), 42.

2. Ibid., 63.

3. "United States Resident Population by State: 1790 – 1850," as of February 8, 2016, http://lwd.dol.state.nj.us/labor/lpa/census/1990/poptrd1.htm.

4. Kramer, *Capital on the Kentucky*, 51.

5. Ibid., 42.

6. Ibid., 53.

7. Ibid., 58–59.

8. Sharon Malinowski, Anna Sheets, and Linda Schmittroth, ed., *UXL Encyclopedia of Native American Tribes Volume 1* (Detroit: UXL, 1999), 186–187.

9. Thomas Clark, *A History of Kentucky* (Ashland: Jesse Stuart Foundation, 1992), 101.

10. Sharon Malinowski, Anna Sheets, Linda Schmittroth, ed., "Mound Builders," *UXL Encyclopedia of Native American Tribes Volume 1* (Detroit: UXL, 1999), 151.

11. Samuel Hopkins, to Walter Alves, January 21, 1812, SC140, Sam Hopkins Papers, 1796-1823, Kentucky Historical Society, Frankfort, KY.

12. *1812 Acts of the Kentucky General Assembly*, State Publications, Kentucky Department for Libraries and Archives (Frankfort, KY), 252–253.

13. John Sugden, *Tecumseh: A Life* (New York: Henry Holt, 1997) 22–23.

14. Norman K. Risjord, *Jefferson's America: 1760-1815* (Lanham: Rowman & Littlefield, 2002), 73–74.

15. Freeman Cleaves, *Old Tippecanoe: William Henry Harrison and His Time* (1939; reprint, Newtown: American Political Biography Press, 1990), 35.

16. William Beall, *Journal of William K Beall*, 1812, 97SC134, Kentucky Historical Society (Frankfort, KY). There are no page numbers on the original manuscript or the accompanying transcription.

17. Cleaves, *Old Tippecanoe*, 53–54.

18. Robert Breckinridge McAfee, *History of the Late War in the Western Country* (1816; reprint, Ann Arbor: University Microfilms, Inc., 1966), 10–12.

19. McAfee, *History of the Late War*, 11.

20. Ibid., 12–13.

21. McAfee, *History of the Late War*, 15.

22. Ibid., 18–20

23. Ibid., 26.

24. Ibid., 29.

25. *1812 Acts of the Kentucky General Assembly*, 252.

26. *Kentucky Gazette*, April 7, 1812 (Lexington, KY).

27. *Kentucky Gazette*, June 30, 1812.

28. Thomas Clark, *A History of Kentucky* (1937; reprint, Ashland: Jesse Stuart Foundation, 1992), 123.

29. Clark, *Kentucky*, 123–124.

30. *1812 Acts of the Kentucky General Assembly*, 252–253.

31. *1812 Acts of the Kentucky General Assembly*, 259.

32. Ellery L. Hall, "Canadian Annexation Sentiment in Kentucky Prior to the War of 1812," *Register of the Kentucky Historical Society* 28 (1930): 372.

33. Clark, *Kentucky*, 67.

34. George Morgan Chinn, *Kentucky: Settlement and Statehood: 1750-1800* (Frankfort: Kentucky Historical Society, 1975), 325.

35. Hall, "Canadian Annexation," 373.

36. Ibid., 377.

37. Robert V. Remini, *Henry Clay: Statesman for the Union* (New York: W.W. Norton, 1991), 76–77.

38. Aylett Hawes, to Col. James Taylor, January 12, 1812, Mss8, James Taylor Papers, Kentucky Historical Society (Frankfort, KY).

39. James Wallace Hammack Jr., *Kentucky & the Second American Revolution: The War of 1812* (Lexington: University Press of Kentucky,1976), 9.

40. McAfee, *History of the Late War*, 49.

41. *1812 Acts of the Kentucky General Assembly*, 11.

42. Ibid., 7.

43. Ibid., 21.

44. John R. Elting, *Amateurs to Arms!: A Military History of the War of 1812* (Boston: De Capo Press, 1995), 9.

45. Elting, *Amateurs*, 9.

46. *1812 Acts of the Kentucky General Assembly*, 33–35.

47. Robert S. Todd Regimental Orders, 1811, May 8, 2012MS018, Special Collections, University of Kentucky (Lexington, KY).

48. Elting, *Amateurs*, 8.

49. Sam Hopkins, to Walter Alves, June 8 1813, SC140, Sam Hopkins Papers, 1796–1823, Kentucky Historical Society (Frankfort, KY).

50. Elting, *Amateur*, 24.

51. McAfee, *History of the Late War*, 50.

52. Anderson Chenault Quisenberry, *Kentucky in the War of 1812* (Frankfort: Kentucky State Historical Society, 1915), 22; and McAfee, *History of the Late War*, 49.

53. Harry M. Ward, *Charles Scott and "The Spirit of '76"* (Charlottesville: University of Virginia Press, 1988), 191.

54. *1811 Journal of the Kentucky House of Representatives*, State Publications, Kentucky Department for Libraries and Archives (Frankfort, KY), 9.

55. *1811 Journal of the Kentucky House of Representatives*, 10.

56. Ibid.

57. Ibid., 11.

58. Ibid., 17.

59. Ibid., 77-78.

60. *1811 Journal of the Kentucky House of Representatives*, 238.

61. G. Glenn Clift, *Remember the Raisin! Kentucky and Kentuckians in the Battles and Massacre at Frenchtown, Michigan Territory, in the War of 1812* (Frankfort: Kentucky Historical Society, 1961), 15.

62. *Kentucky Gazette*, September 18, 1812.

63. *Kentucky Gazette*, March 20, 1800; and *Kentucky Gazette*, January 30, 1800.

64. Clark, *Kentucky*, 73–74.

65. *Kentucky Gazette*, May 5, 1812.

66. *Kentucky Gazette*, May 26, 1812.

67. Ibid.

68. Irving Brant, *The Fourth President: A Life of James Madison* (Norwalk: Eastern Press, 1970), 481.

69. Brant, *Forth President*, 476–477.

70. Ibid., 489.

71. Ibid., 496–497.

72. *Kentucky Gazette*, July 7, 1812.

73. Ibid.

74. Ibid.

75. Remini, *Henry Clay*, 93.

76. *Kentucky Gazette*, June 30, 1812.

77. Hammack, *Second American Revolution*, 13.

78. *Kentucky Gazette*, July 14, 1812.

79. *Kentucky Gazette*, November 24, 1812.

80. William Wood, ed. *Select British Documents of the Canadian War of 1812* (Toronto: Champlain Society, 1920), 6.

81. Lt. James Bryson, to Governor Charles Scott, August 10, 1812, folder 20, box 1, Governor Charles Scott Papers, Kentucky Department for Libraries and Archives, (Frankfort, KY).

82. James Taylor, *James Taylor Reminiscences, 1846*, Mss. A T243k, Filson Historical Society, Louisville, KY, 39.

83. Wood, *British Documents*, 10–11.

84. Ibid., 3.

CHAPTER TWO: DANGER IN DETROIT

1. "United States Resident Population by State: 1790 – 1850," as of February 8, 2016, http://lwd.dol.state.nj.us/labor/lpa/census/1990/poptrd1.htm.
2. Beall, *Journal.*
3. Beall, *Journal.*
4. Taylor, *James Taylor Reminiscences, 1846*, Mss. A T243k, Filson Historical Society, (Louisville, KY), 39.
5. Beall, *Journal.*
6. Taylor, *Reminiscences,* 40–41.
7. Ibid.
8. Ibid.
9. Ibid.
10. Beall, *Journal.* Some places in Beall's journal spell the ship's name *Cayahaga.*
11. Ibid.
12. Ibid.
13. Ibid
14. Ibid.
15. Ibid.
16. Ibid.
17. Quisenberry, *Kentucky in the War,* 22–23.
18. McAfee, *History of the Late War,* 59.
19. Ibid., 60.
20. Ibid.
21. Ibid., 61–62.
22. Ibid., 63–64.
23. Ibid., 64.
24. Ibid., 68.
25. McAfee, *History of the Late War,* 70.
26. *Kentucky Gazette,* November 17, 1812.
27. McAfee, *History of the Late War,* 76.
28. *Liberty Hall,* August 25, 1812.
29. Wesley B. Turner, *Encyclopedia of the War of 1812,* "Isaac Brock" (Santa Barbara: ABC-CLIO, 1997).
30. Major Richardson, K.S.F., *War of 1812: Containing A Full and Detailed Narrative of the Operations of the Right Division of the Canadian Army* (n.p., 1842), 7.
31. Richardson, *Operation of the Right Wing,* 8.
32. Taylor, *Reminiscences,* 45.
33. Ibid.
34. Richardson, *Operation of the Right Wing,* 35.
35. Ibid., 9.
36. *Kentucky Gazette,* September 29, 1812.
37. Ibid.
38. Ibid.
39. McAfee, *History of the Late War,* 85.
40. Ibid., 86.
41. *Kentucky Gazette,* September 29, 1812.
42. *Kentucky Gazette,* September 22, 1812.

43. *Kentucky Gazette*, September 29, 1812.

44. Ibid.

45. Ibid.

46. *Kentucky Gazette*, July 21, 1812.

47. *Kentucky Gazette*, July 14, 1812.

48. Ward, *Charles Scott*, ix.

49. *Kentucky Gazette*, August 11, 1812.

50. John Depauw, letter to Isaac Shelby, June 26, 1812, 1F62M-590, Isaac Shelby Papers, 1765-1911, Special Collections, University of Kentucky (Lexington, KY).

51. Mark Hardin to Shelby, April 10, 1812, 1F62M-590, Isaac Shelby Papers, 1765–1911, Special Collections, University of Kentucky (Lexington, KY).

52. Ibid.

53. *Kentucky Gazette*, July 14, 1812.

54. Lowell H. Harrison, ed. *Kentucky's Governors: 1792-1985*, (Lexington: University Press of Kentucky, 1985), 2.

55. Sylvia Wrobel and George Grider, *Isaac Shelby Kentucky's First Governor and Hero of Three Wars* (Danville: Cumberland Press, 1974), 105 and 107.

56. *Kentucky Gazette*, August 25, 1812.

57. G. Glenn Clift, *Remember the Raisin! Kentucky and the Kentuckians in the Battles and Massacre at Frenchtown, Michigan Territory, in the War of 1812* (Frankfort: Kentucky Historical Society, 1961), 17.

58. Charles Scott, to Major Thomas Martin, August 3, 1812, folder 20, box 1, Governor Charles Scott Papers, Kentucky Department for Libraries and Archives (Frankfort, KY).

59. Clift, *Remember the Raisin*, 17.

60. Ibid., 6.

61. *Liberty Hall*, August 25, 1812 (Cincinnati, OH).

CHAPTER THREE: FORTS WAYNE AND HARRISON

1. G. Glen Clift, ed. "War of 1812 Diary of William B. Northcutt," *Register of the Kentucky Historical Society* 56 (1958): 167.

2. Clift, "Northcutt," 165–166.

3. Ibid.

4. Ibid.

5. Ibid., 167.

6. Ibid.

7. Elias Darnell, Timothy Mallary, John Davenport, *A Journal, Containing an Accurate and Interesting Account of the Hardships, Sufferings, Battles, Defeat and Captivity of Those Heroic Kentucky Volunteers and Regulars, Commanded by General Winchester, In the Years 1812-13. Also, Two Narratives, by Men That Were Wounded In the Battles on the River Raisin and Taken Captive by the Indians* (1813; reprint, Berea: Oscar Rucker, II, 1970), 6.

8. *Liberty Hall*, August 25, 1812.

9. Ibid., 7.

10. *The Kentucky Gazette*, September 29, 1812.

11. Quisenberry, *Kentucky in the War*, 23.

12. John Payne, to Charles Scott, August 25, 1812, folder 71, box 4, Governor Isaac Shelby Papers, Kentucky Department for Libraries and Archives (Frankfort, KY).

13. McAfee, *History of the Late War*, 111–112.

14. Clift, "Northcutt," 167.

15. Ibid., 167–168.
16. John S. Gano, to John Payne, August 24, 1812, folder 71, box 4, Governor Isaac Shelby Papers, Kentucky Department for Libraries and Archives (Frankfort, KY).
17. Harold Allison, *The Tragic Saga of the Indiana Indians* (Washington: Graphic Design of Indiana, 1987), 201–202.
18. Joseph Pierce, to John Payne, August 24, 1812, folder 71, box 4, Governor Isaac Shelby Papers, Kentucky Department for Libraries and Archives (Frankfort, KY).
19. Darnell, *An Accurate and Interesting Account*, 8.
20. *Liberty Hall,* August 25, 1812.
21. Clift, "Northcutt," 168–169.
22. Ibid., 169.
23. Ibid.
24. *Kentucky Gazette*, September 1, 1812.
25. Thomas Bodley, to Isaac Shelby, August 26, 1812, folder 71, box 4, Governor Isaac Shelby Papers, Kentucky Department for Libraries and Archives (Frankfort, KY).
26. Darnell, *An Accurate and Interesting Account*, 9–10.
27. Ibid., 10–11.
28. Benjamin Graves, *Major Benjamin Graves Order Book, 1812*, September 10, 1812, SC1056, Kentucky Historical Society (Frankfort, KY), 10.
29. Darnell, *An Accurate and Interesting Account*, 11–12.
30. McAfee, *History of the Late War*, 125.
31. Ibid., 126–127.
32. Clift, "Northcutt," 170.
33. Graves, *Order Book*, September 22, 1812. Most of the book does not have page numbers and future entries will be identified by dates and physical location.
34. J.E. Kaufmann and H.W. Kaufmann, *Fortress America: The Forts that Defended America, 1600 to the Present* (Cambridge: De Capo Press, 2004), 157.
35. John Forgy, *Kentucky Encyclopedia*, "Zachary Taylor" (Lexington: University Press of Kentucky, 1992).
36. Allison, 182.
37. *Kentucky Gazette*, October 13, 1812.
38. Ibid.
39. Allison, 183–185.
40. Ibid.
41. Ibid.
42. Ibid.
43. *Kentucky Gazette*, October 13, 1812.
44. Ibid., 18.
45. Walker Reid, to Isaac Shelby, September 18, 1812, folder 71, box 4, Governor Isaac Shelby Papers, Kentucky Department for Libraries and Archives (Frankfort, KY).
46. Quisenberry, *Kentucky in the War*, 26.
47. Glenn Clift (ed.), "War of 1812 Diary of William B. Northcutt." *Register of the Kentucky Historical Society* 56 (1958): 169.
48. Clift, "Northcutt," 169.
49. Graves, *Order Book*, September 26, 1812.
50. Graves, *Order Book*, September 27, 1812.
51. Ibid.
52. Graves, *Order Book*, , October 1, 1812.

53. Graves, *Order Book*, October 3, 1812.

54. Ibid.

55. Graves, *Order Book*, Camp Defiance, October 17, 1812.

56. Ibid., Camp Defiance, October 21, 1812.

57. Ibid., Fort Defiance, October 31 1812.

58. Ibid., Camp at Fort Winchester, November 1, 1812.

59. Ibid., Camp 3rd on the Miami, November 18, 1812.

60. Ibid., Camp 3rd on the Miami, November 27, 1812.

61. Ibid., Camp 3rd on the Miami, November 24, 1812.

62. Ibid., Camp 3rd on the Miami, December 1, 1812.

63. Ibid., Camp 3rd on the Miami, December 7, 1812.

64. Ibid., Camp 3rd on the Miami, December 10, 1812.

65. *Kentucky Gazette*, September 1, 1812.

66. Shelby To Do List, August 26, 1812, folder 71, box 4, Governor Isaac Shelby Papers, Kentucky Department for Libraries and Archives (Frankfort, KY).

67. Governor Isaac Shelby letter to William Henry Harrison, August 28, 1812, Governor Isaac Shelby Letter Book A, Page 1, Kentucky Department for Libraries and Archives (Frankfort, KY).

68. *Kentucky Gazette*, September 8, 1812.

69. *1812 Journal of the Kentucky House of Representatives*, State Publications, Kentucky Department for Libraries and Archives (Frankfort, KY), 203.

70. Ibid.

71. Ramsey, letter to Isaac Shelby, September 1812, folder 71, box 4, Governor Isaac Shelby Papers, Kentucky Department for Libraries and Archives (Frankfort, KY).

72. Ibid.

73. *Kentucky Gazette*, September 8, 1812.

74. Ibid.

75. Leon Hamilton, letter to Isaac Shelby, September 14, 1812, folder 71, box 4, Governor Isaac Shelby Papers, Kentucky Department for Libraries and Archives, (Frankfort, KY).

76. Vevay Petition. September 14, 1812, folder 71, box 4, Governor Isaac Shelby Papers, Kentucky Department for Libraries and Archives (Frankfort, KY).

77. McAfee, *History of the Late War*, 114.

78. Ibid., 116.

79. Ibid., 117.

80. Isaac Shelby, to Henry Knox, January 10, 1794, Isaac Shelby Miscellaneous Papers, 1786–1819 (Location Info), Filson Historical Society (Louisville, KY).

81. Isaac Shelby, letter to Secretary of War, January 10, 1794, Isaac Shelby: Miscellaneous Papers 1786–1819, Filson Historical Society (Louisville, KY).

CHAPTER FOUR: BATTLE FOR THE NORTHWEST

1. McAfee, *History of the Late War*, 130.

2. Clift, "Northcutt," 171.

3. Ibid., 172.

4. Ibid., 171.

5. McAfee, *History of the Late War*, 130.

6. Ibid., 157.

7. Isaac Shelby, letter to Sam Hopkins, September 8, 1812, Letter Book A, Page 16,

Governor Isaac Shelby Papers, Kentucky Department for Libraries and Archives (Frankfort, KY).

8. James W. Hammack Jr., *Kentucky Encyclopedia*, "Samuel Hopkins." (Lexington: University Press of Kentucky, 1992).

9. Isaac Shelby, letter to Sam Hopkins, September 8, 1812, Letter Book A, Page 16, Governor Isaac Shelby Papers, Kentucky Department for Libraries and Archives (Frankfort, KY).

10. Ibid.

11. *Kentucky Gazette*, September 22, 1812.

12. McAfee, *History of the Late War*, 158–160.

13. Ibid.

14. Ibid.

15. *Kentucky Gazette*, November 10, 1812.

16. Ibid.

17. Isaac Shelby, letter to William Henry Harrison, September 26, 1812, Letter Book A, Page 25, Governor Isaac Shelby Papers, Kentucky Department for Libraries and Archives (Frankfort, KY).

18. Ibid.

19. 1812 Journal of the Kentucky Senate, State Publications, Kentucky Department for Libraries and Archives (Frankfort, KY), 19.

20. Ibid., 20.

21. Isaac Shelby, to William Blount, October 31, 1812, Letter Book A, Page 31, Governor Isaac Shelby Papers, Kentucky Department for Libraries and Archives (Frankfort, KY).

22. Isaac Shelby, to William Henry Harrison, November 7, 1812, Letter Book A, Page 34, Governor Isaac Shelby Papers, Kentucky Department for Libraries and Archives (Frankfort, KY).

23. Isaac Shelby, to Sam Hopkins, November 9, 1812, Letter Book A, Page 35–36, Governor Isaac Shelby Papers, Kentucky Department for Libraries and Archives (Frankfort, KY).

24. Ibid., 36.

25. Ibid., 36–37.

26. Clift, "Northcutt," 172.

27. Ibid., 173.

28. Ibid., 174.

29. Darnell, *An Accurate and Interesting Account,* 22.

30. Ibid., 22–23.

31. Ibid., 24–25.

32. Ibid., 29.

33. Ibid., 23.

34. Clift, "Northcutt,"172.

35. Ibid., 174.

36. Ibid., 175.

37. Ibid., 176.

38. Ibid., 176–177.

39. Ibid., 253.

40. Clift, "Northcutt," 253.

41. Ibid., 254–255.

42. Ibid., 257–258.

43. Ibid., 258–259.

44. Ibid., 259.

45. Ibid., 260–261.

46. Ibid., 261.

47. Ibid., 260–261.

48. Ibid., 262.

49. Ibid., 264.

50. G. Glen Clift, ed., "War of 1812 Diary of William B. Northcutt," *Register of the Kentucky Historical Society* 56 (1958): 256–257.

51. Circular, folder 72, box 4, Governor Isaac Shelby Papers, Kentucky Department for Libraries and Archives (Frankfort, KY).

52. John Bradshaw, to Isaac Shelby, October 14, 1812, folder 72, box 4, Governor Isaac Shelby Papers, Kentucky Department for Libraries and Archives (Frankfort, KY) and Abraham Hite, to Isaac Shelby, October 31, 1815, folder 72, box 4, Governor Isaac Shelby Papers, Kentucky Department for Libraries and Archives (Frankfort, KY).

53. *The Kentucky Gazette*, October 27, 1812.

54. Abraham Hite, to Isaac Shelby, October 31, 1812, folder 72, box 4, Governor Isaac Shelby Papers, Kentucky Department for Libraries and Archives (Frankfort, KY).

55. Thomas Bodley, to Isaac Shelby, November 9, 1812, folder 72, box 4, Governor Isaac Shelby Papers, Kentucky Department for Libraries and Archives (Frankfort, KY).

56. Thomas Bodley, to Isaac Shelby, November 11, 1812, folder 72, box 4, Governor Isaac Shelby Papers, Kentucky Department for Libraries and Archives (Frankfort, KY).

57. Darnell, *An Accurate and Interesting Account*, 26.

58. McAfee, *History of the Late War*, 173–174.

59. Ibid., 174.

60. Ibid., 183.

61. Darnell, *An Accurate and Interesting Account*, 32–33.

62. Ibid., 34.

63. McAfee, *History of the Late War*, 185.

64. Darnell, *An Accurate and Interesting Account*, 34–35.

65. McAfee, *History of the Late War*, 184.

66. Ibid., 187.

67. Ibid., 166.

68. Wesley B. Turner, *Encyclopedia of the War of 1812*, "Isaac Brock" (Santa Barbara: ABC-CLIO, 1997).

CHAPTER FIVE: THE RIVER RAISIN

1. Darnell, *An Accurate and Interesting Account*, 36.

2. Robert Logan, to Jane Allen, January 17, 1813, 55M54:1:2, Allen-Butler Family Papers, Special collections, University of Kentucky (Lexington, KY).

3. *Kentucky Gazette*, February 2, 1813.

4. Ibid.

5. Ibid., December 29, 1812.

6. Quisenberry, *Kentucky in the War*, 33.

7. McAfee, *History of the Late War*, 203.

8. Darnell, *An Accurate and Interesting Account*, 39–42.

9. Robert Logan, to Jane Allen, January 17, 1813, 55M54:1:2, Allen-Butler Family Pa-

pers, Special collections, University of Kentucky (Lexington, KY).

10. Darnell, *An Accurate and Interesting Account,* 40

11. Darnell, *An Accurate and Interesting Account,* 40–42.

12. Ibid., 42.

13. Ibid., 40–42.

14. Quisenberry, *Kentucky in the War,* 38.

15. Darnell, *An Accurate and Interesting Account,* 43.

16. Quisenberry, *Kentucky in the War,* 38–39. Darnell suggests Winchester's headquarters was only one half mile away. In either case, it was a considerable distance from his men.

17. Taylor, *Reminiscences,* 40–41.

18. Logan Esarey, ed., *Governor's Messages and Letters Volume 2* (Indianapolis: Indiana Historical Society, 1922), 318.

19. McAfee, *History of the Late War,* 210–211.

20. Darnell, *An Accurate and Interesting Account,* 45–46.

21. Ibid.

22. Ibid.

23. Darnell, *An Accurate and Interesting Account,* 47.

24. Ibid.

25. McAfee, *History of the Late War,* 217.

26. Ibid.

27. Quisenberry, *Kentucky in the War,* 40.

28. Taylor, *Reminiscences,* 42.

29. Quisenberry, *Kentucky in the War,* 42.

30. Richardson, *Operation of the Right Wing,* 84.

31. Quisenberry, *Kentucky in the War,* 40.

32. Clift, *Remember the Raisin,* 76.

33. *Kentucky Gazette,* April 20, 1813.

34. Quisenberry, *Kentucky in the War,* 43.

35. Darnell, *An Accurate and Interesting Account,* 72–73.

36. Ibid.

37. Darnell, *An Accurate and Interesting Account,* 74–75.

38. Ibid.

39. Darnell, *An Accurate and Interesting Account,* 76–77.

40. Ibid., 78–79.

41. McAfee, *History of the Late War,* 222–223.

42. Darnell, *An Accurate and Interesting Account,* 59.

43. Ibid., 62.

44. Ibid., 63.

45. Footnote, Darnell, *An Accurate and Interesting Account,* 64–66.

46. Ibid.

47. Ibid.

48. Ibid.

49. Ibid.

50. Darnell, *An Accurate and Interesting Account,* 66–67.

51. McAfee, *History of the Late War,* 246.

52. Isaac Shelby, letter to William H. Harrison, February 9, 1813, Letter Book A, Page 41–42, Governor Isaac Shelby Papers, Kentucky Department for Libraries and Archives (Frankfort, KY).

53. Richardson, *Operation of the Right Wing*, 83–84.

54. Ibid., 82–83.

55. Ibid., 80–81.

56. Antal, 72.

57. Ibid., 178.

58. Ibid., 179.

59. Ibid., 175–176.

60. Ibid., 178.

61. McAfee, *History of the Late War*, 247.

62. Remini, *Henry Clay*, 101–102.

63. *Kentucky Gazette*, September 8, 1812.

CHAPTER SIX: SAVING FORT MEIGS

1. McAfee, *History of the Late War*, 251–252.

2. Ibid., 252.

3. B. Parke, to Isaac Shelby, March 19, 1813, folder 73, box 4, Governor Isaac Shelby Papers, Kentucky Department for Libraries and Archives (Frankfort, KY).

4. Theophilus Skinner, to Isaac Shelby, June 4, 1813, Letter Book B, Page 25, Governor Isaac Shelby Papers, Kentucky Department for Libraries and Archives (Frankfort, KY).

5. William Russell, letter to Isaac Shelby, April 11, 1813, folder 74, box 4, Governor Isaac Shelby Papers, Kentucky Department for Libraries and Archives (Frankfort, KY).

6. McAfee, *History of the Late War*, 253.

7. Larry Nelson, "Dudley's Defeat and the Relief of Fort Meigs during the War of 1812," *Register of the Kentucky Historical Society* 104, (2006): 9.

8. McAfee, *History of the Late War*, 256.

9. Ibid., 257.

10. Isaac Shelby, letter to James Taylor, March 24, 1813, Letter Book A, Page 69, Governor Isaac Shelby Papers, Kentucky Department for Libraries and Archives (Frankfort, KY).

11. Captain Peter Dudley Company Order Book, 1813, May 6,1813, SC762, Kentucky Historical Society (Frankfort, KY) 12.

12. Isaac Shelby, to Secretary of War, March 20, 1813, Letter Book A, page 59–60, Governor Isaac Shelby Papers, Kentucky Department for Libraries and Archives (Frankfort, KY).

13. Ibid.

14. Isaac Shelby, to Secretary of War, March 20, 1813, Letter Book A, page 61, Governor Isaac Shelby Papers, Kentucky Department for Libraries and Archives (Frankfort, KY).

15. Ibid., 62.

16. Quisenberry, *Kentucky in the War,* 34.

17. William Henry Harrison, to R.J. Meigs, April 28, 1813, Letter Book B, Page 23, Governor Isaac Shelby Papers, Kentucky Department for Libraries and Archives (Frankfort, KY).

18. Ibid.

19. McAfee, *History of the Late War*, 260–261.

20. Ibid., 263.

21. John B. Campbell, to Isaac Shelby, May 7, 1813, Letter Book B, Page 19, Governor Isaac Shelby Papers, Kentucky Department for Libraries and Archives (Frankfort, KY).

22. Quisenberry, *Kentucky in the War,* 54–55.

23. Ibid., 55–56.
24. Quisenberry, *Kentucky in the War*, 57.
25. Ibid.
26. Antal, 225.
27. Quisenberry, *Kentucky in the War*, 57.
28. Ibid., 58–59.
29. *Kentucky Gazette*, June 1, 1813.
30. *Kentucky Gazette*, May 18, 1813.
31. McAfee, *History of the Late War*, 274.
32. John B. Campbell, letter to Isaac Shelby, May 7, 1813, Letter Book B, page 20, Governor Isaac Shelby Papers, Kentucky Department for Libraries and Archives, (Frankfort, KY).
33. Captain Peter Dudley, May 9, 1813, Captain Peter Dudley Order Book, 19-20, SC 762, Kentucky Historical Society (Frankfort, KY).
34. McAfee, *History of the Late War*, 276–277.
35. Quisenberry, *Kentucky in the War,* 58–59.
36. McAfee, *History of the Late War*, 278.
37. Isaac Shelby, letter to Henry Clay, May 16, 1813, 67M213 Special Collections, University of Kentucky (Lexington, KY).
38. Ibid.
39. Ibid.
40. Ibid.
41. Ibid.
42. Ibid.
43. Ibid.
44. *Kentucky Gazette*, June 1, 1813.
45. *Kentucky Gazette*, May 18, 1813.
46. Joshua Bartlett, letter to Isaac Shelby, March 1, 2013, folder 73, box 4, Governor Isaac Shelby Papers, Kentucky Department for Libraries and Archives, (Frankfort, KY).
47. William H. Harrison, letter to Isaac Shelby, June 20, 1813, Letter Book B, Page 26, Governor Isaac Shelby Papers, Kentucky Department for Libraries and Archives (Frankfort, KY).
48. Ibid.
49. McAfee, *History of the Late War*, 318–319.
50. Ibid., 320–321.
51. Ibid., 322.
52. *Kentucky Gazette*, September 7, 1813.
53. McAfee, *History of the Late War*, 324–325.
54. Ibid.
55. Ibid.
56. McAfee, *History of the Late War*, 326–327.
57. Ibid.
58. Ibid.
59. David Curtis Skaggs, *Encyclopedia of the War of 1812*, "Fort Stephenson" (Santa Barbara: ABC-CLIO, 1997).
60. Ibid., *War*, 328–329.
61. Richardson, *Operation of the Right Wing*, 95.

62. Ibid., 108.

CHAPTER SEVEN: VICTORY AT THE THAMES

1. McAfee, *History of the Late War*, 336.
2. Shelby Circular to Regimental Commanders, July 31, folder 74, box 4, Governor Isaac Shelby Papers, Kentucky Department for Libraries and Archives (Frankfort, KY).
3. Isaac Shelby, letter to William H. Harrison, Letter Book A, Page 9, Governor Isaac Shelby Papers, Kentucky Department for Libraries and Archives (Frankfort, KY).
4. James Harlan, letter to Isaac Shelby, August 10, 1813, folder 75, box 4, Governor Isaac Shelby Papers, Kentucky Department for Libraries and Archives (Frankfort, KY).
5. H. Anderson, letter to Isaac Shelby, August 11, 1813, folder 76, box 4, Governor Isaac Shelby Papers, Kentucky Department for Libraries and Archives (Frankfort, KY).
6. Young Ewing, letter to Isaac Shelby, August 13, 1813, folder 76, box 4, Governor Isaac Shelby Papers, Kentucky Department for Libraries and Archives (Frankfort, KY).
7. Isaac Shelby, letter to William Henry Harrison, August 11, 1813, Letter Book A Page 151, Governor Isaac Shelby Papers, Kentucky Department for Libraries and Archives (Frankfort, KY).
8. Joshua Bartlett, letter to Isaac Shelby, August 15, 1813, folder 76, box 4, Governor Isaac Shelby Papers, Kentucky Department for Libraries and Archives (Frankfort, KY).
9. Richardson, *Operation of the Right Wing*, 114.
10. James Simrall, letter to Rebecca Simrall, September 26, 1813, Simrall family papers A S613, Filson Historical Society, Louisville, KY.
11. D. Trimble, letter to Isaac Shelby, August 18, 1813, Letter Book B, Page 115, Governor Isaac Shelby Papers, Kentucky Department for Libraries and Archives (Frankfort, KY).
12. Isaac Shelby, letter to Son, August 6, 1813, UK Special Collections Isaac Shelby Papers, 1765–1911, 68M105, Special Collections, University of Kentucky, Lexington KY.
13. Ibid.
14. Ibid.
15. Shelby to Tommy Shelby June 17, 1813, UK Special Collections Isaac Shelby Papers, 1765–1911, 68M105, Special Collections, University of Kentucky, Lexington KY.
16. Isaac Shelby, letter to Presley Gray and William Mitchison August 30, 1813, Letter Book A, Page 155, Governor Isaac Shelby Papers, Kentucky Department for Libraries and Archives (Frankfort, KY).
17. Isaac Shelby, letter to George Walker, August 25, 1813, Letter Book A, Page 147, Governor Isaac Shelby Papers, Kentucky Department for Libraries and Archives (Frankfort, KY).
18. Isaac Shelby, letter to William H. Harrison, August 1, 1813, Letter Book B, page 108, Governor Isaac Shelby Papers, Kentucky Department for Libraries and Archives (Frankfort, KY).
19. Isaac Shelby, letter to Ephraim McDowell, September 10, 1813, Isaac Shelby Papers, 1765–1911, 1F62M-590, Special Collections, University of Kentucky.
20. Ibid.
21. Ibid.
22. Ibid., 74.
23. McAfee, *History of the Late War*, 354.
24. Borneman, 132–133.
25. Richardson, *Operation of the Right Wing*, 119.

26. Quisenberry, *Kentucky* in the War, 89.

27. McAfee, *History of the Late War*, 363–364.

28. Ibid.

29. James Simrall, letter to Rebecca Simrall, September 26, 1813, Simrall family papers A S613, Filson Historical Society, Louisville, KY.

30. James Simrall, letter to Rebecca Simrall, September 20, 1813, Simrall family papers A S613, Filson Historical Society, Louisville, KY.

31. Richardson, *Operation of the Right Wing*, 119.

32. Ibid.

33. Ibid., 120.

34. Ibid.

35. McAfee, *History of the Late War*, 364–365.

36. Turner, letter to Isaac Shelby, September 24, 1813, folder 81, box 5, Governor Isaac Shelby Papers, Kentucky Department for Libraries and Archives (Frankfort, KY).

37. McAfee, *History of the Late War*, 382.

38. Quisenberry, *Kentucky in the War*, 102.

39. McAfee, *History of the Late War*, 376–377.

40. Ibid., 370.

41. Ibid., 374–375.

42. Ibid., 380.

43. McAfee, *History of the Late War*, 376–377.

44. Ibid., 381.

45. Ibid., 372.

46. Ibid., 382.

47. Ibid., 386.

48. Ibid., 386–387.

49. Bennett H. Young, *The Battle of the Thames in Which Kentuckians Defeated the British, French, and Indians, October 5, 1813* (Louisville: John P. Morton and Company, 1903), 62.

50. McAfee, *History of the Late War*, 388–389.

51. Young, *Battle of the Thames*, 73.

52. McAfee, *History of the Late War*, 392.

53. Young, *Battle of the Thames*, 76.

54. McAfee, *History of the Late War*, 392.

55. Young, *Battle of the Thames*, 84.

56. McAfee, *History of the Late War*, 392.

57. Ibid., 394.

58. Quisenberry, *Kentucky in the War*, 96.

59. James Simrall, letter to Rebecca Simrall, October 8, 1813, Simrall family papers A S613, Filson Historical Society, Louisville, KY.

60. McAfee, *History of the Late War*, 400.

61. Quisenberry, *Kentucky in the War*, 44.

62. McAfee, *History of the Late War*, 400.

63. Quisenberry, *Kentucky in the War*, 98.

64. McAfee, *History of the Late War*, 400.

65. Antal, 358.

66. Ibid., 236.

67. Hickey, 309.

68. Hickey, 309.

CHAPTER EIGHT: FIRE AND FEDERALISTS

1. Isaac Shelby, letter to Secretary of War, November 19, 1813, Letter Book A, page 158, Governor Isaac Shelby Papers, Kentucky Department for Libraries and Archives (Frankfort, KY).
2. Robert McAfee, Mss. A M113 4 "Company Memorandum Book & Journal of Robt B McAfee's Mounted Company in Col Rh. M. Johnson's Regiment, Filson Historical Society (Louisville, KY), 146.
3. William Duval, to Andrew Hynes, November 28, 1813, 2011MS098:1:6, Special Collections Library, University of Kentucky, Lexington, KY.
4. William Duval, to Andrew Hynes, January 5, 1814, 2011MS098:1:6, Special Collections Library, University of Kentucky, Lexington, KY.
5. Secretary of War, to Isaac Shelby, August 21, 1813, Letter Book B, page 30, Governor Isaac Shelby Papers, Kentucky Department for Libraries and Archives (Frankfort, KY).
6. Isaac Shelby, letter to William Boswell, May 5, 1814, Letter Book A, page 187, Governor Isaac Shelby Papers, Kentucky Department for Libraries and Archives (Frankfort, KY).
7. Benjamin Geale, to Piers Geale, John Mason Papers, A281 Box 1, Gunston Hall Plantation, (Mason Neck, VA), Geale was ultimately released with the other prisoners in 1814.
8. Committee, to Isaac Shelby November 30, 1813, Letter Book B, page 35, Governor Isaac Shelby Papers, Kentucky Department for Libraries and Archives (Frankfort, KY).
9. M.D. Hardin, to Isaac Shelby, December 6, 1813, Letter Book B, page 38, Governor Isaac Shelby Papers, Kentucky Department for Libraries and Archives (Frankfort, KY).
10. Isaac Shelby, to Secretary of War, August 13, 1814, Letter Book A, page 194, Governor Isaac Shelby Papers, Kentucky Department for Libraries and Archives (Frankfort, KY).
11. Committee, to Isaac Shelby, November 30, 1813, Letter Book B, page 35, Governor Isaac Shelby Papers, Kentucky Department for Libraries and Archives (Frankfort, KY).
12. Isaac Shelby, to William H. Harrison, January 25, 1814, Letter Book A, page 174, Governor Isaac Shelby Papers, Kentucky Department for Libraries and Archives (Frankfort, KY).
13. Isaac Shelby, to President and Directors of the Bank of Kentucky, December 25, 1813, Letter Book A, page 171, Governor Isaac Shelby Papers, Kentucky Department for Libraries and Archives (Frankfort, KY).
14. Isaac Shelby, resolution from legislature to Kentucky representatives in Congress, January 18, 1814, Letter Book A, page 175, Governor Isaac Shelby Papers, Kentucky Department for Libraries and Archives (Frankfort, KY).
15. Jonathon Ramsey, to Isaac Shelby, July 26, 1814, folder 83, box 5, Governor Isaac Shelby Papers, Kentucky Department for Libraries and Archives (Frankfort, KY).
16. James Elder, to Isaac Shelby, August 22, 1814, folder 83, box 5, Governor Isaac Shelby Papers, Kentucky Department for Libraries and Archives (Frankfort, KY).
17. Isaac Shelby, to Secretary of War, August 3, 1814, Letter Book A, page 189, Governor Isaac Shelby Papers, Kentucky Department for Libraries and Archives (Frankfort, KY).
18. Isaac Shelby, to William H. Harrison, August 8, 1813, Letter Book A, page 141, Governor Isaac Shelby Papers, Kentucky Department for Libraries and Archives (Frank-

fort, KY).

19. Ibid.

20. Mahon, *War of 1812*, 375–377.

21. Ibid. Johnathon Russell is not mentioned in Mahon but served as the fifth negotiator.

22. Henry Clay, to Secretary of War, December 14, 1813, MSS CC, Filson Historical Society (Louisville, KY).

23. *Kentucky Gazette,* January 31, 1814.

24. *Kentucky Gazette,* August 29, 1814.

25. Calvin Colton, ed. *The Private Correspondence of Henry Clay* (New York: A.S. Barnes, 1856), 28.

26. Ibid.

27. *Kentucky Gazette*, December 12, 1814.

28. Ibid.

29. Mahon, *War of 1812*, 294.

30. *Kentucky Gazette*, September 26, 1814.

31. Mahon, *War of 1812*, 294–295

32. Ibid., 298.

33. Ibid., 300–301.

34. Mahon, *War of 1812*, 310.

35. Ibid.

36. *Kentucky Gazette*, September 12, 1814.

37. *Kentucky Gazette*, September 26, 1814.

38. Mahon, *War of 1812*, 378–379.

39. *Kentucky Gazette*, December 26, 1814.

40. Ibid.

41. Duncan McArthur, to Isaac Shelby, July 30, 1814, Letter Book B, page 50, Governor Isaac Shelby Papers, Kentucky Department for Libraries and Archives (Frankfort, KY).

42. Isaac Shelby, to Secretary of War, August 13, 1814, Governor Isaac Shelby Letter Book A, Page 194, Kentucky Department for Libraries and Archives (Frankfort, KY).

43. Sam Hopkins, to Isaac Shelby, August 22, 1814, folder 90, box 5, Governor Isaac Shelby Papers, Kentucky Department for Libraries and Archives (Frankfort, KY).

44. James Allen, to Isaac Shelby, August 23, 1814, folder 83, box 5, Governor Isaac Shelby Papers, Kentucky Department for Libraries and Archives (Frankfort, KY).

45. Quisenberry, *Kentucky in the War*, 112–113.

46. Ibid., 115.

47. Ibid., 117.

48. Ennis Duncan, to Hester Duncan, September 17, 1814, SC87, Ennis Duncan Papers, 1814, 1815, n.d., Kentucky Historical Society (Frankfort, KY).

49. Ennis Duncan, to Hester Duncan, September 28, 1814, SC87, Ennis Duncan Papers, 1814, 1815, n.d., Kentucky Historical Society (Frankfort, KY).

50. Ennis Duncan, to Hester Duncan, October 25, 1814, SC87, Ennis Duncan Papers, 1814, 1815, n.d., Kentucky Historical Society (Frankfort, KY).

51. Ennis Duncan, to Hester Duncan, January 13, 1815, SC87, Ennis Duncan Papers, 1814, 1815, n.d., Kentucky Historical Society (Frankfort, KY).

52. Hester Duncan, to Ennis Duncan, January 5, 1815, n.d., Kentucky Historical Society (Frankfort, KY).

53. Ennis Duncan, letter to Hester Duncan, SC87, Ennis Duncan Papers, 1814, 1815,

January 11, 1815, Kentucky Historical Society (Frankfort, KY).

54. Ibid.

CHAPTER NINE: NEW ORLEANS

1. *1814 Journal of the Kentucky Senate*, State Publications, Kentucky Department for Libraries and Archives (Frankfort, KY), 77-82.

2. *1814 Journal of the Kentucky House of Representatives*, State Publications, Kentucky Department for Libraries and Archives (Frankfort, KY), 18.

3. Isaac Shelby, letter to Secretary of War, November 6, 1814, Letter Book A, Page 213, Governor Isaac Shelby Papers, Kentucky Department for Libraries and Archives (Frankfort, KY).

4. Many histories attribute this act of personal sacrifice to James Taylor of Newport who had served as quartermaster general under Hull. However, this is in error.

5. Ibid.

6. Lowell H. Harrison and James C. Klotter, *A New History of Kentucky* (Lexington: University Press of Kentucky, 1997), 93.

7. Isaac Shelby, to Secretary of War, October 19, 1814, Letter Book A, Page 208, Governor Isaac Shelby Papers, Kentucky Department for Libraries and Archives (Frankfort, KY).

8. Isaac Shelby, to George Trotter, October 19, 1814, Letter Book B, Page 120, Governor Isaac Shelby Papers, Kentucky Department for Libraries and Archives (Frankfort, KY).

9. Abraham Hite, to Isaac Shelby, October 26, 1814, folder 84, box 5, Governor Isaac Shelby Papers, Kentucky Department for Libraries and Archives (Frankfort, KY).

10. Thomas Dudley, to Isaac Shelby, November 4, 1814, folder 84, box 4, Governor Isaac Shelby Papers, Kentucky Department for Libraries and Archives (Frankfort, KY).

11. Isaac Shelby, to Commanding Officer at Vincennes, November 8, 1814, Letter Book B, Page 130, Governor Isaac Shelby Papers, Kentucky Department for Libraries and Archives (Frankfort, KY).

12. James Bryson, to Isaac Shelby, November 21, 1814, folder 84, box 5, Governor Isaac Shelby Papers, Kentucky Department for Libraries and Archives (Frankfort, KY).

13. Quisenberry, *Kentucky in the War*, 134.

14. *Kentucky Gazette*, January 9, 1815.

15. *Kentucky Gazette*, February 20, 1815.

16. Quisenberry, *Kentucky in the War*, 139.

17. *Kentucky Gazette*, January 30, 1815.

18. *Kentucky Gazette*, February 20, 1815.

19. *Kentucky Gazette*, January 30, 1815

20. John Adair, to Andrew Jackson, March 20, 1815, *Letters of General Adair and General Jackson: Relative to the Charge of Cowardice Made by the Latter Against the Kentucky Troops at New Orleans*, 3. Filson Historical Society, Louisville, KY.

21. *Kentucky Gazette*, January 30, 1815.

22. Ibid.

23. Ibid.

24. *Kentucky Gazette*, February 20, 1815.

25. *Kentucky Gazette*, January 30, 1815.

26. Lowell H. Harrison and James C. Klotter, *A New History of Kentucky* (Lexington: University Press of Kentucky, 1997), 94.

27. Mahon, *War of 1812*, 368.

28. *Kentucky Gazette*, January 30, 1815.

29. Ibid.

30. *Kentucky Gazette*, January 30, 1815.

31. Most other sources maintain that the Kentucky militia arrived on the fourth of January.

32. Ibid.

33. Ibid.

34. Ibid.

35. *Kentucky Gazette*, February 20, 1815.

36. John Adair, to Andrew Jackson, March 20, 1815, Rare Pamphlet 973.5239 A191 1816, *Letters of General Adair and General Jackson: Relative to the Charge of Cowardice Made by the Latter Against the Kentucky Troops at New Orleans*, Filson Historical Society (Louisville, KY), 1.

37. Ibid.,1–2.

38. Adair seems to contradict himself in stating that around 400 men crossed the river but then referring to only 175 as being present at the attack. It is probably that these men represented the armed portion of Davis' men.

39. Ibid., 2.

40. Ibid.

41. Ibid.,1–2.

42. Ibid.

43. Ibid., 3.

44. Ibid.

45. Ibid.,1–2.

46. Sentence of the Court of Inquiry, February 19, 1815, *Letters of General Adair and General Jackson*, 37.

47. Andrew Jackson, letter to John Adair, July 23, 1817, *Letters of General Adair and General Jackson*, 7.

48. Ibid., 8.

49. John Adair, to Andrew Jackson, October 21, 1817, *Letters of General Adair and General Jackson*, 15.

50. Ibid., 16.

51. *1815 Journal of the Kentucky Senate*, State Publications, Kentucky Department for Libraries and Archives, (Frankfort, KY), 303.

CHAPTER TEN: PEACE AT LAST

1. Secretary of War, to Isaac Shelby, January 30, 1815, Letter Book B, Page 54–56, Governor Isaac Shelby Papers, Kentucky Department for Libraries and Archives, (Frankfort, KY).

2. John Francisco, to Isaac Shelby, January 21, 1815, folder 86, box 5, Governor Isaac Shelby Papers, Kentucky Department for Libraries and Archives (Frankfort, KY).

3. George Trotter, to Isaac Shelby, February 10, 1815, folder 87, box 5, Governor Isaac Shelby Papers, Kentucky Department for Libraries and Archives (Frankfort, KY).

4. Circular, January 25, 1813, folder 86, box 5, Governor Isaac Shelby Papers, Kentucky Department for Libraries and Archives (Frankfort, KY).

5. *Kentucky Gazette*, January 9, 1815.

6. Samuel McDowell, letter to unknown, November 22, 1814, Mss. C M, Samuel McDowell Letters, 1783–1814, Special Collections, Filson Historical Society (Louisville,

KY).

7. John Thomas, to Isaac Shelby, February 10, 1815, folder 87, box 5, Governor Isaac Shelby Papers, Kentucky Department for Libraries and Archives, (Frankfort, KY).

8. Secretary of War, to Isaac Shelby, February 13, 1815, Letter Book B, Page 67–68, Governor Isaac Shelby Papers, Kentucky Department for Libraries and Archives (Frankfort, KY).

9. Peter Voorhies, to Isaac Shelby, February 14, 1815, folder 87, box 5, Governor Isaac Shelby Papers, Kentucky Department for Libraries and Archives (Frankfort, KY).

10. Remini, *Henry Clay*, 113.

11. Mahon, *War of 1812*, 380.

12. Quisenberry, *Kentucky in the War*, 123.

13. Ibid.

14. "Treaty of Peace and Amity between His Britannic Majesty and the United States of America." NARA [Online version, http://ourdocuments.gov/doc.php?flash=true&doc =20&page=transcript, National Archives and Records Administration, August 14, 2015.]

15. Ibid.

16. *1815 Journal of the Senate*, December 13, 1815, State Publications, Kentucky Department for Libraries and Archives (Frankfort, KY), 60.

17. Ibid., 61–62.

18. Isaac Shelby, to the Federal Government, February 8, 1817, Isaac Shelby Papers, 1765–1911, 1F62M-590, Special Collections, University of Kentucky (Lexington, KY).

19. *Kentucky Gazette*, August 19, 1816.

20. Ibid.

21. *1815 Journal of the Senate*, December 13, 1815, 111.

22. Quisenberry, *Kentucky in the War*, 70.

23. Ibid., 45.

24. Ibid., 46–47.

25. "River Raisin Battlefield," as of August 14, 2015, http://www.riverraisinbattlefield. org.

26. Quisenberry, *Kentucky in the War*, 93.

27. Ibid., 152–153.

28. Hickey, 6 and 11.

29. Hickey, 314–315.

30. Cleaves, *Old Tippecanoe*, 336 and 342.

31. Malcolm Muir Jr., *Encyclopedia of the War of 1812*, "William Hull" (Santa Barbara: ABC-CLIO, 1997).

32. *Kentucky Encyclopedia*, "Richard Mentor Johnson" (Lexington: University Press of Kentucky, 1992).

33. *Kentucky Gazette*, May 8, 1818.

34. Melba Porter Hay, *Kentucky Encyclopedia*, "Henry Clay" (Lexington: University Press of Kentucky, 1992).

35. *Kentucky's Governors*, ed. Lowell H. Harrison (Lexington: University Press of Kentucky, 1985), 21.

36. Ward, *Charles Scott*, 195.

37. Richardson, *Operation of the Right Wing*, 127.

38. Sandor Antal, *Encyclopedia of the War of 1812*, "Henry Procter" (Santa Barbara: ABC-CLIO, 1997).

39. R. David Edmunds, *Tecumseh and the Quest for Indian Leadership*, (New York: Pearson

Longman, 2007), 207.

40. Phippant, to Isaac Shelby, November 16 1818, Isaac Shelby Papers 1765–1911, 1F62M-590, Special Collections, University of Kentucky (Lexington, KY).

41. Robert Pierce Forbes, *The Missouri Compromise and Its Aftermath: Slavery and the Meaning of America* (Chapel Hill: University of North Carolina Press, 2007), 24.

42. Isaac Shelby to Jackson, June 27, 1818, MSS 11 DD 58, Special Collections Library, University of Kentucky (Lexington, KY).

43. Isaac Shelby to Jackson (Undated) Draper MSS 11 DD 70, Special Collections Library, University of Kentucky (Lexington, KY).

44. Isaac Shelby and Jackson to the Chickasaw Nation, Isaac Shelby Papers 1765–1911, 1F62M-590, Special Collections Library, University of Kentucky (Lexington, KY).

45. Isaac Shelby and Jackson to the Chickasaw Nation, Isaac Shelby Papers 1765–1911, 1F62M-590, Special Collections Library, University of Kentucky (Lexington, KY).

46. *Kentucky Gazette*, July 28, 1826.

47. "Governor Isaac Shelby," *Register of the Kentucky Historical Society* 2, (1903): 11–12.

48. *Kentucky Gazette*, August 25, 1826.

49. *1826 Acts*, January 17, 1827, 196.

BIBLIOGRAPHY

ARCHIVAL MATERIALS

Allen-Butler Family Papers, 55M54:1:2. University of Kentucky Special Collections, Lexington, KY.

Beall, William K., Journal. 1812, 97SC134. Kentucky Historical Society, Frankfort, KY.

Benjamin Graves, Major Benjamin Graves Order Book, 1812. SC 1056, Kentucky Historical Society, Frankfort KY.

Dudley, Peter. Company Order Book, 1813. SC762, Kentucky Historical Society, Frankfort, KY.

Duval, William. Papers. 2011MS098, Special Collections, University of Kentucky, Lexington, KY.

Ennis Duncan Papers, 1814–1815. SC87, Kentucky Historical Society, Frankfort, KY.

Geale, Benjamin, to Piers Geale, John Mason Papers, A281 Box 1, Gunston Hall Plantation, Mason Neck, VA.

Governor Charles Scott Papers, 1808–1812. Kentucky Department for Libraries and Archives, Frankfort, KY.

Governor Isaac Shelby Papers, Letter Book A, Kentucky Department for Libraries and Archives, Frankfort, KY.

Governor Isaac Shelby Papers, Letter Book B, Kentucky Department for Libraries and Archives, Frankfort, KY.

Isaac Shelby, letter to Henry Clay, May 16, 1813, 67M213. Special Collections, University of Kentucky, Lexington, KY.

Isaac Shelby: Miscellaneous Papers, 1786–1819, Mss. A S544. Filson Historical Society, Louisville, KY.

James Taylor Papers. Mss8, Kentucky Historical Society, Frankfort, KY.

Sam Hopkins Papers, 1796–1823. SC140, Kentucky Historical Society, Frankfort, KY.

Samuel McDowell Letters, 1783–1814. Mss C.M. Filson Historical Society, Louisville, KY.

Shelby, Isaac. Isaac Shelby Papers, 1765–1911. 1F62M-590, Special Collections, University of Kentucky, Lexington KY.

Shelby, Isaac. Governor Isaac Shelby Papers, 1812–1816. Kentucky Department for Libraries and Archives, Frankfort, KY.

Simrall Family Papers. A S613, Filson Historical Society, Louisville, KY.

Skaggs, David Curtis. *Encyclopedia of the War of 1812*, "Fort Stephenson" (Santa Barbara: ABC-CLIO, 1997).

Letters of General Adair and General Jackson: Relative to the Charge of Cowardice Made by the Latter Against the Kentucky Troops at New Orleans. Filson Historical Society, Louisville, KY.

Robert McAfee, Mss. A M113 4 Company Memorandum Book & Journal of Robt B McAfee's Mounted Company in Col Rh. M. Johnson's Regiment, Filson Historical Society, Louisville, KY.

Isaac Shelby Papers, 1865–1911. 1F62M-590 (Microfilm) Special Collections, University of Kentucky, Lexington, KY.

Shelby, Isaac, to Andrew Jackson. n.d. Draper MSS 11 DD 70 (Microfilm) Special Collections, University of Kentucky, Lexington, KY.

Taylor, James. Reminiscences, 1846, Mss. A T243k, Filson Historical Society, Louisville, KY.

Todd, Robert S. Regimental Orders, May 8, 1811, 2012MS018, Special Collections, University of Kentucky, Lexington, KY.

GOVERNMENT PUBLICATIONS

Acts of the Kentucky General Assembly, 1810–1817; 1826, State Publications, Kentucky Department for Libraries and Archives, (Frankfort, KY).

Journal of the House of Representatives, 1811–1815, State Publications, Kentucky Department for Libraries and Archives, (Frankfort, KY).

Senate Journals , 1811–1815, State Publications, Kentucky Department for Libraries and Archives, (Frankfort, KY).

BOOKS

Allison, Harold. *The Tragic Saga of the Indiana Indians*. Washington: Graphic Design of Indiana, 1987.

Antal, Sandor. *Encyclopedia of the War of 1812*, "Henry Procter." Santa Barbara: ABC-CLIO, 1997.

Antal, Sandy. *A Wampum Denied: Procter's War of 1812*. Ontario: Carleton University Press, 1997.

Borneman, Walter R. *1812: The War that Forged a Nation.* New York: HarperCollins, 2004.

Brant, Irving. *The Fourth President: A Life of James Madison.* Norwalk: Eastern Press, 1970.

Chinn, George Morgan. *Kentucky: Settlement and Statehood: 1750–1800.* Frankfort: Kentucky Historical Society, 1975.

Clark, Thomas. *A History of Kentucky.* 1937. Reprint, Ashland: Jesse Stuart Foundation, 1992.

Cleaves, Freeman. *Old Tippecanoe: William Henry Harrison and His Time.* 1939. Reprint, Newtown: American Political Biography Press, 1990.

Clift, G. Glenn. *Remember the Raisin! Kentucky and Kentuckians in the Battles and Massacre at Frenchtown, Michigan Territory, in the War of 1812.* Frankfort: Kentucky Historical Society, 1961.

Colton, Calvin, ed. *The Private Correspondence of Henry Clay.* New York: A.S. Barnes, 1856.

Darnell, Elias, John Davenport, and Timothy Mallary. *A Journal Containing an Accurate and Interesting Account of the Hardships, Sufferings, Battles, Defeat and Captivity of Those Heroic Kentucky Volunteers.* 1813. Reprint, Berea: O. Rucker, 1970.

Edmunds, R. David. *Tecumseh and the Quest for Indian Leadership.* New York: Pearson Longman, 2007.

Elting, John R. *Amateurs to Arms!: A Military History of the War of 1812.* Boston: De Capo Press, 1995.

Esarey, Logan. ed. *Governor's Messages and Letters Volume 2.* Indianapolis: Indiana Historical Society, 1922.

Forbes, Robert Pierce. *The Missouri Compromise and Its Aftermath: Slavery and the Meaning of America.* Chapel Hill: University of North Carollina Press, 2007.

Forgy, John. *Kentucky Encyclopedia,* "Zachary Taylor." Lexington: University Press of Kentucky, 1992.

Hammack, James W. Jr., *Kentucky Encyclopedia,* "Samuel Hopkins." Lexington: University Press of Kentucky, 1992.

Hammack, James Wallace Jr. *Kentucky & the Second American Revolution: The War of 1812.* Lexington: University Press of Kentucky, 1976.

Harrison, Lowell H. ed. *Kentucky's Governors.* Lexington: University Press of Kentucky, 1985.

Harrison, Lowell H. and James C. Klotter, *A New History of Kentucky.* Lexington: University Press of Kentucky, 1997.

Hay, Melba Porter. *Kentucky Encyclopedia*, "Henry Clay." Lexington: University Press of Kentucky, 1992.

Hickey, Donald R. *The War of 1812: A Forgotten Conflict*. Champaign: University of Illinois Press, 2012.

Kaufmann, J.E. and H.W. Kaufmann. *Fortress America: The Forts that Defended America, 1600 to the Present*. Cambridge: De Capo Press, 2004.

Kentucky Encyclopedia, "Richard Mentor Johnson." Lexington: University Press of Kentucky, 1992.

Kramer, Carl. *Capital on the Kentucky: A Two Hundred Year History of Frankfort and Franklin* County. Frankfort: Historic Frankfort, 1986.

Langguth, A.J. *Union 1812: The Americans Who Fought the Second War of Independence*. New York: Simon & Schuster, 2007.

Mahon, John. *The War of 1812*. Cambridge: DeCapo Press, 1991.

Malinowski, Sharon, Anna Sheets, and Linda Schmittroth, ed. *UXL Encyclopedia of Native American Tribes, Volume 1*. Detroit: UXL, 1999.

McAfee, Robert Breckinridge. *History of the Late War in the Western Country*. 1816; Reprint, Ann Arbor: University Microfilms, Inc., 1966.

Muir, Malcolm Jr. *Encyclopedia of the War of 1812*, "William Hull." Santa Barbara: ABC-CLIO, 1997.

Quisenberry, Anderson Chenault. *Kentucky in the War of 1812*. Frankfort: Kentucky State Historical Society, 1915.

Remini, Robert V. *Henry Clay: Statesman for the Union*. New York: W.W. Norton & Co., 1991.

Richardson, K.S.F. *War of 1812: Containing A Full and Detailed Narrative of the Operations of the Right Division of the Canadian Army*. N.P., 1842.

Risjord, Norman K. *Jefferson's America: 1760-1815*. Lanham: Rowman & Littlefield, 2002.

Sugden, John. *Tecumseh: A Life*. New York: Henry Holt, 1997.

Taylor, Alan. *The Civil War of 1812: American Citizens, British Subjects, Irish Rebels & Indian Allies*. New York: Vintage Books, 2010.

Turner, Wesley B. *Encyclopedia of the War of 1812*, "Isaac Brock." Santa Barbara: ABC-CLIO, 1997.

Ward, Harry M. *Charles R. Scott and the "Spirit of '76."* Charlottesville: University Press of Virginia, 1988.

Wood, William. ed. *Select British Documents of the Canadian War of 1812*. Toronto: Champlain Society, 1920.

Wrobel, Sylvia, and George Grider, *Isaac Shelby: Kentucky's First Governor and Hero of Three Wars*. Danville: Cumberland Press, 1974.

Young, Bennett H. *The Battle of the Thames in Which Kentuckians Defeated the British, French, and Indians, October 5, 1813*. Louisville: John P. Morton and Company, 1903.

NEWSPAPERS

Kentucky Gazette, Frankfort, KY. January 30, 1800; 1812–1815; 1818; 1826.

Liberty Hall, Cincinnati, OH. 1812–1813.

JOURNAL ARTICLES

Clift, G. Glen, ed. "War of 1812 Diary of William B. Northcutt," *Register of the Kentucky Historical Society* 56, No. 2 (1958): 165–181.

Clift, G. Glen, ed. "War of 1812 Diary of William B. Northcutt," *Register of the Kentucky Historical Society* 56, No. 3 (1958): 253–269.

Clift, G. Glen, ed. "War of 1812 Diary of William B. Northcutt," *Register of the Kentucky Historical Society* 56, No. 4 (1958): 325–343.

"Governor Isaac Shelby," *Register of the Kentucky Historical Society* 1, No. 2 (1903): 9–12.

Hall, Ellery L. "Canadian Annexation Sentiment in Kentucky Prior to the War of 1812," *Register of the Kentucky Historical Society* 28 (1930): 372-380.

Harris, James Russell. "Kentuckians in the War of 1812: A Note on Numbers, Losses, and Sources," *Register of the Kentucky Historical Society* 82 No. 3 (1984): 227–286.

Quisenberry, A.C. "Kentucky Troops in the War of 1812," *Register of the Kentucky Historical Society* 10, No. 30 (1912): 47–66.

Quisenberry, A.C. "Kentucky Regulars in the War of 1812," *Register of the Kentucky Historical Society* 12 No. 34 (1914): 13–27.

WEBSITES

U.S. Census Bureau. "United States Resident Population by State: 1790–1850," http://lwd.dol.state.nj.us/labor/lpa/census/1990/pop-trd1.htm.

"River Raisin Battlefield," as of August 14, 2015, http://www.riverraisinbattlefield.org.

"Treaty of Peace and Amity between His Britannic Majesty and the United States of America." NARA [Online version, http://ourdocuments.gov/doc.php?flash=true&doc=20&page=transcript, National Archives and Records Administration, August 14, 2015.

ACKNOWLEDGMENTS

THIS PROJECT began so long ago that it is difficult to recall its exact origin or all of the parties who have played a part along the way. However, there are several people whose knowledge and advice were key to this book reaching completion. At the Kentucky Department for Libraries and Archives, I constantly tapped Research Room Supervisor, Walter Bowman's knowledge of nineteenth-century politics and militia practices. His comprehensive understanding of the nuances of life as it was more than two centuries ago provided context for understanding many of the actions and beliefs expressed by the men and women in this book. Likewise, Archival Services Branch Manager Jennifer Patterson's vast knowledge of archival holdings at the state level provided helpful suggestions on what records still existed and what would be relevant to my research.

Numerous staff members at the Kentucky Historical Society's Research Library were helpful in locating and providing me with access, as well as copies, of invaluable manuscripts and journals in their possession. Matt Harris and the staff at the University of Kentucky's Special Collections were also generous with their time and their materials while I was researching there. During my research trip to Louisville the suggestions of both Jim Holmberg and Jim Pritchard of the Filson Historical Society served to introduce me to new collections I did not know existed and greatly expanded the primary sources at my disposal. Lacey Villiva, and the Linda Baltrusch at Gunston Hall in Mason Neck, Virginia, as well as Sergeant John Trowbridge of the Kentucky Army National Guard (Ret.) were also willing to answer questions when they arose.

Once the sources from the repositories above had been hammered into an actual manuscript I was fortunate enough to receive feedback from Dr. Francis Kolb-Turnbull of the *Tennessee Historical Quarterly* as well as Bruce Franklin of Westholme Publishing who has patiently guided me through the labyrinthine world of publishing.

Finally, I want to express my gratitude to several family members who provided the impetus and support for this project. I owe a good deal to my grandmother, Stella Harris, who fostered in me an unceasing interest and love for the history of Kentucky. Most of all, I want to thank my wife, Daralyn and son Aidan, who willingly sacrificed many weekends and evenings to allow me to finish this project. They remain my inspiration for this and all future endeavors.

INDEX